Criminal Accusation

Accusing someone of committing a crime arrests everyday social relations and unfurls processes that decide on who to admit to criminal justice networks. Accusation demarcates specific subjects as the criminally accused, who then face courtroom trials, and possible punishment. It inaugurates a crime's historical journey into being with sanctioned accusers successfully making criminal allegations against accused persons in the presence of authorized juridical agents. Given this decisive role in the production of criminal identities, it is surprising that criminal accusation has received relatively short shrift in sociological, socio-legal and criminological discourses. In this book, George Pavlich redresses this oversight by framing a socio-legal field directed to political rationales and practices of criminal accusation. The focus of its interrogation is the truth-telling powers of an accusatory lore that creates subjects within the confines of socially authorized spaces. And, in this respect, the book has two overarching aims in mind. First, it names and analyses powers of criminal accusation – its history, rationales, rites and effects – as an enduring gateway to criminal justice. Second, the book evaluates the prospects for limiting and/or changing apparatuses of criminal accusation. By understanding their powers, might it be possible to decrease the number who enter criminal justice's gates? This question opens debate on the subject of the book's final section: the prospects for more inclusive accusative grammars that do not, as a reflex, turn to exclusionary visions of crime and vengeful, segregated, corrective or risk-orientated punishment. Highlighting how expansive criminal justice systems are populated by accusatorial powers, and how it might be possible to recalibrate the lore that feeds them, this ground-breaking analysis will be of considerable interest to scholars working in socio-legal studies, critical criminology, social theory, postcolonial studies, and critical legal theory.

George Pavlich is a Canada Research Chair in Social Theory, Culture and Law and Professor of Law and Sociology at the University of Alberta, Canada.

Criminal Accusation

Political Rationales and Socio-Legal Practices

George Pavlich

Routledge
Taylor & Francis Group
LONDON AND NEW YORK

First published 2018
by Routledge

2 Park Square, Milton Park, Abingdon, Oxfordshire OX14 4RN
52 Vanderbilt Avenue, New York, NY 10017

Routledge is an imprint of the Taylor & Francis Group, an informa business

First issued in paperback 2018

British Library Cataloguing in Publication Data
A catalogue record for this book is available from the British Library

Library of Congress Cataloging in Publication Data
Names: Pavlich, George, 1960- author.
Title: Criminal accusation : political rationales and socio-legal practices / George Pavlich.
Description: Abingdon, Oxon [UK] ; New York : Routledge, 2018. | Includes bibliographical references and index.
Identifiers: LCCN 2017032215 | ISBN 9781138505377 (hbk)
Subjects: LCSH: Malicious accusation—Law and legislation. | Offenses against the person. | Malicious accusation—Political aspects. | Malicious accusation—Social aspects. | Criminal law. | Criminal justice, Administration of.
Classification: LCC K5170 .P38 2018 | DDC 345/.06—dc23
LC record available at https://lccn.loc.gov/2017032215

ISBN: 978-1-138-50537-7 (hbk)
ISBN: 978-0-367-18563-3 (pbk)

Typeset in ITC Galliard Std
by Swales & Willis Ltd, Exeter, Devon, UK

Contents

For Carla and Seth

Preface

There are moments that, on reflection, turn out to be pivotal. Living through them, it might not always seem so; but their influence becomes apparent when subsequent muses place one unexpectedly back in their midst. For me, one such moment occurred in the early 1980s in South Africa at Germiston Magistrate's Court (a city on the outskirts of Johannesburg). Even as some details have faded, I recall vividly the smells of creaking wooden benches, a fan moving rhythmically to dissipate the intense heat, adding noise to the disquiet within that nook of apartheid law. Having survived a near fatal car crash, I was called to give evidence against the man accused of dangerous driving. Against the advice of his lawyer, he offered me a heartfelt apology, and I was not unhappy to learn later that he had been acquitted.

Regardless, while waiting in the courtroom to testify, another case was heard. A police constable led a man, eyes downcast, from the holding cells to the accused's dock. He hailed from a farming community and was visiting the city for a brief period. Apprehended and subsequently charged with possessing a dangerous weapon, his apprehension displayed in silence and a disoriented countenance. A junior prosecutor, showing off his legal learning, read the charges in overly formal, legal idioms. The magistrate then called – via a court interpreter – on the accused to plead, booming his voice from an elevated platform that, despite its modesty, did its best to appear imposing.

The interpreter who spoke isiZulu tried to decode the indictment, but an extended exchange with the accused drew the magistrate's silencing rebuff. The translator explained that the man did not fully understand what this 'meeting' was about, and moreover spoke a dialect of Sesotho that made communication between them difficult. So as not to waste court time, the magistrate entered a 'not guilty' plea on behalf of the accused. The police constable was called to a witness platform and testified that following a routine check, he had found a (diminutive) penknife in the accused's kitbag. He had not seen the man act aggressively, and 'no' he had not asked why he had a small knife. The magistrate turned to the interpreter who then addressed the accused man. His response was muted, but concise: the knife was there to cut the meat ('nama') in the same bag. The magistrate transcribed to paper the translator's words.

I was astounded when he stopped writing abruptly, looked up from his book, judged the accused guilty as charged, and sentenced him to judicially supervised corporal punishment. With inapt alacrity, he adjourned the court for morning tea, subtly gesturing for the young prosecutor to join him. As the courtroom emptied I recall feeling part of – along with the participants and props of apartheid's magisterial rituals – a subterfuge that marked itself as authorized justice. My excoriation was heightened by the thought of the two conspirators drinking tea; did they, or indeed the constable, pause to reflect on the suffering of a visitor metamorphosed into a criminally accused person? I recall too the figure trying to maintain a wider dignity as he shuffled off resignedly to meet his court-imposed fate.

Viscerally appalled at the thought of the man being lashed, I began seriously to query the unpredictable, makeshift and pain-authorizing decisions of criminal law visited upon the unsuspecting in the name of justice. Such musing incubated as I worked my way through graduate studies, before guiding a series of critical explorations into possible replacements: alternative dispute resolution, community mediation, and restorative justice. Later, they propelled inquiry into how contingent perceptions of crime had come to appear essential, with identifiable criminals deemed solely responsible for its commission. This eventually led me to the focus of the following essays: the socio-legally negotiated accusations that provided the inconspicuous and socially obscured entrances to criminalization processes. These entryways helped to assert criminal law's monopolistic claims over criminality and its punishment, and thereby its jurisdiction. I soon realized the complexity at play; there were no panaceas, no simple paradigmatic fixes. After all, emphasizing practical solutions had led some restorative justice practitioners too easily into thorny political pastures wherein they embraced concepts of the very criminal justice that their 'alternatives' claimed to replace.

But my approach was no simple for-or-against story either; instead it acknowledged the fluid paradoxes, promises and powers that enunciated different rationales of justice. It did, even if by implicit trace, hold out for a responsive, hospitable, and socially cognizant justice against the vagaries of individualized criminal justice. My allied focus on criminal accusation led me to chart the political rationalities behind its rituals (through which bloated criminal justice systems are unequally populated), and to contest its failure to emphasize ethical responsibilities that enhance, rather than emaciate, social attachments. By highlighting that accusation's changing rationales and practices, one could problematize and so understand the gatekeeping roles behind growing crime-control arenas. Might it not then be possible to truncate these gateways to criminal justice, and so constrain the size and unequal profiles of regulatory arenas focused on crime and its punishment? That promise no doubt traces the following chapters, although they focus on understanding how historical ideas, powers and rituals of accusation dynamically bridge lore and law, social culpability and judicial guilt, cultural rite and legal right, social order and law's violence.

Re-assembling and re-reading one's work over almost two decades is a sobering experience. Most of the chapters that follow have been published previously:

they have been edited to aid the flow of this collection, yet keeping the basic integrity and probing quality of the original texts. I am grateful to the various publishers for agreeing to their re-publication here. I am also grateful to the University of Alberta for enabling my endeavours, the Social Science and Humanities Research Council for financially supporting this work, and the Canada Research Chairs (CRC) Programme for granting me the time and space required to contemplate and write.

Too many people have contributed to my muses over the years to thank individually here; still, I acknowledge many colleagues across the globe who have – through incisive comment and critical questioning – shaped how I now think. I want especially to thank Peter Fitzpatrick, Ros Sydie, Bryan Hogeveen, Heribert Adam, Kogila Moodley, Pat O'Malley, Colin Perrin, Ivo Aertsen, Bruna Pali, Mark Antaki and Val Napoleon for many insightful conversations about these ideas.

Various members of the Canada Research Chair in Social Theory, Culture and Law team, the Department of Sociology and the Faculty of Law are to be thanked for intellectual challenge and research assistance. Fruitful intellectual collaborations with Matt Unger, Aaron Henry, Jean-Philippe Crete, Megan McKenna and Eric Pentland are appreciated. Sonja Sapach helped with permissions. A special thanks to Mahmood Exiri Fard who provided timely assistance with preparing references for the final manuscript; his thoughtful comments on a draft are much appreciated.

To my extended family – siblings, in-laws, offspring – I offer thanks for the genial responses you collectively nurture. Carla and Seth personify what remains most important to me – my words can but insufficiently gesture toward their generous presence over the years that spawned this book.

June 2017
Victoria, B.C., Vancouver Island

Works previously published: acknowledgements

The following chapters were previously published, and are here published with permission and with the gratitude of the author. Most have been edited to assist with the flow of this book.

Chapter 1:
Accusation: landscapes of exclusion
Pavlich, George. (2006). 'Accusation: landscapes of exclusion'. *The Geography of Law, Landscape and Identity*, edited by W. Taylor, Oxford: Hart Publishing, 85–99 – used by permission of Bloomsbury PLC.

Chapter 2:
Apparatuses of criminal accusation
Pavlich, George. (2016). 'Apparatuses of criminal accusation'. In George Pavlich and Matthew Unger (eds), *Accusation: Creating Criminals*. Vancouver: UBC Press, 21–43.

Chapter 3:
Avowal and criminal accusation
Pavlich, George. (2016). 'Avowal and Criminal Accusation'. *Law and Critique* 27(2): 229–245.

Chapter 4:
The violent rhetoric of accusation: Cicero and the Marcus Ameleus Scaurus case
Pavlich, George. (2018). 'The violent rhetoric of accusation: Cicero and the Marcus Ameleus Scaurus case'. In Joshua Nichols and Amy Swiffen (eds), *Legal Violence and the Limits of the Law*. Abingdon: Routledge, 30–49.

Chapter 6:
Creating crime: accusatory entryways to criminal justice
Pavlich, George. (In process). 'Creating crime: accusatory entryways to criminal justice.' In George Pavlich and Matthew Unger (eds), *Entryways to Criminal Justice: Accusation and Criminalization in Canada*. Edmonton: University of Alberta Press.

Chapter 7:

The lore of criminal accusation

Pavlich, George. (2007). 'The lore of criminal accusation'. *Criminal Law and Philosophy: An International Journal for Philosophy of Crime, Criminal Law and Punishment* 1(1): 79–97.

Chapter 8:

Criminal justice and Cape law's persons

Pavlich, George. (2014). 'Criminal justice and Cape law's persons'. *Social & Legal Studies* 23(1): 55–72.

Chapter 9:

Forget crime: accusation, governance and criminology

Pavlich, George. (2000). 'Forget crime: accusation, governance and criminology'. *Australian & New Zealand Journal of Criminology (Australian Academic Press)* 33(2): 136–152.

Chapter 10:

The emergence of habitual criminals in nineteenth-century Britain: implications for criminology

Pavlich, George. (2010). 'The emergence of habitual criminals in nineteenth century Britain: implications for criminology'. *Journal of Theoretical and Philosophical Criminology* 2(1): 1–62.

Chapter 11:

The subjects of criminal identification

Pavlich, George. (2009). 'The subjects of criminal identification'. *Punishment & Society* 11(2): 171–190.

Introduction

> 'You say further that you do not want to save yourself. But your salvation is not a matter that rests in your hands. If we, your judges, do not do our best to save you, following scrupulously the letter of the law, then we will have failed to save the law. Of course we have a responsibility to society, a grave and onerous responsibility, to shield it from rapists and murderers. But we have an equal responsibility to save you the accused from yourself, in the event that you are or were not yourself, as the law understands being oneself to be. Am I clear?'
>
> (Coetzee, 2016, *The Schooldays of Jesus*. Kindle locations 2063–2068)

This passage from Coetzee's novel draws attention to an often-overlooked idea: judgments of criminal guilt may only be passed on legal persons who are rendered as 'the accused' at entryways to criminal law. At these thresholds, people often find themselves facing mystifying procedures that they negotiate as witnesses, deponents, accusers, or the accused. Such assumed identities are piloted through encounters with law as it calls them to account, and requires them to assert truths about specific events in authorized ways. Such accounts are limited to what given forms of law deem relevant, what its representatives can decipher, and what can be transcribed through the legal parlance of the day. With such matters in mind, the following collection examines the social, cultural and political dimensions of criminal accusation over time, focusing particularly on political rationalities of rituals that define and select – by way of accusation – persons to face law's trials. Today's omniscient criminal justice institutions are contingent upon such accusations; the epigraph reminds us too of their constitutive role in bids to 'shield' social orders under auspices of criminal justice.

The complexities of criminal accusation as a concept are signalled by its etymology. Ancient Greek roots indicate such meanings as to 'charge', to 'categorize', to 'censure' and to 'blame'. The Latin *accusare* suggests a calling of 'someone to account for their actions' (Ayto, 1990: 5), whereas the conjoined Latin *ad* and *causa* references 'to lay one's charge' (Skeat, 1961: 72; Pavlich & Unger, 2016: 3; Antaki, 2016: 49). Relatedly, the Latin noun, *crimen* connotes 'judgment, accusation, illegal act'. It derives from the Latin root *cernere* meaning 'verdict, accusation, crime' (Negrier-Dormont, 1994: 12; Partridge, 1958: 130). This root, in its turn, originates from the Greek '*krinein*' (decide), and shares an etymological heritage with words like *certain*, *categorize*, *crisis*, *critic*, *discrete*, *excrement*, *secret*, *riddle* (Ayto, 1990: 145). This etymology suggests that rituals of criminal accusation respond to cries of distress, call people to account, and categorize them to face possible socio-legal censure. The specific calling here is contoured by cultural precepts of suspicion, blame, censure, and allegations of wrongdoing.

One might then view criminal accusation as embracing a politics of recognition that surfaces when social interactions encounter troubling events. Its rituals and bridging technologies arrest what is usually taken for granted, channelling participants' thoughts to notions of mistrust and culpability. It thereby negotiates who might be recognized as accused *personas* in context, and uses various political technologies to render witness statements in idioms decipherable to law. Of course, visions of crime and wrong are contingent social matters, but they are analogously related by initial accusatory rituals. Using the term 'crime' as a shorthand for wrongs thus conceived, I do not mean to underplay such contingency, whether locally enunciated as public offences, delicts, sins of high order, or crimes. It is but a signal for fluid social processes that detect and define specific wrongs as requiring socio-legal censures of criminal or public law (see Chapter 4). In turn, this highlights the basic role that accusation plays in initiating processes that erect criminal (or analogous) *personas*. That is, all subjects accused of crimes and the like must pause with due deference at gates, where social rites yield to the rights bestowed on law's accused subjects.

These rites and rights took a distinctive form with medieval and modern state administrations in the West; they supported gradually centralized institutions devoted to crime, criminals and their punishment (e.g., Grossi, 2010; Landau, 2002; Garland, 1990). Their monumental growth spawned criminal justice arenas that now assume city-like proportions devoted to selective banning – they delimit social order by defining, categorizing, adjudicating, separating and punishing 'criminals'. Enlightenment promises sought to rationalize the bans, to yield measured responses to crimes (and their punishment), and to seek reasonable societies freed from criminal impulses (e.g., Becarria). Such lofty promises turned into what might seem like – if eliminating crime were the overall goal – a failure of colossal historical proportions. Over several centuries, it did not so much eliminate criminality as succeed in generating vast networks of crime control in the name of a sovereign justice founded upon the creation of criminals, with accusation as a seldom referenced source thereof.

To be sure, socio-legal studies and critical criminology have offered trenchant critiques of resulting criminal justice institutions, homing in on the inequities of policing, court processes and mass incarceration (see Reiner, 2007). Some noted the detrimental effects of burgeoning 'crime-control industries' and cultures that promoted, as a standard reflex, the criminalization and punitive control of locally defined wrongdoing (Christie, 1994). Such industries monopolized legal definitions and responses to 'crime', and they flourished by expanding their budgetary, operational and bureaucratic reach. Other critics catalogued how growing crime-control arenas unequally identified, judged and censured 'criminal' individuals (Alexander, 2010), calling for the abolition of prisons (e.g., Matthiesen, 1974), or at least the need for significantly altered restorative justice 'lenses' (e.g., Zehr, 2015). Still others, such as Foucault (1995: 277) and Reiman (2005), wryly detected (in the latter's terms) a 'pyrrhic defeat' at play that seized success from the jaws of its failure. They pointed to the political success of creating power relations that managed unequal social limits, despite – or even because of – a failing to arrest crime through punishment or correction. Such power yielded a pervasive undemocratic governance 'through' crime (Simon, 2007), punitive 'cultures of control' (Garland, 2002), duplicitous risk-based controls (O'Malley, 2010), as well as vast and vastly unequal punishment institutions contoured by age, class, race, and gender (Alexander, 2010; Wacquant, 2009; Reiner, 2007).

As trenchant as these criticisms of an expanding criminal justice system undoubtedly are, they pay scant attention to the founding accusations that populate criminal justice arenas in the first place. It is through versions of accusation that criminalization became possible. Consequently, the following chapters focus attention on the political rationalities, rituals and practices by which accusation deploys gateways that open or close access to subsequent criminalizing trials. More specifically, they problematize accusations focused on selecting potential criminals for socio-legal censure. Approaching such selections as a problem to be investigated, this collection examines influential lineages of criminal accusation. It thereby focuses on complex social, political and cultural foundations of criminalization – even as these paradoxically work within the criminal justice arenas they spawn. Unveiling the political logic of such entrances promises insight into their inconspicuous hold, and the prospect of considering how to contain the flow of people brought into criminalizing networks in the first place. To be sure, judgments of 'criminal' guilt and criminalization begin in murky and aleatoric social waters from whence accusations surface. Inequitous selections of who precisely to criminalize operate without question when hidden. Consequently, overlooking them eclipses their constitutive role in sustaining criminalizing institutions. In other words, the sheer size, disproportionate population profiles, and quantum of resources dedicated to criminal justice exclusions might be altered by constraining the accusation-based gateways through which criminalized populations initially flow.

Conceptual approach to criminal accusation

How then should one approach criminal accusation conceived as a political matter that supports vast and unequal criminal justice populations? As is evident throughout, I do not consider criminal (or analogous) accusation to contain a singular, necessary, fixed, or discoverable 'essence'. It is always contingently formed, but that does not preclude analysis of its operations. To contest visions of accusation that blithely exercise power in support of deterministic visions of crime and punishment requires a critical unveiling and formulation of a problem. In that quest, and interpreting Foucault's (1977) anti-methodological appropriation of Nietzsche's 'genealogical' approach, one might agree with Koopman's (2013: 1) sense that we are here concerned with 'problems' that do not 'come with supposed solutions readily apparent' and which are 'submerged'. We might also note, as does Saar (2002: 232), that genealogical approaches problematize power formations as 'a mode of writing history', a critique and a 'textual practice'. Transposing these ideas to governmental analysis, Walters (2012: 116) usefully alerts us to how such genealogies trace the 'emergence' of phenomena (such as criminal accusation) by separating out sometimes forgotten 'lines of descent', and developing 'counter-memories' that highlight vanquished knowledges (or the silenced casualties of given powers). In short, 'Whatever its style, emphasis or source, genealogy uses historical knowledge to reveal that who and what we are is not fixed or eternal, not a matter of destiny or grand design, but a series of contingent becomings' (2012: 115).

Working off such interpretations, and recognizing genealogy as a way to 'diagnose' limits to our present (see Garland, 2014), the following chapters variously problematize visions of current criminal accusations in the service of crime and punishment. They turn to erstwhile discourses not to conjure a 'history of the past in terms of the present'; but rather to use historical analysis to contest what is taken for granted in the present – possibly a 'history of the present' (Foucault, 1995: 21). The exemplary archives of accusation addressed suggest 'lines of descent' for the emergence of a preoccupation with crime and its control; this sets rudimentary limits to how we live amid a criminal justice colossus today.

What kind of critique does this genealogy embrace? I have elsewhere detailed the genre of critique framing much of my work (e.g., Pavlich, 2013, 2000); but suffice here to note that it does not echo dominant, modern, critical grammars that require critics to judge social contexts against absolute criteria, pointing assured paths to progress (see Chapter 9). Rather, the 'governmental' grammar of critique I embrace is far less clear-cut, involving interpretative separations that question what is presented as necessary. Such genres deconstructively (not destructively) open specific political rationales and practices to meaning horizons beyond what they set as necessary or absolute social limits. As with Foucault's (1984) re-appropriation of Kant's critiques as a 'limit attitude' toward the present, this critique does not simply judge what is; it interpretatively opens to horizons beyond what is currently asserted – via limits erected by current power–knowledge relations – as necessary being (e.g., see Garland, 2014).

Furthermore, the following analyses make copious reference to examples of criminal accusations across time and place. The chosen illustrations are meant to elucidate different facets of the phenomenon of criminal accusation and its contextual political rationalities/practices. Agamben's (2009) essay 'What is a paradigm?' indicates how examples are neither inductively nor deductively locatable in paradigmatic sets. Instead, one contingently extracts examples with the promise of rendering an encompassing phenomenon intelligible. The examples are analysed beside (para-) a phenomenon (-digm), say criminal accusation: they are examined as parts of a wider phenomenon. Like Foucault's use of Bentham's panopticon to illustrate disciplinary power, an example can help to explicate, 'the intelligibility of the set to which it belongs and which at the same time it constitutes' (Agamben, 2009: 2). Yet, while examples exemplify a set, they also stand as singular instances that defer to others. In what follows, they are used to highlight singular exercises of power that form elements of the phenomenon of criminal accusation over time. Hence, the criminal cases described should be read simultaneously in their singularity (i.e., as depicting specific moments of criminal accusation) and as exemplary elements of the wider phenomenon (political rationalities of criminal accusation).

Finally, most of the chapters address criminal accusation through 'political rationalities' that tie it to initiating claims of criminal jurisdiction – whether in ancient Greece, the Roman Republic, early medieval Norwich, Flanders, modern Britain, or in colonies such as the Cape and Canada. They evoke a concept of 'political rationality' primarily through a reading of Foucault's ambiguous references to that idea. Without revisiting its complexities (but see Walters, 2012: 25–27), Foucault's work refers to a liberal 'mentality' that from the eighteenth century sought 'to rationalize the problems posed to governmental practice by phenomena characteristic of a set of living beings forming a population: health, hygiene, birthrate, life expectancy, race' (2008: 317).

But he also claims that 'rationality' has far wider political reach, tracing all political schemes, 'institutions' and 'ideas' (Foucault & Dillon, 1980: 4). Indeed, he suggests that 'all human behaviour is scheduled and programmed through rationality' such that 'there is a logic in institutions and in behaviour and in political relations' (1980: 4). Political rationalities are thus neither good, nor bad; they are, however, always capable – when left unexamined – of yielding atrocious forms of violence. On this view:

> What is most dangerous in violence is its rationality. Of course violence is terrible. But the deepest root of violence and its permanence come out of the form of rationality we use. The idea has been that if we live in a world of reason, we can get rid of violence. This is quite wrong. Between violence and rationality there is no incompatibility. My problem is not to put reason on trial, but to know what is this rationality so compatible with violence.
>
> (1980: 4)

One way to reveal concealed political rationalities is to generate genealogies behind their contingent beginnings, and so problematize taken-for-granted power relations that operate quietly in shadows. While political efficiencies might be gained from covert exercises of power, the ethico-political costs to 'being with' others through open collectives is potentially fatal. To arrest this possibility, the ensuing genealogies of criminal accusation highlight (instances of) political rationalities that have surfaced over centuries. It critically charts accusatory entryways that lie in assumptive shadows, especially when they operate as unexamined foundations for criminal justice.

Finally, while socio-legal practices of criminal accusation differ significantly over time and place, one might discern a fluid 'grammar' that specifies 'what kind of object' accusation is – its 'essence' (Wittgenstein, 1980: #373, #371). For Wittgenstein, the grammar of accusation does not simply supply instructions for correct uses of words in language games ('surface grammar' #664); they are traced by local conventions, and these imply a 'given' form of life. Thus, what makes it possible to even speak of accusation across time is not a universal essence, but rather fluid agreements on how to 'use' words within and across language games – a kind of 'depth grammar' that implies what it is to 'mean' something (#664). Thus, to understand what we mean by 'criminal accusation', it is not enough to achieve, 'only agreement in definitions' (#242); rather, the agreement is traced by underlying, and largely inscrutable, conventions. To clarify, Wittgenstein asks of himself, 'So you are saying that human agreement decides what is true and what is false?' In response, he views such agreement as basic to a form of life: 'It is what human beings say that is true and false; and they agree in the language they use. That is not agreement in opinions but in form of life' (#241).

Criminal accusation's modes of address then ensue from a grammar traced out of a historical form of life. That grammar is neither simply an ontology, nor a technical procedure; it appears through indeterminate and ethically charged patterns of association that have tied themselves fundamentally to a politics of criminalization and punishment. In refusing that pervasive grammar, my work tries to 'amend' accusation fundamentality, and perhaps to enable a rupture – even if contra Wittgenstein – in the attendant form of life. Here one glimpses accusation's ethical dimensions. Its grammar sets up ethical responsibilities within a form of life that generates the co-appearance of accused and accuser, as well as the co-appearance of order and disorder (Nancy, 2000). Here one might briefly note an overlap with Levinas (1998: 112) who recognizes accusation to be a 'pre-conceptual' grammar through which unformed, ethically created, selves appear. He points out that the very appearance of a self is predicated on a fundamental and prior accusation – a calling to account – by an amorphous collective into which an undefined potential is born. The face of the other, that is, calls 'me' to account (accuses me); 'my' subsequent responses to their accusations fashion a responsible, indeterminate, but ethical self that is primordial to ontology. Here we encounter Levinas' pre-conceptual sense of accusation as a founding social moment; it demands that we recognize a fundamental responsibility to others who call us to account as a matter of self-definition, a form of life. But from this pre-conceptual foundation, diverse, contingent *concepts* of accusation become possible; as does the possibility of reframing ethical imperatives for different forms of accusation not attached to dominant fixations with crime and criminals.

Explorations into realms of criminal accusation

The following essays were written over a span of some 18 years for different venues, and hence predictably do not develop a single argument. They do, however, explore diverse elements of the political rationales and techniques through which criminal accusation has over centuries initiated legal trials, censured public wrong and had ordering collective effects. Using several examples and cases, they pull out common and discontinuous threads of accusation over time, but all by way of providing limit critiques of how we presently do things. Themes recur, overlap and sometimes are re-examined from different angles; not all repetition is excised so that chapters can be read individually. At the same time, the essays are grouped thematically (rather than chronologically) in four related sections: orientating conceptual traces; cultural grammars of criminal accusation; accusation and colonial law; and amending accusation.

1 Conceptual traces

The two opening chapters set the conceptual stage for a genealogical counter-memory that recovers influential ideas, practices and logics behind the contingent formation of Western ideas and rituals of criminal accusation. The varied renditions of accusation do not indicate an essential being but a contingent political becoming. The latter emerges through diverse political ideas and rituals that accuse subjects of crime; these are forged historically, as are the accusing and accused subjects fashioned by – and who serve as the vehicles of – its power relations. Chapter 1 recognizes that criminal accusation has been hosted by different discursive 'landscapes of exclusion' that arrest familiar flows of everyday life, and initiate authorized practices that attach stranger identities to selected persons – all are recognizable to contemporary legal idioms. It offers interpretations of accusation through scholastic reasoning (Aquinas), art exemplars (Gerhard David) and the opening lines of Plato's accounts of Socrates' accusation. The chapter reads 'lost traces of accusation into the present', and confronts current limits that emphasize criminalization and its punishment.

The more recently written Chapter 2 develops themes raised here, but focuses on the contingent political rationalities of three intersecting and influential discursive 'apparatuses' of criminal accusation. Referencing Foucault (2014, but see also 2015), it highlights how sovereign, disciplinary and risk-based logics of power have interacted to create expansive and unequal entrances to criminalizing institutions. Such contingent lines of descent provide a marker for genealogical interventions that reframe a present political problem; namely, one that does not see accusation as necessarily serving crime and its punishment. It restates the problem thus: deciphering prevalent apparatuses of criminal accusation allows us to confront their interactive expansion at entrances to criminal justice, and thereby to curb the latter's size and inequities. This problematization calls for us to imagine open, and less individualistically focused, uses for accusation. In short, the genealogical discussions of both chapters elucidate criminal accusation as a contingent mode of address within political rationalities that – despite significant differences – create gateways to regulate criminal justice's population flows. Such modes of address call particular sorts of subjects to account (accused persons) before other legal persons (accusers, justices of the peace, etc.); but the contours of that calling make it possible for all such 'beings' to co-appear historically.

2 Cultural grammars of criminal accusation

Underscoring contingent expressions of criminal accusation, Chapters 3 to 5 reference ancient examples of its grammars, rites and rituals. They show how erstwhile political rationalities called subjects to account through modes of address that formed around particular events; they arrested everyday meanings and 'recognized' new identities that followed from suspicion, perceptions of criminal (or analogous public – see Chapter 4) wrong, and blame. Returning in more detail to Socrates' trial in Athens, Chapter 3 references Foucault's (2014) ideas on avowal to explore what kind of truth-telling was demanded by contemporary accusatory processes, and how these released patterns of subjection and subject formation as public accusers and accused. The discussion shows how Socrates' seemingly odd defence could be read as a basic refusal; it refused the compunction to conform to the avowals and subjections required of law's accused persons in contemporary Athens. Even faced with death, Socrates remained true to the philosophical identity to which he had dedicated his life.

Chapter 4 turns to the accusation of Scaurus for extortion in the late Roman Republic to detail emerging rationales and practices of criminal accusation required for rhetorical practices considered 'proper' to accusers, the accused and mediating authorities, respectively. It details what Cicero and others meant when saying that accusation has a distinctive rhetorical form: a violence that used words to frame carefully planned character attacks. This chapter recalls the key role that accusation plays in the enunciations of 'public' wrong, and by analogous extension 'crime'. The Roman Republic (and indeed Socrates' Athens) did not rely on abstract codes to define criminal wrongdoing; instead rituals of accusation authorized certain kinds of accusers, accused persons and mediating legal agents to negotiate public wrong (and delict) requiring censure. Accusation's key political role in the formulation of public wrong highlights criminology's 'big mistake': to emphasize the ontology of crime, and to eclipse how calling people to account through local accusatory rituals generates specific 'criminals'.

Chapter 5's genealogy takes us to mid-twelfth-century Norwich where Thomas of Monmouth issued an early blood libel accusation against a Jewish community. Criminal accusation directed to an ethno-religious group reflects its capacity for divisive and extreme social ordering, the cultural grammar of which is unearthed through a reading of Thomas's surviving text. That grammar appears through perceived disruptions of events that participants find confusing, and challenges familiar meaning grids. When criminal accusation is mobilized to deal with such confusion, participants make sense of the events through rituals that demand avowals of wrong and culpability, 'heard' by locally designated authorities. The cultural grammar of this mode of address ensures that perceived wrongs are framed in ways decipherable to local justice. Thomas's account highlights the divisive, highly dangerous and socially injurious potential of accusatory processes that declare limits through rhetorical forms of avowal, legal transcriptions of events and the use of public fame. His contingent politics conceals the noxious bordering and social division that his treacherous accusations license, indicating thereby a broader danger that attends to Western grammars of accusation.

3 Imperial accusations and settler-colonial law

The following three chapters tap colonial examples of criminal accusation from Western Canada, the Cape of Good Hope, and offer imperial contrasts through cases from nineteenth-century Britain. In so doing, they extend the previous analysis of criminal accusation's political logic and the ethics of the bordering/ ordering that produced settler-colonial social formations. They highlight the indeterminate contingencies by which accusations form entrances to colonial and imperial law, and how the latter declare various kinds of criminal jurisdiction.

Referencing Nietzsche to conceptualize dominion entryways to criminal justice in late nineteenth-century Western Canada, deployed largely by police and justices of the peace, Chapter 6 locates the 'lowly beginnings' of crime as formed through settler-colonial processes of accusation. The latter translated multifaceted social events into narrowly transcribed records made decipherable to colonial law's idioms. The imposition of criminalization over indigenously occupied arenas not only displaced people and customs, but denied indigenous legal forms. It claimed a monopoly over the definition and control of criminal wrongdoing. This chapter suggests that emerging settler practices helped to forge colonial images of how to accuse others of crime, and consequently what and who dominion law deemed as 'criminal'. It describes accusatory entrances to criminalizing juridical processes, showing how they at once asserted criminal jurisdiction, deployed criminal law by laying down accusatory gauntlets, and formed a bridge between changing social relations and settler claims to legal right.

Discussing emerging colonial ideas and powers, I intentionally do not limit – as might be the case in conventional jurisprudence – the analysis to criminal procedure. Chapter 7 thus discusses a socio-cultural lore of criminal accusation, explicitly recognizing the demotic and local syntax of negotiated meanings that initiate, and so form gateways to criminalizing processes. However, I eschew traditions that capture folklore as signatory to unchanging social forms. Instead, a changing historical lore of criminal accusation is located within fluid social and ethical forms. This vision of lore, referencing Nancy (2000), is shown to be tethered not to universal cultures, but to local, ethical, and political rationales that define how to be with others.

Indeed, a multiplex politics that calls subjects to account for crimes is neither ethically, nor socially, indifferent. Addressing subjects as accusers, accused or mediating authorities calls each *persona* into being. By the narrowed responses required of each, specific kinds of subject identities appear. Without echoing Althusser's (2001) visions of ideological state apparatuses, one might nevertheless recall his insight that 'hailing' subjects recursively generates both their subjectification and subjection; it might even be that law never gets its person, because it structurally 'misrecognizes' the indeterminate dynamism that is always in excess of narrow juridical framings of the accused, accuser, judge, criminal, etc. (Martel, 2016). However, as Chapter 7 argues, the 'co-appearance' of accuser and accused is tied to prescriptions of order and disorder; refusing imperial accusations of crime is to contest the ethical precepts therein. It also suggests that culturally fixating on 'criminals' turns our gaze to 'problem' individuals who 'disrupt' purported communal orders, thereby diverting our eyes from the criminogenic dimensions of societies themselves. Social disorder is deftly cast as an individual responsibility to be detected, juridically identified and removed in chains: thus framing the 'crime' problem as an individual matter. This chapter then calls for us to 'amend' a lore of accusation that supports such political rationalities and to imagine other governmental possibilities.

Chapter 8 explores links between local conceptions of legal persons, criminal accusation and the creation of sovereignly sanctioned, crime-focused law in the late eighteenth-century Cape of Good Hope. An early foreshadowing of apartheid logics, authoritatively sanctioned accusations of crime were differentially applied through local 'distinctions of person'. The ensuing 'categories of persons' (e.g., 'burghers', 'slaves', etc.) assigned people to hierarchical visions of social order, determining which subjects could be accused of what crimes, how, and what forms of punishment were deemed appropriate to each. The 'atrocity' of crimes was in part determined in relation to these distinctions, as were initiating accusations of crime and the consequent punishments. The social order was upheld by a criminal law that claimed to operate exclusively in an imperial sovereign's name. If this justice displaced indigenous forms of law, it did not do so simply at the command of an imperial sovereign. Rather, it was through this 'crime-focused' justice – and initiating criminal accusations – that colonial images of sovereignty were publicly, and repeatedly, projected. Settler-colonial sovereignty was thus constitutively tied to performances of criminal justice and the accusations upon which it rested – a political logic that tenaciously endures through current fixations on crime and the sovereign limits it enables.

4 Amending crime-focused accusations

The final chapters of the collection variously refuse the ontological framings of crime and criminals that dominate mainstream criminology. Chapter 9 calls on us to 'forget crime' conceived as a being with discoverable essence, and to return to a forgotten etymology of criminology as a *logos* of *crimen* that references how we accuse, or call people to account. It challenges mainstream criminology to release its attachments to realism, modern genres of critique centred on founded judgement, and to engage governmental spaces that do not assume crime and criminals as ontologically fixed. So, instead of targeting crime and criminals as objects of technocratic criminological study, the chapter reaches for a 'post-disciplinary' discourse to focus on how and why subjects are called to account for 'criminal' actions, emphasizing the power and ethical dimensions of accusations that initiate criminalizing processes.

Part of this argument is developed further in Chapter 10's discussion of how the 'criminal' appeared in nineteenth-century British discourses as a distinctive being. Notions of 'criminal class', 'criminal character' and 'criminal habits' were merged to produce a concept of the 'habitual criminal' as a distinctive being. The latter provided founding contours for positivist criminology's assertions of 'the criminal' as an absolute sort of human being (*anthro*). By contrast, the chapter's genealogy references such a 'person' as a contingent ethical, political and social invention. It appeals to criminology to attend to the 'justice of creating criminals', and to consider the ethical effects of calling criminal persons to accusatorial account as if they existed in advance of criminal law's interventions. Finally, Chapter 11 echoes this appeal by exploring two influential, even if rather different, late nineteenth-century, criminal identification techniques (Galton's composite portraits, and Bertillon's anthropometry). It seeks explicitly to re-politicize both practices of criminal identification and their role in forms of criminalization whose effect is to create – rather than discover – criminals. It challenges the legitimacy commonly ascribed to mainstream criminology as a supposedly neutral science, calling for 'just governance' that rescinds an exclusionary reflex to create criminals. It insists on the importance of recognizing the ethics and politics behind their creation, and the concealed visions of how to be with others that they imply.

The refusals of mainstream criminology in this section, and the resultant appeal to address much wrongdoing beyond lexicons of crime and punitive control, criminals and their punishment, echo a general questioning of a pervasive political rationality of criminal accusation that stands at entrances to criminalizing processes. Working through the political logic of these processes involves neither calling pre-formed individuals to account, nor fixed accusers who make allegations, nor unchanging legal authorities who hear. Rather, it is precisely through the deployment of historically sanctioned ideas and rituals of accusation that specific identities of accuser, accused and mediating authority emerge.

In this sense, the politics of criminal accusation is always contingent. Its underlying ethical commitments are imitated by modes of address that call people to account, and define communal questions of how to 'be with others'. By beckoning selected subjects to account, it hails them into a kind of historical being. It borders and orders by targeting categories of persons to account for 'crimes'; it accuses through contingent rituals, rites and responses that render complex life forms decipherable to narrow legal idioms. To question a political logic that initiates the creation of criminals as a reflex is also to question the resultant, distended, criminal justice arenas. Amending a technical grammar of criminal accusation that admits individual persons to criminal law's trials is a way to pursue alternative uses of accusation not tied to crime, exclusion and punishment. That sort of accusation might align itself with a basic ethical responsibility to be with others in ways that enhance rather than destroy sociality. The following chapters serve as a preface to further study of such questions as this: what rationalities and rituals of accusation might turn away from individualized 'criminal suspects' in attempts to enhance encompassing associational patterns that encourage social attachments and limit social bans?

References

Agamben, G. (2009). *The Signature of all Things: On Method*, New York: Zone Books.
Alexander, M. (2010). *The New Jim Crow: Mass Incarceration in the Age of Colorblindness.* New York: New Press.
Althusser, Louis (2001). Ideology and the state. In *Lenin and Philosophy and other Essays.* New York: Monthly Review Press, 85–126.
Antaki, M. (2016). 'Declining accusation', in G. Pavlich & M. Unger (eds), *Accusation: Creating Criminals.* Vancouver: UBC Press, pp. 44–72.
Ayto, J. (1990). *Dictionary of Word Origins.* New York: Arcade Publishers.
Christie, N. (1994). *Crime Control as Industry: Towards Gulags, Western Style* (2nd edn). London: Routledge.
Coetzee, J. M. (2016). *The Schooldays of Jesus.* London: Penguin Random House (Kindle Edition).
Foucault, M. (1977). *Language, Counter-memory, Practice: Selected Essays and Interviews.* Ithaca, NY: Cornell University Press.
——. (1984). 'What is Enlightenment?', in P. Rabinow (ed.), *The Foucault Reader.* New York: Pantheon, pp. 32–55.
——. (1995). *Discipline and Punish: the Birth of the Prison* (2nd edn). New York: Vintage Books.
——. (2008) *Society Must Be Defended: Lectures at the Collège de France, 1975–1976.* New York: Palgrave Macmillan.
——. (2014). *Wrong-doing, Truth-telling: The Function of Avowal in Justice.* F. Brion, B. E. Harcourt & S. W. Sawyer, trans. Chicago, IL: University of Chicago Press.
——. (2015). *On the Punitive Society: Lectures at the Collège de France, 1972–1973.* UK: Palgrave Macmillan.
Foucault, M., & Dillon, M. (1980). Conversation with Michel Foucault. *The Threepenny Review*, 1 (Winter/Spring), 4–5.
Garland, D. (1990). *Punishment and Modern Society: A Study in Social Theory.* Oxford: Clarendon Press.
——. (2002). *The Culture of Control: Crime and Social Order in Contemporary Society.* Chicago: University of Chicago Press.
——. (2014). What is a 'history of the present'? On Foucault's genealogies and their critical preconditions. *Punishment & Society*, 16(4), 365–84.
Grossi, P. (2010). *A History of European Law.* Chichester: Wiley-Blackwell.

Koopman, C. (2013). *Genealogy as Critique: Foucault and the Problems of Modernity.* Bloomington, IN: Indiana University Press.
Landau, N. (2002). *Law, Crime, and English Society, 1660–1830.* Cambridge: Cambridge University Press.
Levinas, E. (1998). *Otherwise than Being: Or Beyond Essence.* Pittsburgh, PA: Duquesne.
Martel, J. (2016). 'Guilty without accusation: legal passions and the misinterpellation of subjects in Althusser and Kafka', in G. Pavlich & M. Unger (eds), *Accusation: Creating Criminals.* Vancouver, BC: UBC Press, pp. 131–51.
Mathiesen, T. (1974). *The Politics of Abolition.* Oslo: Scandinavian University Books.
Nancy, J.-L. (2000). *Being Singular Plural.* Stanford, CA: Stanford University Press.
Negrier-Dormont, L. (1994). Criminology: foundations and efficacy. *International Criminal Police Review*, 450, 10–15.
O'Malley, P. (2010). *Crime and Risk.* Los Angeles, CA: Sage.
Partridge, E. (1958). *Origins: A Short Etymological Dictionary of Modern English.* London: Routledge and Kegan Paul.
Pavlich, G. (2000). *Critique and Radical Discourses on Crime.* Aldershot: Ashgate.
——. (2013). 'Dissociative grammar and constitutional critique?', in K. van Marle & S. Motha (eds), *Genres of Critique: Law, Aesthetics and Liminality.* Stellenbosch: Sun Press, pp. 31–48.
Pavlich, G., & Unger, M. (eds). (2016). *Accusation: Creating Criminals.* Vancouver, BC: UBC Press.
Reiman, J. (2005). *The Rich Get Richer and the Poor Get Prison.* New York: MacMillan.
Reiner, R. (2007). *Law and Order: An Honest Citizen's Guide to Crime and Control.* Cambridge: Polity.
Saar, M. (2002). Genealogy and subjectivity. *European Journal of Philosophy*, 10, 231–45.
Simon, J. (2007). *Governing through Crime.* New York: Oxford University Press.
Skeat, W. W. (1961). *A Concise Etymological Dictionary of the English Language.* Oxford: Clarendon Press.
Wacquant, L. J. D. (2009). *Punishing the Poor: the Neoliberal Government of Social Insecurity.* Durham, NC: Duke University Press.
Walters, W. (2012). *Governmentality: Critical Encounters.* New York: Taylor & Francis (Kindle Edition).
Wittgenstein, L. (1980). *Philosophical Investigations.* Worcester: Basil Blackwell Publishers.
Zehr, H. (2015). *Changing Lenses: Restorative Justice for Our Times.* Kitchener, Ontario: Herald Press.

Chapter 1

Accusation

Landscapes of exclusion

Situated in cultural horizons infatuated with images of crime, one easily forgets that criminality is created through complex processes that impart criminal identities (Christie, 1994). Moreover, criminal justice traditions descending from the English common law are built on accusatorial foundations (Pollock & Maitland, 1898; O'Connor, 1984). In general, one might say that all forms of exclusion involve the creation of otherness and are thus related – one way or another – to precipitating moments of accusation. Over the centuries, vastly different landscapes have hosted versions of accusation; all arrest the ordinary flows of everyday social life, initiating processes that are licensed to attach stranger identities to designated subjects. In this sense, accusation could be viewed as a moment where accusers draw on local cultural resources to allege that there are criminal outsiders within a given context. It involves a process that, if successful, precipitates exclusion, othering and simultaneously ensconces never completed boundaries around what is included.

Accusation per se could be approached from many different interpretative horizons. There is much to be said, for example, about the diverse architectural spaces expressly designed to hear accusations. The following discussion, however, focuses specifically on general *conceptual landscapes* of accusation, but it does so in a very particular way. It aims to theorize accusation by reflecting on the underlying binary oppositions – friendship and enmity, inclusion and exclusion, sameness and otherness, inside and outside, good and evil, commonality and difference, legal and illegal – through which accusation is articulated. Against a culture of crime, which so dominates criminal exclusion, one finds here an attempt to envision accusation as the foundation of Western bids to exclude others. Specifically, I shall refer (perhaps defer) to four related archives in narrating accusation: etymological traces; Aquinas' *Summa Theologica*, Question #68; Gerard David's painting *The Judgment of Cambyses* (left and right panels); and Plato's opening line in the *Apology*. In one sense, this archive is of course limited; but then comprehensiveness is neither possible nor necessarily a desirable aim. My intended yield is rather different: to insert a reading of lost traces of accusation into the present.

Remembering an etymological bequest: to 'accuse'

In a bid to gain control over his kingdom, King Henry instructed, in the *Assize of Clarendon*, his justices to search the land to discover

> whether there be in their hundred or will any man accused or notoriously suspected of being a robber, murderer or thief, or anyone who is receiver of robbers or murderers or thieves since the Lord King has been King. And let the justices inquire among themselves and the sheriffs among themselves.
>
> (Cited in O'Connor, 1984: 354)

This snippet suggests the importance of accusation to the king's attempts to identify and exclude enemies of the realm (see also Chapters 2 and 5). From this, one might sense that by identifying otherness, a given order thereby silently defines its included subjects. One way to open this silence is to return to the etymology of the *crimen* that lies buried in many Western discourses on criminal exclusion (e.g., criminology). A Latin noun, *crimen* connotes 'judgment, accusation, illegal act'. It derives from the Latin root *cernere*, meaning 'verdict, accusation, crime' (Negrier-Dormont, 1994: 12; Partridge, 1958: 130). In turn, this root comes ultimately from the Greek word '*krinein*' (decide), and shares this etymological line of descent with other words including *certain*, *crisis*, *critic*, *discrete*, *excrement*, *secret*, *riddle* (Ayto, 1990: 145). It is also most instructive to recall, as does Ayto, that the Latin noun *crimen* 'passed via Old French *crimne* (later *crime*) into English, where traces of the original meaning "accusation" survived until the 17th-century' (145). After that, with the successful emergence of social sciences such as criminology, layers of new meaning were attached to *crimen* and the intimate links with accusation were lost. One effect is the almost exclusive ways in which *crimen* is now taken to mean crime, or offence; the apparent amnesia has also allowed crime to be reified as an ontologically distinct entity *sui generis*, capable of bearing the inscrutable weight of the essences and necessities that criminologists ascribe to it.

However, I want to argue that there is value in returning to earlier images that associated *crimen* with accusation. We might then recover *crimen* as referring to moments that arrest everyday life flows, and mobilize institutions to create strangers from within the midst of a given order. This imagery recalls the etymology of the word 'accuse', which derives from the Old Latin *acusare*, 'to call someone to account' (Ayto, 1990: 5). Calling someone to account obliges the accused to enunciate an account of a self in relation to a specified set of events. The obligation takes place in structured institutional landscapes that demand particular ways of speaking, problems to be resolved, licensed discourses, and so on. Although the landscapes are as various as they are unique, all demand that accuser and accused speak out about a perceived set of events in front of a witnessing gathering. This echoes Klein's (1966: 372) claim that accusation is etymologically related to a 'cry of distress' (in the sense of a 'hue and cry'), to moments that raise a social alarm.

Such etymologies connote images of accusation as a unique moment in which taken-for-granted flows of everyday life in each context are disturbed by cries of distress that call specific subjects to account for themselves. The accusatorial bell tolls to initiate a confessional technology of self-accounting that is quite different from everyday political technologies through which self-identities are negotiated. Accusation signals the opening of procedures to identify and/or judge the alleged otherness of the accused. These identifications and judgments are political assertions of limit formation, forging boundaries by calling subjects to account and defining their identities as inside or outside, same or other, included or excluded. Accusation's etymology permits one to grapple with traces of a heritage that demarcates inclusion through discourses of the excluded. The common is not other, not strange, and not the enemy – the negations fortify a unity through neg(oti)ations from within.

Scholastic thinking: against Aquinas on accusation and the common good

Article 1. Whether people are bound to accuse, as distinct from judging, for the 'common good'?

Objection 1. 'Accusation is ordered for the common good which it aims at procuring by means of knowledge of the crime. Now no man ought to injure a person unjustly in order to promote the common good' (Question #68, Article 3, Response). Considering this, two issues arise. First, 'a man ought not to proceed to accuse except of what he is quite certain about, wherein ignorance of fact has no place' (Question #68, Article 3, Response). Second, 'in the case of a crime that conduces to the injury of the Commonwealth, a man is bound to accusation, provided he can offer sufficient proof, since it is the accuser's duty to prove' (Question #68, Article 1, Response). These considerations apply to all accusations, even when accusations are levelled against 'superiors'. Overall, then, accusation initiates a series of events designed to punish those who defy the common good; therefore, members of a common good are bound to accuse in appropriate circumstances.

Objection 2. 'When the process in a criminal case goes by way of accusation, the accuser is in the position of a party, so that the judge stands between accuser and accused for the purposes of the trial of justice' (Question #68, Article 2, Response). It is necessary to make an accusation in writing because 'words are so various that it is difficult to remember each one . . . a slight difference of words changes the sense . . . the certainty of judgment requires that the accusation be drawn up in writing' (Question #68, Reply to Objection 1, Article 2). The accuser is distinct from the judge, for 'a man cannot be accuser, witness and judge at the same time' (Question #67, Article 3, Reply to Objection 3). Therefore, the accuser makes accusations to another subject, who will rely on words to make judgments on the status of accusation. These judgments are impartial; they are also made on the strength of formal accusations in the interests of the common good.

Objection 3. 'He who accuses wrongfully sins both against the person of the accused and against the Commonwealth' (Question #68, Article 4, Reply to Objection 2). When accusers fail to prove indictments, they must face serious consequences: 'Consequently it is just that he who by accusing a man has put him in danger of being punished severely, should himself suffer like punishment' (Question #68, Article 4, Response). Since accusation is necessary for the common good, no false accusation or calumny can be tolerated. The common good is to be enunciated and protected through accusation. Therefore, people are bound to truth in their accusations if they are to protect the common good.

On the contrary, accusations in the name of crime often fragment a given image of the common good by delimiting identities of inclusion from those to be excluded. This accusatorial fragmentation of erstwhile common goods might sometimes produce yet another common good, but accusation is never the slave of one overarching common good. Moreover, historical contexts decide and no amount of writing, or formality, can secure certainty of judgment. Also, especially in contexts characterized by an 'ambient uncertainty', where universal absolutes are doubted, the distinction between truthful and false accusations emerges more overtly as a political battle than an impartial epistemological discussion (Bauman, 1997).

Response. Accusation is the initiating instrument in processes of social exclusion. It can take many forms, including accusations of heresy, crime, deceit, etc. Accusation is designed to arrest the flows of everyday experience and to negotiate passages between the included (as deemed by local power–knowledge formations) and excluded. The process is not so much a defence of the common good; it is the very means of creating, erecting, sustaining and entrenching an image of what is 'common', shared; it is also a way of enunciating what is taken to be good in context. Accusation is, therefore, an act of creation rather than a passive response to clear-cut, universally understood transgressions. It is the means of creating new identities; in so doing – whether accusations lead to exclusion or not – accusation defines and fortifies given images of a common unity (community?). It is an attempt to gather limits, to close off a realm of the common by designating threats, enemies within. It is coupled with institutions through which accused subjects are identified, judged or somehow marked as other, as outside, as excluded.

Reply to Objection 1. The common good does not order anything. The common good is partly created through accusatorial processes that set up limits around domains of the included, of the common, and isolate the constructed enemy, the stranger. The onus is then on both accuser and accused to account for given events to persuade appointed representatives of the common good. If the accuser succeeds, instruments of extradition are assembled to judge, name and formulate consequences. Accusation, that is, propels events that usually culminate in judgments designating local borders of what is deemed common and distinguishing this from what lies outside. Accusation is concerned with creating outsiders from within, thereby fashioning both what is included, and what is not.

It involves a creative sequence of events, characterized by proactive bids – it is not a reactive response to a static ontological scene. In its quest to name parameters of absence, taxonomies of exclusion, accusation is implicated in formulating a common good. It operates as a spy, an advance intelligence-gathering process, mobilized in support of specific formulations of a common grouping. At the same time, it creates discourses of exclusion in the name of specific 'common' unities.

Accusation is never an impartial voyeur; it is always involved in local negotiations of what is deemed 'common' by locally active political agents and groups. In contexts where there are multiple claims to what is common, where multiple political agents permit political diversity to be championed over universal claims to what is common, then accusatorial processes abound. If definitions of a specific common good are shaped by accusation, then practices of accusation can be expected to multiply in direct proportion to the number of images that successfully allege unity of interest, commonness, etc. Being bound to a given definition of a common good might well encourage the included to accuse, to preserve the integrity of existing images of commonality. But this posture is difficult to sustain where multiple conceptions of commonality collide without an overarching sense of what is common to all people.

Therefore, one is not bound to accuse in service of one common good, as Aquinas might allege; rather, one is bound to accuse if one wishes to create, sustain, preserve and continue the appearance of a common good. The order is not decreed by some inherent common good, but is delimited by specific power–knowledge regimes in the interests of unifying subjects for a purpose.

Reply to Objection 2. The separation of accuser and judge might be procedurally important in bids to enunciate and preserve a common good. As such, accusation and judgment are complementary processes. For its part, accusation is a beginning, an assembling of events into a framework ordered by its focus on inclusion/exclusion. Regardless of whether the story is written, spoken, or related through media, what counts is its persuasive force. The medium is not a neutral means of communicating a persuasive message. To paraphrase McLuhan's phrase: 'the medium is the message'. That is, the successful accusation is not simply an accurate representation of events (re-presentation through another medium); rather, language violently creates events, and the medium is very much part of the potentially persuasive force of any attempt to render events present. The beauty of the medium, the poetry of the narration, is relevant to the potential success of socially enunciated accusations. Therefore, it is not necessary to make accusations in writing – so long as they persuade in context, the force of accusatorial decree remains intact.

Reply to Objection 3. Under postmodern conditions, semblances of the common are fragmented into many relative, uncertain domains of inclusion and exclusion; there are diverse 'common' domains (communities) and various senses of the good (see Bauman, 1997). In this light, except for rare cases, the idea of false accusation is rendered problematic. False accusations are not inherently decidable; rather they stand as undecided textual dialogues, contested images negotiated between the diverse and fragmenting regimes of truth. On the terrain of false accusation lies a battle that always waits to be named, a battle that in outline involves the politics of deciding what is common, what is friendly, and separates an amorphous inside from what is a threat, excluded, other, etc. Calumny is ultimately a struggle within regimes of truth; that is, a strategic bid in epistemological warfare involving self-identities in a politics of truth that helps to define the friend and to mark it off from the foe. Falseness implies a truth, and different regimes of truth will dictate different regimes of falseness. Therefore, false accusers sin not so much against an inherently stable commonwealth, but rather against the precepts of given truths enunciated in the services of, and in the creation of, a given truth system.

The accused's skin as exemplum: excreting Sisamnes

Traces of an old myth about the importance of the impartial administration of justice, frequently ascribed to Herodotus and retold by several others (e.g., Valerius Maximus), remain in the archives of our present. The details of their retelling vary but the bald plot goes something like this. Cambyses, the king of Persia, discovers the existence of a corrupt judge by the name of Sisamnes.[1] Witnesses accuse Sisamnes of taking a bribe for a judgment. Upon discovery, and in response to the accusation, Cambyses acts with uncharacteristic severity by ordering that the judge be flayed. His skin is to be placed on the future seat of judgment for the new judge; and Sisamnes' son, Otanes, is to occupy his father's seat. Otanes must sit in judgment, being reminded tangibly of his father's transgressions by the flayed skin.

Elements of both Herodotus' and Valerius Maximus' accounts are recounted in two panels painted by a Flemish artist, Gerard David (one panel is dated 1498). David painted the panels for the alderman's chamber in the town hall of Bruges, and as one commentator notes, they were designed to add formal ornamentation to the chamber but also incarnated a medieval rhetorical device known as an exemplum (see van der Velden, 1995). In brief, the device served the purpose of recalling an event or personage in history to prove a given argument. The specificity of the exemplum provided a way of backing up a given narrative, symbol, image, claim, etc. In the context of David's paintings, entitled *The Judgment of Cambyses*, a literary exemplum was centred on the impartiality of justice and a didactic exemplar designed to show the spectacular responses to corrupt magistrates for those attending the alderman's hall in the town of Bruges. The splendour of the paintings adds to the dignity of the setting, and reinforces the solemn importance of administering justice impartially.

For present purposes, however, the panels also give some insight into the importance of accusation for the justice of that time. Turning first to the left panel, the painting provides a temporal narrative of events, beginning at the top left of the painting and moving down (forward) to the present. To the rear left of the painting, beneath the covered doorway, David captures the event of Sisamnes taking a bribe in return for a favourable judgment to an accused subject. To the left, two small characters witness the events, huddled perhaps in dismay at the flagrant corruption of Sisamnes. The leaping dog signals a disquiet of the otherwise ordinary setting, and anticipates a disruption of the everyday, ordinary flow of medieval social life. Moving down the picture, and forward through time, one sees the symbols of the accusation in the raised swords that have been alerted to, and are now responding to, the accusation. Sisamnes in the centre of the picture is called to account, in the presence of his accusers, and must face the judgment of Cambyses.

The moment of Sisamnes' accusation has, over centuries, become the subject of many works of art (see van der Velden, 1995). One painted in 1619 by Jan Tengnagel is particularly striking, indicating the sheer violence and anger pervading the setting.[2] The courtiers frame the moment of Cambyses' accusation and then judgment, adding their public weight to the accusation. One character consults a text; Sisamnes' law books lie scattered in a dishevelled pile beside him, suggesting an intrusion that has disrupted the ordinary flow of his life. His head is downcast, with his hand gesturing shame and humility as he accounts for himself in response to Cambyses' fury and aggressive judgmental stance. This speaks to the way accusation disrupts contextual flows of sociality, requires accusers to enunciate their accusations publicly, and demands that the accused provide some account for the events at hand. Both accuser and accused must appeal to discourses that are available to those present, who constitute themselves in context as the border patrols that decide on where lines between insider and outcast must be drawn. It is they who must be persuaded, and this requires appeals to discourses of the included – appeals to discourses outside of that are likely to provoke hostility.

The right panel of David's painting shows just how severe the consequences of Cambyses' accusation and judgment are for Sisamnes, who endures the pain of his skin being flayed. In the foreground of the painting, signifying the immediate present, the flayers do their awful work, knives in action or held between the teeth as they prise open the skin. Reversing the temporal construction of the left panel, as one moves up the right panel the narration speaks to future events, ending with Otanes taking his seat at the chair of justice, cloaked by his father's flayed skin.

The rhetorical *exemplum* of both paintings centres on the impartial administration of justice, and makes clear the disadvantages of tending toward a corrupt judicial life. However, there are further, even allegorical, elements regarding accusation to be recovered from both the story and the paintings. Let us turn briefly to three of these.

First, there is the precipitating gesture of accusation in which the witnesses cast aspersions, arrest the everyday and familiar social being, to allege publicly that a given subject has committed something that must be met with an accusation. The accuser(s) alleges his/her inclusion within a given formation by declaring the presence of something (an act), or someone (a subject), that must be called to account, and who may subsequently be absented from the order. The accuser assumes a unique position as active subject who takes a stand in favour of initiating processes of exclusion for the accused. For whatever reasons, and emotion (revenge, anger, jealousy, moral indignation, etc.) is often central here, accusers do the precipitating work of arresting everyday social flows, and prepare the way for the possibility of the accused being re-identified as an outsider, stranger, criminal, etc.

David's painting (left panel) captures the emotions of the accusers in some detail. He represents the solemn, the angered, the morally righteous, the sympathetic, the king's regal certitude – all help to define Sisamnes as a judge who has crossed limits that require his expulsion. The public gathering hears the accusation (for accusers cannot initiate a grand process in private), and the accusation is made in the presence of witnesses. Accusations must be heard, must be witnessed, and so demand a confessional response from the accused. Those who bear witness to and entertain an enthusiasm for the limits are both created and reinforced through the public accusation. The fear in accused Sisamnes' eyes suggests a life disturbed, reflecting the extent to which the accuser interrupts the habitual iterations of actions that enable an accused to function as someone who possesses an insider identity. The process of accusation demands that accused subjects forgo familiar, everyday conceptions and techniques of self-creation, and reflect on themselves using different accounts of self that address specific accusatorial demands.

Second, the accusation proceeds by expulsion, by reflection on an act, and the experience of alleging the presence of an absence. The accusation does more than allege, it names the absence, names the otherness against which it takes a stand. The discursive horizons of that stand are framed from within present horizons of inclusion, usually around moral, normative, legal, religious, scientific precepts, or a combination of these. Accusations made in the name of crime, however, typically include reference to some or other legal precept.

In addition, David's panels suggest an interesting allegory through which to understand accusation as an initiating moment in the exposure and expulsion of the accused from domains of a 'common' life. There is perhaps much to be made of his selection of this story that centres on the flayed skin as both a spectacular punishment, and symbol for deterrence. Why the skin? The skin constitutes its own form of limit, a limiting case that contains an interior from that which is exterior. Like other limits, it is porous, blurred, changeable, and subject to rupture; nevertheless, so long as it remains relatively intact, it serves to contain, to separate – imperfect though this might be – the inside from the out. Expelling Sisamnes' insides from his skin through flaying, and the pain this exacts, allegorically reflect moments of exposure; after being called to account, the successfully accused is exposed as a stranger in the heart of a collective. His skin-deep affiliation with what is created as 'common' is recovered; the entrails are extracted and destroyed as other. But the skin, which provided the judge's public representation of the just order, is preserved and displayed on Otanes' seat of judgment. There are multiple symbols at play, including the allegorical presence of what remains when an accused is expelled from the midst; even then the other is reclaimed, represented and mobilized in the service of continually creating/preserving given images of an order.

Accusing Socrates: the other identity

> How you have felt, O men of Athens, at hearing the speeches of my accusers, I cannot tell; but I know that their persuasive words almost made me forget who I was – Such was the effect of them; and yet they have hardly spoken a word of truth.

Encountering these, Socrates' opening words of Plato's *Apology*, from a different meaning horizon, signals key aspects of how accused subjects experience accusation. Chapter 3 details Socrates' trial, but for now let us focus on the opening line of Plato's account. It starts with a glimpse of the supreme court of Athens, comprising around 501 jurors appointed by lot. In Socrates' case, the representative of three accusers, Meletus (in the prologue of *Euthyphro*, Socrates describes him as 'a hook-nosed man with long hair, and a scanty beard') reads an indictment charging Socrates with impiety and corrupting the minds of youth. The *Apology* opens with Socrates' account of, and defence against, the charges; as part of this, he subjects his accusers to cross-examination. According to processes of the time, the jurors then decide on guilt in relation to an accusation after the accused has spoken. If the accused is found guilty, a penalty is proposed. The accused is then given a chance to propose an alternative punishment. In its second judgment, the court either accepts or rejects this appeal, and the last word is then given to the accused (see Guardini, 1962). In the opening words, we encounter the first of the three speeches Socrates makes to the court. There is a density to the irony of the opening lines, and from them we can exact several features of the accused's experience.

How you have felt, O men of Athens . . . The opening appeal betrays the 'calling to account', whereupon the accused is required to defend him/herself against publicly enunciated accusations in an equally public forum. The public address is directed to the 'men' of Athens, the (patriarchal) powers that be and who imagine themselves to constitute a common unity, defenders of the common good. The public exhortations are made before a 'public' that has political clout; they are not made before, say, the beggars outside the city walls. Socrates directs a defence against his accusers to the jurors, and they must judge the merits of the accusation. The stakes are high; a guilty verdict will impart upon Socrates consequential exclusions, including exile or death. He must address himself directly to an imagined order, and using the language of the allegedly common unity, to defend publicly the charge that he has somehow betrayed that order. He responds to the call to account for his past actions in a language that is understandable to his accusers. He does not speak in the language of the other, in the language of, say, unreason, or even in the impious language of an atheist. His is a discourse that resolutely appeals to the law of what should be common, even if he thinks that his accusers have betrayed the order by their trumped-up charges.

That Socrates should open with an allusion to *how you have felt* is revealing. The process is ultimately about feeling, emotion; this contrasts with usual images of justice as involving impartial, unemotional processes. Plato's account expressly acknowledges the feelings surrounding the accusatorial process. We might even say that Socrates engages his enemies, using the language of a friend who acknowledges their capacity to feel, and their ability to understand. Moreover, he appeals as though the accusers and judges were sympathetic to him, as though his accounting for himself would fall on ears that wanted to hear, learn and understand. The 'as though' is an important part of the accuser being called to account, for those who accuse require the accused to speak in a 'common' language on the assumption that 'hearing' the speeches of the accusatorial process might sway people in his/her favour.

Yet from the very outset, Socrates is aware of the distance between himself and those who have listened to his accusers; he dolefully indicates that he 'cannot tell' how they felt and later in the text recognizes that he stands outside the flow of much common discourse. As he listens to the accusations made against him, he follows the logic, gets caught up in the discursive currents of their persuasive power, drifts along in accusatorial seas that open participants up to creations of otherness and thus negotiate limits around what is seen as common in context.

Then comes a revealing admission: such is the power of the accusations that Socrates freely admits, *their persuasive words almost made me forget who I was.* What are we to make of this? To begin with, there is the question of persuasive words. The accusers have offered a persuasive defence of their indictments, which are centred on bringing to public attention the identity of an alleged impostor, a stranger within. The identity that is brought before the public trial is that of an impious man, an atheist, a clever manipulator, who is intent on destroying the common traditions of Athenian society, and corrupting the youth by enticing them to think in new ways. At stake here, so the accusers' reasoning goes, is the integrity of Athens, and its ability to survive intact into future generations. The public construction of this identity is established by 'persuasive words'.

From Plato's words, we see how accusers are required to draw on existing cultural resources, construct convincing interpretations of events, draw on plausible rhetorical devices of the day, persuade others, etc., if they are to make their accusations stick. The possibility of a successful social enunciation is precisely what accusers must engage if they are to succeed in their bids to accuse. Hence, as Socrates notes, he is obliged – before he responds to his three present accusers – to confront the spirit of a far older group of accusers who have already laid the groundwork by casting his long-established reputation as sage, or philosopher against the sophists, in dubious shadows of impious behaviour. This provides a pervasive cultural and discursive resource for his current accusers to tap into when making their accusations. But the point is this: accusers must make their claims within linguistic horizons that allow interpretations to be persuasively cast over events, thus licensing the accusations.

However, Socrates denies that the identity created by his accusers can appropriately be attributed to him. No doubt, the dramatic enthusiasm generated by the public occasion surrounding the accusation is difficult to evade, even for the accused. He almost forgets who he 'was', momentarily displaces the 'I' who he has over many years developed as a kind of self. Socrates' interpretation of self is at odds with the interpretations offered by his accusers, even if the clash is not absolute, or clear-cut. Socrates, too, recognizes the persuasiveness of their words. Stated differently, one might say that his sense of self is assembled through different interpretative lenses from those of his accusers. For them, he is a stranger (even enemy) in their midst, hell-bent on destroying the traditional unity; Socrates, by contrast, works on himself to forge a self who leads the humble, even poverty-stricken, life of a philosopher in perpetual search of one thing – the truth, at whatever cost. The details of the differences and attempts to create Socrates' true identity in this context are recoverable from the text, but all speak to a fundamental clash in the accusatorial process: the attempt to construct, versus the attempt to refute, the accused's identity as 'other' and so worthy of exclusion.

Here one glimpses the plight of the accused whose identity is publicly constructed as a foreign type, of another sort, whose continued presence in 'common' limits poses a threat to the integrity of a perceived order. The accusations are paraded before representatives of this imagined order, using the language, rhetoric, persuasive techniques, advocacy, processes, norms, etc., that are meaningful – understandable – from within that order. It also involves tapping into the regimes of traditions, knowledge and myths that are the order. The accused must hear the nuances of the accusations, and mount a defence against them by responding with an alternative account of him/herself.

This account, however, is directed publicly to the representatives of the imagined order, not the accusers. To make an impact, it must appeal to discursive devices sanctioned by that order. Those accused of being other cannot appeal to their alleged identity of otherness to make a case for inclusion (except in limited cases of insanity, which typically lead to exclusion anyway). If the accused accepts the identity of otherness, and responds through the language, norms, etc., of that identity, s/he thereby confirms the accusation. All that one can do, if the accused is to avoid being excluded, is to formulate a convincing refusal, using the language of the imagined order on whose behalf an accusation is made, of the identity proffered by an accuser.

This is a foundation of accusation, and one that Socrates does not embrace. He clings onto his 'othered' identity as philosopher and puts forward a spirited defence of this before the assembled jurors. He uses a language that is partially understandable to them, by focusing on the language of truth. But his conception of truth, as noted in his indictment, further confirms the point made by his accusers. In the end, despite the tragic consequences, his speech successfully persuades 220 of the 500 jurors. His fate, initiated by the accusatorial process against him, then ultimately hangs in the balance of 30 men's votes; and it is to them that history owes the image of Socrates drinking the last of his life from a cup of hemlock.

Despite the outcome, we would do well to recall that accusations are always negotiated rather than enforced. And even when they are judged and decided, the accused self might – as does Socrates – choose the possibility of serious violence, even death, over subjugation to an identification prescribed and decided upon by accusers and judges. Furthermore, the accused, in being called to account, is forced to arrest the ordinary sort of work that s/he does on her/himself in constructing self-identities. The very act of public accusation invites an unusual form of public confession, in the presence of witnesses, and this entices work and conceptions of self that are not ordinarily part of everyday iterations. It is perhaps appropriate to address precise 'ethical' work at hand at the moment of accusation, and I leave this discussion recognizing that such are the demands for further analysis on accusation. I have noted a refusal in Socrates' words, a defiance that does not so much evade the accusations made against him, as involve a realization that selves are always the product of ethical work done by selves on selves in given social contexts. He realizes that at the conjuncture of his life as he faces his accusers, a unique form of selfhood is required of him. Many words have addressed the limitations of the defence enunciated in Plato's *Apology*, but few ponder Socrates' attempt to distil a noble self in the face of extraordinary pressures for him to accept the enunciations of his accusers. He does this by contesting the discourse (the legacy) that his current accusers draw upon, showing the absurdity of his accusers' contradictory assertions, and then – perhaps most especially – resigns his fate to drinking the hemlock to remain true to the philosophical identity that he has habitually cultivated in the course of his life. The brave defiance of that gesture, which is captured in a painting by Jacques Louis David,[3] inspires an important critique that refuses to be governed through forms of accusation. That heroic refusal still has currency among the growing spaces of accusation that assemble communities nowadays.

Notes

1 Gerard David, *The Judgment of Cambyses* (left and right panels). Bruges, Groeningemuseum.
2 Jan Tengnagel, *The Judgment of Cambyses*, 1619. The Hague, private collection.
3 Jacques Louis David, *The Death of Socrates*, 1787. Metropolitan Museum of Art, New York.

References

Ayto, J. (1990). *Dictionary of Word Origin*. London: Bloomsbury.
Bauman, Z. (1997). *Postmodernity and its Discontents*. New York: New York University Press.
Christie, N. (1994). *Crime Control as Industry: Towards Gulags, Western Style*. London: Routledge.
Guardini, R. (1962). *The Death of Socrates*. New York: Meridian Books.
Klein, D. (1966). *A Comprehensive Etymological Dictionary of the English Language*. Amsterdam: Elsevier.
Negrier-Dormont, L. (1994). Criminology: foundations and efficacy. *International Criminal Police Review*, 450, 10–15.

O'Connor, D. (1984). The transition from inquisition to accusation. *Criminal Law Journal*, 8, 351–72.

Partridge, E. (1958). *Origins: A Short Etymological Dictionary of Modern English.* London: Routledge and Kegan Paul.

Plato. (1948). *Euthyphro, Apology, and Crito and the Death Scene from Phaedo.* F. J. Church, & R. D. Cumming (eds). New York: The Liberal Arts Press.

Pollock, F., & Maitland, F. (1898). *The History of English Law before the Time of Edward I.* Cambridge: Cambridge University Press.

Thomas Aquinas, St. (1981). *Summa Theologica.* Westminster: Christian Classics.

van der Velden, H. (1995). Cambyses for example: the origins and function of an *exemplum iustitiae* in Netherlandish art of the fifteenth, sixteenth and seventeenth centuries. *Simiolus*, 23, 5–39.

Chapter 2

Apparatuses of criminal accusation

Introduction

The previous chapter refers to the co-appearance of accusers, the accused and the common good through rituals of criminal accusation. Working through this idea, the following chapter focuses on fluid political ideas that have, over centuries, shaped changing modes of criminal accusation, and given rise to varied entrances to criminalizing processes. The start of these processes involved calling someone to account – or laying one's charge formally – through power–knowledge relations centred on changing notions of crime. Such relations recursively positioned accusation as an unseen, though privileged, gateway to criminal justice arenas (Negrier-Dormont, 1994). I propose in this chapter to work with Foucault's (1980) concept of an apparatus (*dispositif*) to signal the ideas and relational arrangements that enabled historically what it is to accuse another of a criminal wrong. These apparatuses are meant to signal relations between 'heterogeneous' elements consisting of 'discourses, institutions, architectural forms, regulatory decisions, laws, administrative measures, scientific statements, philosophical, moral, and philanthropic propositions – in short, the said as much as the unsaid' (1980: 194). My basic claim is that as gatekeepers to crime-control networks, apparatuses of criminal accusation historically consolidate relations between elements to initiate (potentially at least) criminalization processes (Ericson & Baranek, 1982). There are often several authorized accusatory apparatuses in specific contexts; but their cumulative action regulates the flows of subjects into crime-control systems (Hamilton, 2009; Naffine, 2009; Dayan, 2013), and directly affects the profile of these populations (Brown, 2009; Wacquant, 2009; Simon & Sparks, 2013).

Referring particularly to Western (especially English) archival reverberations, my aim here is to sketch broad lines of descent behind accusatorial apparatuses that now control entryways to vast criminal justice arenas. To say that the chapter provides a detailed historical analysis of specific institutions (as per Thompson, 1975; Herrup, 1987; King, 2003; Hay, 2011) would mistake its more limited attempt to name fluid, but influential, apparatuses of criminal accusation. It will locate three paradigmatic rationales of governance within which accusations of crime variously surfaced: (i) in the name of a sovereign, (ii) against images of abnormal criminality, or (iii) as ways to manage insecure populations. Its reference here is clearly to another aspect of Foucault's work. Specifically, it references political truths within three exemplary paradigms: *sovereignty*, *discipline* and *biopolitics*. However, transposed to contexts of criminal accusation, as elsewhere, these paradigms do not follow chronologically. Instead, they appear as hybrid historical apparatuses that in concert have driven such consequential tendencies as: massively expanded criminal justice systems; disproportionate and unequal class, race and gender profiles of penal populations; and a punitive culture that – as a reflex – responds to crime in exclusionary ways (Garland, 2002). Complex regulatory gateways, arising from such interacting rationalities of criminal accusation have, that is, surfaced through decisions that regulate the corresponding size, forms and profile of criminal justice systems in historical context.

The limited aim of what follows then is to conceptualize relations in the manner of an admittedly well-trodden and already noted 'history of the present', but directed toward criminal accusation. The intent here is to

> detect those things which have not yet been talked about, those things that, at the present time, introduce, show, give some more or less vague indications of the fragility of our system of thought, in our way of reflecting, in our practices.
>
> (Foucault, 2007: 137)

Even if gesturing toward the fragility of accusatorial apparatuses that feed dominant forms of criminal justice is demanding, O'Malley points out the importance of so doing (2010: Chapter 4). After all, the deployment of governmental forms is always unstable, yielding both dangers and opportunities. Naming contingent political rationalities behind concepts that commonly appear as fixed realities (e.g., 'crime') is an important step to accentuating their 'fragility'. Equally, locating the political exigency of current apparatuses of accusation highlights their pivotal role as entry points to criminal justice arenas (see Chapters 3 and 11).

Sovereign apparatuses of accusation

With echoes of ancient Greek and Roman justice forms (see Chapters 3 and 4), early medieval apparatuses of accusation depended largely on private accusers to call other subjects to account for criminal wrongdoing (Grossi, 2010). Associated rituals typically involved accusers avowing to an appointed authority that another had committed a crime (Goebel, 1976). Such measures placed limits on blood feuds and echoed Roman law (see Chapter 4) where elements of a sovereignly organized mode of accusation emerged:

> When the accuser made a formal accusation before the proper *quaesitor* (the chairman of the individual court) and the *quaesitor* accepted it, the latter enrolled the name of the accused in the register of those scheduled to face criminal trial. The accuser had to swear that he was not making his accusation out of malice (*iuramentum calumniae*).
>
> (Peters, 1989: 14)

From such Roman incarnations, sovereignly sanctioned processes formally recognized the identities of accused and accuser through legal processes administered by delegated officials. While the gatekeeping roles of the latter became more prominent over the course of the second and third centuries ACE (see Peters, 1989: 16), the accuser continued to play a pivotal role in calling someone to account for many centuries (Whitman, 2008: 97ff.; Grossi, 2010; Goebel, 1976). Indeed, as Whitman points out, even in the early middle ages, 'Normal criminal procedure . . . hinged on the appearance of an accuser, who brought the charge, offered to prove it, and took the consequence for failure to do so' (2008: 74).

That accuser's position was transformed by the growth of monarchic administrations and changing criminal justice agencies (Gorski, 2009). In England, for example, Stephen (1883: 244) describes the emergence of, 'three modes of trial in criminal cases, namely, trial by ordeal, trial by battle, and trial by jury'. Alongside these, he saw the development of 'three modes of accusation, namely, appeal or accusation by a private person, indictment or accusation by a grand jury, and informations which are accusations either by the Attorney-General or by the Master of the Crown Office' (Stephen, 1883: 244).

Private accusations mostly served orally-based, local forms of government where groups were required to account for one another — tithings, compurgation, raising the hue and the cry, the use of *posse comunatis* and so on (Hitchcock & Shoemaker, 2006). Framed as a moral contest between good and evil, criminal indictments required the accused to undergo tests (ordeal, battle) as deific indications of guilt or innocence; but an onus was placed on accusers and witnesses to prove claims — they faced severe fines and even mortal consequences if accusations were rejected (Stephen, 1883: 245). In view of such risks to life and limb, it is not surprising that few subjects were willing to initiate accusations. Indeed, as Whitman argues, 'In general, trustworthy oral declarations – whether accusations, witness testimony, confession or oaths – were hard to come by . . . Bringing an accusation was potentially a foolhardy undertaking' (2008: 74). Yet, without a precipitating accuser, the juridical apparatus of battles and ordeals faced a potential crisis, as did the order that sanctioned, and arranged, them (op. cit.). Perceptions of a looming crisis in such justice propelled a reliance on the other techniques by which to identify potentially criminal offenders.

Pope Innocent III, for example, responded to the crisis by authorizing a new way to arraign wrongdoing: the inquisition (Whitman, 2008: 132). Echoing Roman *quaestiones* that investigated criminal matters of public interest, the inquisitions ratified representatives of church authority – the inquirers – to initiate and conduct their own investigations (see Harries, 2007: 16ff.; Peters, 1989). Throughout the twelfth and thirteenth centuries, criminal accusation also formed part of an expanding jurisdiction of English royal courts in attempts to secure the king's peace (Shoemaker, 1991: 19). An emerging political logic empowered judges to proceed, '*ex officio* either of his own mere motion, or on the suggestion of a promoter (*inquisitio cum promovente*); he collects testimony against the suspect, testimony which the suspect does not hear; it is put in writing' (Pollock & Maitland, 2010: 357). Sworn 'communal accusations' were made in the name of a sovereign by sanctioned representatives who subordinated private accusers to the emerging accusatorial apparatus (Whitman, 2008). The novelty of this process attracted some criticism; as Pollock and Maitland suggest, 'A new accusatory process was being tried, and for a while men were not certain that it was as just or as cogent as the appeal in which the accuser risked his body' (2010: 276).

In the event, however, testing accusations through ordeals gradually disappeared, or was reserved for cases without a formal accuser, witnesses, confessions or person of high status to allege the commission of a wrong (Whitman, 2008). The emerging sovereignty-based apparatuses of accusation retained attachments to moral ideas of religious good and satanic forces of evil, but now required accusers or witnesses to provide information (depositions) to locally delegated authorities (reeves, sheriffs, justices of the peace). If charges were drawn up, they were decided by people comprising grand juries rather than God-inspired ordeals (Gorski, 2009; Stephen, 1883: 244). In other words, this shift introduced an emphasis on accusations framed around written documents and a growing reliance on local representatives to administer justice (Gorski, 2009; Landau & Beattie, 2002). Since relatively elite social strata tended to occupy these positions, the rising apparatuses of accusation entrenched social hierarchies and permitted its agents the discretion to decide on the truth of accusations (King, 2003: 66ff.), to benefit from some accusations (op. cit., 235), and in some cases to escape accusations (196ff., 210).

The resulting apparatuses of accusation were frequently tied to the haphazard exercise of a hierarchically ordered sovereign power that Foucault (1979) famously describes. Its awe-inspiring juridical potency and spectacular penalties sought to etch the sovereign's overwhelming power onto public minds. Here, criminal accusation opened selected subjects to face the calculated brutality of this power and its public punishments. The latter were supposed to deter by spectacularly demonstrating the sovereign's vengeful might unleashed on those who dared to break the peace (see Gatrell, 1994). In such political contexts, new political technologies of accusation replaced the likes of compurgation and ordeal by establishing the 'truth' of accusations through written depositions (Reeves, 1869: 34), witness testimony, the authorized judgments of delegated officials, grand juries, etc., all working 'by the King's authority' (Whitman, 2008: 132). Much has been written on the significant growth and increasing administrative centralization of sovereign-law models of criminal law over seventeenth-century England (for an overview see Oberwittler (1990)). However, as sovereign philosophies of rule framed themselves around moral orders with the king as the injured party of crimes (Tuck, 1993), so accusatorial apparatuses were increasingly organized around the delegated powers of constables, justices of the peace (magistrates) and grand juries, all placed in the service of vengeance-based legal force (Girard, 2005: 70; King, 2003: 18ff.; Landau, 1984).

Each of these gateways afforded considerable discretion. King's (2003: 1–14) analysis of English eighteenth-century property crimes, for instance, shows how pre-trial arenas offered the accused several potential ways of escaping trial: informal mediations, support from witnesses and constables (2003: 62), summary hearings before justices of the peace, and, if charges were compiled, grand jury hearings. Equally, however, an initial reliance on such gateways suggests the extent to which criminal accusation depended on local communal input:

> The initial response to alleged crimes in early modern England combined communal and official participation. Since by the seventeenth century private complaints in criminal matters (appeals) had been virtually replaced by public accusations (indictments), public officials should have been in charge of investigations. However, while some part of detection was played by constables, observing, investigating and accusing suspects seemed to have remained as much a private concern as a governmental duty.
>
> (Herrup, 1987: 68).

In other words, at this stage in the development of sovereignty paradigms, apparatuses of accusation required collaboration: neither 'private individuals' nor 'public officials completely controlled the legal process' (Herrup, 1987: 92). However, the combined effect of both cleared the way to more centralized forms of state control over accusatorial processes. But the emerging system was far from transparent and, as King (2003: 1–2) points out, accused subjects mostly

> found themselves propelled on an often bewildering journey along a route which can best be compared to a corridor of connected rooms or stage sets. From each room one door led on towards eventual criminalization, conviction and punishment, but every room also had other exits. Each had doors indicating legally acceptable ways in which the accused could get away from the arms of the law, while some rooms also have legal candles through which the accused might sometimes be smuggled to safety. Each room was also populated by a different and socially diverse group of men and woman, whose assumptions, actions, and interactions, both with each other and with the accused determined whether or not he was shown an exit or thrust on at the corridor.

The accusatorial arenas of early modern justice in England, by contrast, often aspired to more formalized justice processes, but witnesses, accusers and accused parties still played a key role in instigating accusations. However, justices of the peace or local constables became increasingly important to regulated accusations via 'amateur and communal' (Herrup, 1987: 68) offices that displaced verbal techniques (like the hue and cry) and required written charges: 'A written warrant sworn before a justice of the peace and issued to a constable was replacing the traditional verbal alarm' (Herrup, 1987: 70).

This prominence of written records no doubt recalled elements of Roman law (Stein, 2005), but it also encouraged new forms of 'documentality' (see Ferraris & Davies, 2013) around sovereignty-based criminal accusations; e.g., depositions, witness statements, drafted testimony, accounts of procedures, hearing minutes, justices of the peace record books, charges, writs, case records, verdicts and so on (Herrup, 1987). These newly forming apparatuses enabled, for example, indictments to be heard before grand juries where final decisions were made on whether the accused's docket constituted a 'true bill' requiring a trial, or whether it was false – an *ignoramus* – requiring that no further action be taken (Herrup, 1987: 93; King, 2003). Juries of the day often included accusers and witnesses, suggesting a continued appreciation that judges should have intimate knowledge of suspects and criminal events (Whitman, 2008: 133). If such developments introduced formal elements to procedures of criminal accusation, they also enabled a form of sovereignty that administered 'charges' following from initial suspicions and accusations.

This sketch is admittedly and impossibly broad, but let us recall its aim – merely to signal select aspects of emerging apparatuses of criminal accusation that appeared within a wider, sovereignty-focused political paradigm. It is worth reiterating that late medieval and early modern processes of accusation authorized both communal and official agents (e.g., accusers, witnesses, constables, justices of the peace, sheriffs, grand jurors) to expand the king's peace (Langbein, 2003; Foucault, 2000). As legally ratified accusers, these agents served a vengeance-based justice by identifying, in moral terms, those 'criminal' persons who had enabled 'evil' to enter communities and dared to break the king's peace (Gatrell, 1994). Evil of this sort could not be allowed to taint good order, and its purveyors were often sacrificed in the name of the sovereign (Foucault, 2000: 54; Girard, 2005). In this morally charged order, the sovereign – in addition to victims – surfaced as the one who was wronged by crimes, demanding fierce revenge from offenders (Foucault, 1979; Osmond, 1990). Served by religious and moral epistemes asserting a divine right of kings (Andersen *et al.*, 2013), sovereign accusation authorized representatives to open or close gates to the force of royal courts. It also enabled: centrally authorized social hierarchies to administer justice (Hay, 2011); quasi-inquisitional technologies of criminal identification (inquiries, detection, interrogation, torture, justice of the peace or magistrate examinations, witness depositions (King, 2003: 21), etc.); and, new institutions (e.g., grand juries) to replace ordeals and battles to establish 'true' accusations.

Such accusatorial apparatuses formed part of sovereign powers that depended on visibility to ensure deterrence in contexts where direct regulatory intervention was sporadic. Yet this paradigm of power was tested by the limited triumphs of rebels and outlaws who contested the king's authority (see Gorski, 2009) – as indicated by growing numbers of riots that overshadowed the intended symbolism of public executions (Gatrell, 1994). Yet, another political logic had already surfaced in the military contexts, and in measures to ward off plagues. Such power was said to avoid the weaknesses of monarchical sovereignty in urban contexts, especially its tendency to exercise power haphazardly. In response, as Foucault's (1979: 2000) famous analysis argues, the time had come to embrace an immense expansion of disciplinary powers that promised continuous and inconspicuous regulation. The latter would reshape sovereignty politics and associated apparatuses of accusation.

Modern discipline and criminal accusation

Foucault's (2014, 2000) lectures on truth-telling and avowal helpfully show how, over millennia, different juridical forms inspired novel accusatorial apparatuses. For example, alongside the urban concentrations of people, expansive industrial capitalism, and growing state administrations, modern (eighteenth-century) rituals of criminal accusations appeared. They certainly embraced elements of medieval sovereignty's accusatorial forms, but they also incorporated novel adaptations (see also Emsley, 2010; Wiener, 1994). Indeed, for Foucault, the 'content of the laws, the set of penally sanctioned acts, was radically altered' (2000: 52–53). New kinds of knowledge framed emerging notions of crime, criminals and criminality outside of strictly moral precepts. For instance, influential commentators such as Bentham (1890) and Beccaria (1996) partially echoed moral versions of crime as a 'penal infraction' violating the state's laws, but they also argued that it broke an implicit social contract and so threatened the integrity of rational societies. As such, rational, humanistic and enlightenment responses to crime supplemented moral or vengeance-based truths of past approaches. The net effect was to endorse 'a clear and simple definition of crime. A crime is not something related to sin or transgression; it is something that harms society; it is a social injury, a trouble, a disturbance for the whole of society' (Foucault, 2000: 53).

Social defence here called for reason-based trial processes and punishments (e.g., banishment or transportation, labour that forced individuals to act in ways useful to society, and imprisonment in penitentiaries). Victorian criminal justice also focused on corrective penitentiaries to reclaim criminals (Garland, 1991; Ignatieff, 1989), while simultaneously seeking to shape wills before they produced criminal behaviour (Wiener, 1994).

Within this emerging political ethos, new apparatuses of criminal accusation developed beyond sovereign inquisitional discourses. As Foucault (2000: 59) put it:

> [W]e have in contrast to the great knowledge of the inquiry – organized in the middle of the middle ages through the appropriation of the judicial system by the state, consisting in assembling the means to reactualize events through testimony – a new knowledge of a completely different type, a knowledge characterized by supervision and examination, organized around the norm, through the supervisory control of individuals throughout their existence.

Such disciplinary knowledge championed defensive social strategies within and outside sovereign-law, enabling human sciences (e.g., psychiatry, psychology, criminology and sociology) to play a key role in judging and reforming individuals against the norms of a 'disciplinary society' (Foucault, 2000: 69).

As ideas around criminal investigation in defence of society supplanted older forms of sovereign inquiry, so specific accusatorial apparatuses surfaced around new forms of truth-telling to identify 'dangerous' criminal individuals and selves (Foucault, 2014: 210ff.). In the process, emerging apparatuses became party to a wider 'inversion of spectacle into surveillance or of the birth of a society of panopticism' that exercised power continuously and invisibly to protect normal society from its enemies within (Foucault, 2000: 72). In these expansive social control networks, criminal accusation apparatuses occupied various gatekeeping positions. While accusations might still have referred to legal codes, they called subjects to account in ways that evoked disciplinary truths through which criminal individuals not only broke the law but also transgressed basic social norms. The resulting criminal identifications also rested, that is, on normalizing judgements around disciplinary techniques (Gould, 2008; Rafter, 2008). As well, they indicated pastoral confessional technologies of self that required criminals to confess (legally accepted) truths about 'their crimes' (Foucault, 2014: 216). Discouraging criminals from offending was here thought to require 'swift and certain' apprehension, thus endorsing a rising call for systematic police investigation (Hitchcock & Shoemaker, 2006).

In 1829, for example, Robert Peel's idea of a metropolitan police force gained popularity, especially after the apparent successes of the famous Bow Street Runners (Durston, 2012). Even if not universally or immediately accepted, these emerging forms of police relied on distinctive ways to call 'criminals' (especially of the 'habitual' or 'dangerous class' sort) to account; namely, by referring to the truth of disciplinary sciences (e.g., medical jurisprudence, eugenics, medicine, criminology, sociology, psychology and psychiatry) and emerging forensic disciplines (see Chapter 11; Sengoopta, 2003; Cole, 2001; Levasseur, 1995). From the middle of the nineteenth century, scientific identification technologies claimed to represent identity through bodily measurements stored in and retrievable from complex classification systems (see Wiener, 1994). Bertillon's anthropometry was, of course, the paradigm for such identification techniques (Sengoopta, 2003); however, disciplinary accusation also sought to predict which criminal 'types' threatened society (Emsley, 2010; Wiener, 1994). Drawing on emerging disciplines (e.g., physiognomy, medical jurisprudence, phrenology, penology and later anthropology, psychology, criminology, sociology and eugenics), the new forms of accusation claimed to predict likely offenders:

> The entire penal regime of the nineteenth century became a control over not so much what individuals did – was it lawful or unlawful? – as over what they might do, what they were capable of doing, what they were liable to do, what they were immanently about to do.
>
> (Foucault, 2000: 56–7).

Consequently, modern apparatuses of accusation increasingly sought to predict criminality by identifying biological, psychological and/or eugenic 'types' through new forms of knowledge that claimed to identify causes of criminality (Gould, 2008; Rafter, 1997).

So, where criminal *actions* tended to be at the centre of sovereign apparatuses of accusation, disciplinary forms adopted ideas of *character* with particular vigour. In Weiner's (1994: 46) words:

> It was less the actions than the characters of offenders on which attention came to focus . . . crime was essentially seen as the expression of a fundamental character defect stemming from a refusal or inability to deny wayward impulses or to make proper calculations of long-run self-interest.

The aim here was to prevent crime by deciphering observable character templates from known criminals to predict whether specific individuals would commit crimes (Pick, 1989; Rafter, 1997). Hence one finds Galton searching for criminal types through his composite portraits and fingerprints of 'known criminals', just as Lombroso's criminal anthropology claimed to have found a biological basis for declaring 'born criminals' – both examples suggest how predictive modes of accusation came to be enunciated in disciplinary horizons.

These apparatuses of criminal accusation also conceived of social defence beyond criminal law per se, and evoked the value of scientific truths for neutralizing 'criminal' threats (Pratt, 1995; Steadman, 2000). Specifically, these apparatuses of accusations embraced statistical norms to delineate normal from abnormal (criminal) individuals – the latter were then subjected to enhanced (neutralizing) regulation. For example, reading Treilhard's 1808 treatise on criminal procedure, Foucault (2000: 75) detects new prosecutorial roles where the, 'main, primary function must be that of supervising individuals even before the infraction has been committed'. As his interpretation suggests, rather than simply following the reactive precepts of criminal law, the modern prosecutor's role became 'above all, a gaze, an eye constantly trained on the population', and one that coordinated other gazes – the attorney general, police, emperor, etc. Together, the 'great pyramid of gazes constituted the new form of the judicial process' and helped proactively to support surrounding justice systems (Foucault, 2000: 73). In many ways, one might say that elements of sovereign power could persist precisely because of disciplinary orderings that reconciled average individuals with normal social orders, and identified collective threats in advance of any attacks on society (Foucault, 1979). In that ethos, criminal accusation assumed renewed significance via identification techniques undergirded by disciplinary truths. These techniques allowed accusatorial powers to extend their reach beyond law to social networks directed at controlling individuals, thereby aligning sovereign-law with local normalized orders (Golder & Fitzpatrick, 2010).

In combination, developments like this cultivated new judges of normality: disciplinarily credentialed accusers deemed capable of identifying and containing the threats posed by criminal persons. Located throughout modern society, 'expert' accusatorial judges of abnormality examined rather than inquired, and their examinations worked off norms of expected or desired variability. Judges that distinguished between the normal, law-abiding individual and the abnormal criminal individual comprised a regime of normative social ordering that supported sovereign legality – now working together to safeguard newly ordered modern societies (Foucault, 1979). Both legal agents (against law) and social scientists (against norms) judged the truth about criminals in defence of a social order. In this context, 'one is constantly punishing and rewarding, evaluating and classifying' (Foucault, 2000: 83). As a result, approved criminal accusers were less private or communal subjects and increasingly demanded juridical and disciplinary expertise. Their truths became the primary mechanism for accusations of crime designed to protect society (Foucault, 2014).

Through such changes, the lines between classical sovereign legality and disciplinary normality blurred as state agents (police, prosecutors, judges, correctional facilities, etc.) relied on norms to fashion legitimate accusations of criminality (Golder & Fitzpatrick, 2010). As 'law and order' became a definitive mantra of the times, so normative legality and legally sanctioned norms infused a rising politics of recognition, and inflected acts of criminal accusation with both legal and normative force. At the same time, a biopolitics that had previously surfaced in Roman law attached itself to both sovereign and disciplinary political models, leading to disastrous social forms (e.g. eugenics and Nazism) and a rising 'biometric citizenship' that supplanted disciplinary prediction with actuarial knowledge regimes (Ajana, 2012, 2013; Magnet, 2011). Criminal accusation was developed in ways that would enable even further expansion of entry nodes to criminal justice institutions.

Biopolitical criminal accusations

Reflecting on biometric technologies developed by Bertillon and Galton, Agamben understands the rise of a 'decisive transformation of the concept of identity' (2011: 48; see also Chapter 11). 'For the first time in the history of humanity,' he tells us,

> identity was no longer a function of the social 'persona' and its recognition by others but rather a function of biological data, which could bear no relation to it. Human beings removed the mask that for centuries had been the basis of the recognizability in order to consign their identity to something that belongs to them in an intimate and exclusive way but with which they can in no way identify. No longer do the 'others', my fellow men, my friends or enemies, guarantee my recognition.
>
> (2011: 50)

For him, the pervasive use of biometric instruments across populations replaced previous (social) ways of identifying persons; others perceive a rather subtler alliance with erstwhile identification practices (Cole, 2001; Rose, 2007; Toom, 2012). In either case, biometric technologies have become central to our everyday lives; not only to the shifting contours of criminal justice arrangements. Our identities are today frequently 'confirmed', and consequently shaped, by instruments designed to code, analyse data on vast scales, store and recognize enduring corporeal traces: fingerprints, retinal shapes, DNA profiles, blood vessel patterns, voice contours, face shapes, and so on (Ergin, 2008; Hannah, 2014; Lyon, 2008; Magnet, 2011). In addition, biologically informed psychometric technologies purportedly profile personality traits, or cognitive structures, in 'sciences' such as forensic psychology or biocriminology (Arrigo, 2000; Rafter, 2008).

For Agamben, these technologies tie persons to biological and/or psychological traces of identity, with asocial recognitions reducing them to forms of bare, determined, and apolitical existence. The result is the production of biopolitical apparatuses of accusation that work within altered – biometrically or psychometrically inspired – political paradigms (see Ajana, 2013). These apparatuses include such elements as forensic, actuarial, police investigation and community crime-prevention discourses (Arrigo, 2000; Simon, 2007; Wood and Shearing, 2007). The resulting forms of knowledge champion biometric technologies (e.g. genetic profiling, neuroimaging) as pivotal ways of recognizing subjects at risk of committing future crimes (Rafter, 2008). Consequently, alongside criminal investigations initiated in the name of sovereigns and social orders, biopolitical apparatuses of accusation now form part of attempts to govern crime through such initiatives as intelligence-led policing (Sheptycki, 2007), risk-based governance of security (Wood & Shearing, 2007), crime control or prevention (O'Malley 2010: Chapter 2), and risk-reduction community, restorative or family service programs (Steadman, 2000). Just as disciplinary forms of criminal accusation transposed medieval sovereign apparatuses away from moral wickedness to sciences of individual characters and selves, so accusations issued through biopolitical logics revise anthropometry and criminal anthropology actuarially.

Operating beyond statistical abstractions, biopolitical apparatuses of accusation increasingly depend on virtual nodes directed at populations and actuarially calculated risks to an amorphous 'security' (Simon & Sparks, 2013). No longer defined by the panoptic surveillance of unseen gazes that defend society, biometric logics of recognition involve simulations of accusation within predefined digital universes. These operate at a distance from their algorithmic architects, without necessarily depending on corporeal accusers, or accusing corporally conceived individuals (Bogard, 1996). These 'simulated' forms of accusation depend on new forms of data mining, metadata analysis and the creation of profiles to contain risk and achieve an amorphous 'security' without explicit reference to normal societies or their welfare (Murphy, 2007).

The emerging apparatuses of criminal accusation tend to be grounded upon three elements: the creation of algorithmic templates from biometric profiles that use inductive, actuarial calculations to impute 'known' categories of persons (not so much individual criminals, but groupings of predefined criminal populations); technologies to extract biometric (or allied psychometric) profiles from specific persons in retrievable digital formats as traces (simulations) of identity (Kruger, Magnet & van Loon, 2008); and rapid computer searches to match profiles with virtual identities, selecting subjects who meet algorithmically specified conditions (Ajana, 2013; Magnet, 2011). The result is to generate lists of accusable persons who are then translated back to corporeal forms by arresting corporeal bodies to face specific criminal justice interventions. In sum, digitized, biopolitical apparatuses of accusation serve as virtual entry points arrayed in the service of risk-reduction initiatives; the latter are populated by the figurative flick of algorithmic switches. To be sure, such accusatory procedures may still refer to transcribed and sworn testimonies of firsthand witnesses, police interviews, normative judgements and other information recorded through criminal investigations. Increasingly, however, these documents are incorporated as profiles in biometric databases that virtual searches use to identify – on the basis of risk calculation (O'Malley, 2010) – which subjects likely do, or probably will, threaten 'security'.

Here, apparatuses of criminal accusation work less off morally framed rituals of sovereignty that distinguish good from evil, or disciplinary diagnoses of criminal individuals. Instead, they occupy liminal spaces anchored to a Boolean logic of ones and zeros arranged in ways that enable actuarial projections and profiles. These accusations might share a broad emphasis on locating 'criminal' threats, but the biopolitical paradigms within which they are situated centre around risk-reduction strategies founded on applied, actuarial knowledge. The aim here is to preselect biometric data clusters as criteria for profiles to locate the 'probable' identity profiles of specific 'criminals' (e.g., see Lines, 2015). By crunching massive amounts of data, employing methods associated with 'big data' analysis, the biometric recognition of criminally accused subjects works through digital technologies in simulated regimes, underwritten by forensic sciences bound to actuarial knowledge (Magnet, 2011). For example, in criminal investigations conducted by elite police, government agencies or forensic scientists, biopolitical accusations are increasingly predicated on data sourced from concealed regulatory horizons via supercomputers that use lightning-speed correlations to identify specific people (Lines, 2015; Ajana, 2010, 2013).

Within this political logic, virtual gatekeepers ply a computer-generated trade whose digital gates open or close binary electrical circuits to populate regulatory horizons. Admission to biopolitical regulatory horizons does not then require accusations directed to criminal acts, or abnormally dangerous characters: simply being the bearer of biometric traits pre-judged as risky is enough to gain entry to different levels of criminal justice programming, whether preventive or rehabilitative. The pre-judgments that define criminal profiles are often forged from surveys, or experiences of practitioners in the 'field' (see Lines, 2015). These profiles are then legitimized through the façades of an actuarial science that inductively projects the probability of future occurrences from putatively 'known' past events (Ajana, 2013).

The selection methods used to decide which traits to include in profiles are politically most effective when inscrutable. Yet such decisions prejudge many lives; unseen software programmers, data analysts, practitioners and consultants create closed systems to simulate regulatory worlds that identify matches. One might even say that biopolitical regimes of truth behind such accusatory apparatuses often work in shadows, inductively claiming the 'known' as a basis for what will probably happen in future. This logic allows policy analysts, governmental agents, administrative criminologists, public health officers, police executives, social/community workers, actuarial calculators, lawyers, and judges to work together off probabilistic prediction and to evoke different responses, or degrees of force, for differently calibrated levels of criminal risk (Ajana, 2010; Dean, 2010). Those accused are considered neither as evil, sinful persons, nor as abnormal individual characters; they are enunciated as carriers of threatening or risky criminogenic profiles (Lines, 2015; see also Chapter 11).

Biopolitical apparatuses of accusation, therefore, do not require clearly enunciated cut-off points to judge whether an accused subject should be admitted to state-sponsored criminal justice systems. Rather they provide multiple entryways to changing regulatory arrangements of state, community, police, governmental, restorative and legal 'programs' that manage profiles of algorithmically enunciated risks to security. In such regulatory horizons, arrays of authorized digital gatekeepers open or close Boolean pathways to identify likely suspects for given criminal investigations, or predict whether given profiles are likely to offend (Chapter 11). Echoing anthropometrical and positivist criminological approaches, biopolitical identification taps genetics, biology, forensics, social-psychology, biocriminology and neuroscience (Rafter, 2008; Rose, 2007, 2010). It offers probabilistic rather than absolute assessments.

In parentheses, it might be useful to note that were biopolitical logics of accusation to frame criminality as completely determined by genetics, neurology and the like, then criminal law would face the prospect of redundancy. That is, if criminality was fully determined by an a priori make-up, then criminal law's enduring culpability logic – that holds specific persons accountable for voluntary chosen acts – would be undermined. However, one should be cautious here for, as Morse (2007) indicates, some determinism (e.g., cognitive state, social background) has always accompanied notions of free will and criminal culpability. Even so, a politics of *bios* usually inserts uncertain environmental (social, cultural, administrative, etc.) variation as a foundation of persons, thus securing an indeterminate element at the heart of partly determined beings and thus continuing to assert the need for criminal law (Freeman, 2011; Naffine, 2009; Rafter, 2008). In short, persons accused of possessing predefined combinations of biological, psychological and/or social traits that are considered criminogenic risks could, by this political logic, become prime targets for biopolitical accusation and management in advance of any offending behaviour, mostly in the name of crime management, control or prevention strategies.

In any case, biopolitically framed apparatuses of accusations reflect a logic that calls for multiple and variously coordinated governance nodes – all directed to deciphering profiles said to be at risk of offending. The political rationale seems to question enlightenment attachments to criminal law, but not simply to return accusatorial powers to private parties or normative experts. Instead, biopolitical apparatuses of criminal accusation increasingly govern through technologies that channel criminal profiles to be managed through various programs and responses, including criminal trials. They appear as administrative clearinghouses rendering criminal law as one among many governmental techniques, forming parts of a wider amoral, non-normative management of populations that reduces subjects to basic elements of 'known traits'.

Agamben (1998) and Esposito (2008) have variously pointed to the dangers lurking behind governance with a propensity to reduce persons to politically enervated forms of life (*zoe*). Behind such worries are the horrors of eugenic programs that produced 'bare lives' and sanctioned a repugnant politics of death – as was found in Nazi concentration camps. But there is an added layer to critiques directed at criminal accusation: within the predefined boundaries of inaccessible, virtual worlds of crime management it is difficult – short of rewriting computer codes and rejecting a vast supporting infrastructure – to entertain fundamental voices of dissent, or to question the foundations of systems at play. The reduction at hand is doubled: not only are pulsing lives reduced to depoliticized biological traits selectively traced in biometric records, but they are further reduced to hypostatized bits of machine code to be fed into a predefined digital language amenable to the correlations of biopolitical accusatorial apparatuses. This poses a significant challenge for those wishing to give some indication of the contingent fragility of a politics framing such apparatuses. But this is precisely the scale of what is required to name and engage the subtle admission of subjects who find themselves entangled within virtual thresholds of criminal accusation – it is precisely here that subjects are chosen for entry into an actuarially inflected 'governance through crime' (Simon, 2007).

Conclusion

Reflecting across the apparatuses, one should not misread the heuristic distinctions proposed as marking chronological shifts from sovereign-law to discipline to biopolitical forms of criminal accusation. Rather these political logics are always enmeshed, contemporaneously shaping, complementing and undermining one another in trilateral patterns that form and counter-form over time (Foucault, 2000: 219). By highlighting differences and overlaps between the apparatuses, one might note how, in combination, their political logics have underscored hybrid accusatorial entrances that today isolate criminally accused subjects through moral, normative and virtual selections. In tandem, such heterogeneous apparatuses of criminal accusation have developed greater nodes and entryways to ever-expanding criminal justice horizons. One might then say that political logics of sovereignty-based criminal accusation have endured precisely because of, rather than despite, disciplinary modifications that reframed subjects as law-abiding individuals. Equally, a rising 'biopolitical sovereignty' has directed accusation to the creation of 'biometric citizens'; it has also sometimes inflected these with conservative moral discourses around controlling and 'getting tough' on wayward criminals, rather than considering their welfare or reform (Agamben, 1998; Ajana, 2013; Garland, 2002).

The very form of vengeful medieval sovereignty politics may have been attenuated (though not annihilated) by a new focus on rationales centred on the surveillance of populations; but a punitive edge continues to drive the collection of biometric metadata so that states can identify actuarially defined risks and threats to – with reformed echoes of modern discipline – the security of a society. Similarly, biometric logics of criminal accusation echo disciplinary reductions to biological types, but work much more stringently off actuarial probability profiles than statistically calibrated norms that demarcate abnormal types of individuals. The norms and profiles behind different sorts of criminal accusation still shape sovereignly defined illegalities of criminal codes. However, biopolitical logics extend a disciplinary escape from juridical contexts by expanding the array of responses (restorative, clinical, pharmacological, etc.) beyond those available within the criminal law and networks that surround a wilful and rational individual whose criminality must be controlled in the name of sovereign justice. Criminal justice arenas are thus anchored to various, and simultaneously operating, nodes of criminal accusation to regulate flows of persons into the 'system'. One might also note that by identifying specific persons as targets for criminal law's intervention, accusation helps to define that law's jurisdiction (Dorsett & McVeigh, 2012).

Of course, much more is required to enunciate the historical overlaps and effects of apparatuses of criminal accusation facing us today, or indeed to confront a current obsession with crime control, criminal causes, forensic identification and the punitive vengeance of moral sovereigns. Yet, the previous analysis has at least alluded to the apparatuses of three basic political rationalities, the combined legacy of which has shaped criminal accusation's role as gatekeeper that selects accused subjects to face variously organized forms of criminal justice. In concert, these rationalities admit subjects to criminal justice systems that govern with vestiges of sovereign trials and disciplinary social control networks, but also countless risk-reduction and crime-prevention initiatives. The amalgam has produced a continuously, nay massively, expanding and disproportionately populated crime control and penal industry (Christie, 2001; Wacquant, 2009). Yet even if criminal justice industries appear unshakeable, criminal accusation highlights their contingent moments of entry, inviting us to focus on the initial selection processes for criminalization and an ensuing populating of criminal justice networks. What are the prospects for more open, democratized and potentially inclusionary accusations? Might accusation be turned away from moral subjects, correctable individuals or biological bits and bytes to iniquitous social formations? Could systems and institutions face bordering enunciations through different grammars of accusation? Through such questions one glimpses how a more direct engagement with gatekeeping mechanisms could help to interrogate the subtle – and often eclipsed – apparatuses that fuel disproportionate criminal justice expansions. The latter's dependence on accusatory entry points for their perpetuation is exactly what the previous discussion has attempted to highlight. If nothing else, this should render apparatuses of criminal accusation basic to resisting the expanding and unequal flows of current criminal justice horizons.

References

Agamben, G. (1998). *Homo Sacer: Sovereign Power and Bare Life*. Stanford, CA: Stanford University Press.

——. (2011). *Nudities*. Stanford, CA: Stanford University Press.

Ajana, B. (2010). Recombinant identities: biometrics and narrative bioethics. *Journal of Bioethical Inquiry*, 7(2), 237–58.

——. (2012). Biometric citizenship. *Citizenship Studies*, 16(7), 851–70.

——. (2013). *Governing through Biometrics: The Biopolitics of Identity*. London: Palgrave Macmillan.

Andersen, P., Salonen, K., Sigh, H. M., & Vogt, H. (2013). *Law and Disputing in the Middle Ages: Proceedings of the Ninth Carlsberg Academy Conference on Medieval Legal History 2012*. Copenhagen: Djoef Publishing.

Arrigo, B. A. (2000). *Introduction to Forensic Psychology: Issues and Controversies in Crime and Justice*. San Diego, CA: Academic Press.

Beccaria, C. (1996). *Of Crimes and Punishments*. New York: Marsilio Publishers.

Bentham, J. (1890). *Theory of Legislation*. London: Trübner.

Bogard, W. (1996). *The Simulation of Surveillance: Hypercontrol in Telematic Societies*. Cambridge: Cambridge University Press.

Brown, M. (2009). *The Culture of Punishment: Prison, Society, and Spectacle*. New York: New York University Press.

Christie, N. (2001). *Crime Control as Industry*. London: Routledge.

Cole, S. (2001). *Suspect Identities: A History of Fingerprinting and Criminal Identification*. Cambridge, MA: Harvard University Press.

Dayan, C. (2013). *The Law Is a White Dog*. Princeton, NJ: Princeton University Press.

Dean, M. (2010). Power at the heart of the present: exception, risk and sovereignty. *European Journal of Cultural Studies*, 13, 459–75.

Dorsett, S., & McVeigh, S. (2012). *Jurisdiction*. New York: Routledge.

Durston, G. (2012). *Burglars and Bobbies: Crime and Policing in Victorian London*. Newcastle: Cambridge Scholars.

Emsley, C. (2010). *Crime and Society in England, 1750–1900*. Harlow: Longman.

Ergin, M. (2008). Biometrics and anthropometrics: the twins of Turkish modernity. *Patterns of Prejudice*, 42(3), 281–304.

Ericson, R. V., & Baranek, P. M. (1982). *The Ordering of Justice: A Study of Accused Persons as Dependants in the Criminal Process*. Toronto, ON: University of Toronto Press.

Esposito, R. (2008). *Bíos: Biopolitics and Philosophy*. Minneapolis, MN: University of Minnesota Press.

Ferraris, M., & Davies, R. (2013). *Documentality: Why It Is Necessary to Leave Traces.* New York: Fordham University Press.
Foucault, M. (1979). *Discipline and Punish: The Birth of the Prison.* New York: Vintage Books.
——. (1980). *Power/Knowledge: Selected Interviews and Other Writings, 1972–1977.* New York: Vintage Books.
——. (2000). *Power.* New York: The New Press.
——. (2007). *The Politics of Truth.* Los Angeles, CA: Semiotext(e).
——. (2014). *Wrong-Doing, Truth-Telling: The Function of Avowal in Justice.* F. Brion & B. E. Harcourt (eds). Chicago, IL: The University Of Chicago Press.
Freeman, M. (ed.). (2011). *Law and Neuroscience: Current Legal Issues.* Oxford: Oxford University Press.
Garland, D. (1991). *Punishment and Modern Society: A Study in Social Theory.* Chicago, IL: University of Chicago Press.
——. (2002). *The Culture of Control: Crime and Social Order in Contemporary Society.* Chicago, IL: University of Chicago Press.
Gatrell, V. (1994). *The Hanging Tree: Execution and the English People, 1770–1868.* New York: Oxford University Press.
Girard, R. (2005). *Violence and the Sacred.* New York: Continuum.
Goebel, J. (1976). *Felony and Misdemeanor: A Study in the History of Criminal Law.* Philadelphia, PA: University of Pennsylvania Press.
Golder, B., & Fitzpatrick, P. (2010). *Foucault and Law.* Farnham: Ashgate.
Gorski, R. (2009). 'Justices and injustices? England's local officials in the Later Middle Ages', in J. C. Appleby & P. Dalton (eds), *Outlaws in Medieval and Early Modern England Crime, Government and Society, c.1066–c.1600.* Farnham: Ashgate, pp. 55–74.
Gould, S. J. (2008). *The Mismeasure of Man.* New York: W.W. Norton.
Grossi, P. (2010). *A History of European Law.* Malden, MA: Wiley-Blackwell.
Hamilton, S. N. (2009). *Impersonations: Troubling the Person in Law and Culture.* Toronto, ON: University of Toronto Press.
Hannah, M. G. (2014). Biometrics: bodies, technologies, biopolitics. *Cultural Geographies*, 21(1), 161–2.
Harries, J. (2007). *Law and Crime in the Roman World.* Cambridge: Cambridge University Press.
Hay, D. (2011). *Albion's Fatal Tree: Crime and Society in Eighteenth-century England.* London: Verso.
Herrup, C. B. (1987). *The Common Peace: Participation and the Criminal Law in Seventeenth-century England.* Cambridge: Cambridge University Press.
Hitchcock, T., & Shoemaker, R. B. (2006). *Tales from the Hanging Court.* London: Hodder Arnold.
Ignatieff, M. (1989). *A Just Measure of Pain: The Penitentiary in the Industrial Revolution, 1750–1850.* London: Penguin.
King, P. (2003). *Crime, Justice, and Discretion in England, 1740–1820.* Oxford: Oxford University Press.
Kruger, E., Magnet, S., & van Loon, J. (2008). Biometric revisions of the 'body' in airports and US welfare reform. *Body & Society*, 14(2), 99–121.
Landau, N. (1984). *The Justices of the Peace, 1679–1760.* Berkeley: University of California Press.
Landau, N., & Beattie, J. M. (2002). *Law, Crime and English Society, 1660–1830.* Cambridge: Cambridge University Press.

Langbein, J. H. (2003). *The Origins of Adversary Criminal Trial.* Oxford: Oxford University Press.

Levasseur, C. (1995). Managing social insecurity: politics as the focus in building the modern welfare state. *Revue internationale d'action communautaire/International Review of Community Development*, 33(73), 47–60.

Lines, K. (2015). *Crime Seen*. Toronto, ON: Random House.

Lyon, D. (2008). Biometrics, identification and surveillance. *Bioethics*, 22(9), 499–508.

Magnet, S. (2011). *When Biometrics Fail: Gender, Race, and the Technology of Identity.* Durham, NC: Duke University Press.

Morse, S. J. (2007). Criminal responsibility and the disappearing person. *Cardozo Law Review*, 28(6), 2545–75.

Murphy, E. (2007). The new forensics: criminal justice, false certainty, and the second generation of scientific evidence. *California Law Review*, 95(3), 721–97.

Naffine, N. (2009). *Law's Meaning of Life: Philosophy, Religion, Darwin, and the Legal Person*. Portland, OR: Hart.

Negrier-Dormont, L. (1994). Criminology: foundations and efficacy. *International Criminal Police Review*, 450 (Sept.–Oct.), 10–15.

Oberwittler, D. (1990). Crime and authority in eighteenth century England: law enforcement on the local level. *Historical Social Research*, 15(2), 3–34.

O'Malley, P. (2010). *Crime and Risk*. Los Angeles, CA: Sage.

Osmond, R. (1990). *Mutual Accusation: Seventeenth-century Body and Soul Dialogues in their Literary and Theological Context*. Toronto: University of Toronto Press.

Peters, E. (1989). *Inquisition*. Berkeley: University of California Press.

Pick, D. (1989). *Faces of Degeneration: A European Disorder*. Cambridge: Cambridge University Press.

Pollock, F., & Maitland, F. M. (2010). *The History of English Law before the Time of Edward I*. Indianapolis, IN: Liberty Fund.

Pratt, J. (1995). Dangerousness, risk and technologies of power. *Australian & New Zealand Journal of Criminology*, 28(1), 3–31.

Rafter, N. H. (1997). *Creating Born Criminals.* Urbana, IL: University of Illinois Press.

——. (2008). *The Criminal Brain: Understanding Biological Theories of Crime*. New York: New York University Press.

Reeves, J. (1869). *A History of English.* London: Reeves and Turner.

Rose, N. (2007). *Politics of Life Itself: Biomedicine, Power, and Subjectivity in the Twenty-first Century.* Princeton, NJ: Princeton University Press.

——. (2010). 'Screen and intervene': governing risky brains. *History of the Human Sciences*, 23(1), 79–105.

Sengoopta, C. (2003). *Imprint of the Raj: How Fingerprinting Was Born in Colonial India*. London: Macmillan.

Sheptycki, J. (2007). High policing in the security control society. *Policing*, 1(1), 70–9.

Shoemaker, R. B. (1991). *Prosecution and Punishment: Petty Crime and the Law in London and Rural Middlesex, c.1660–1725*. Cambridge: Cambridge University Press.

Simon, J. (2007). *Governing Through Crime: How the War on Crime Transformed American Democracy and Created a Culture of Fear*. New York: Oxford University Press.

Simon, J., & Sparks, R. (2013). *The SAGE Handbook of Punishment and Society.* Thousand Oaks: Sage.

Steadman, H. J. (2000). From dangerousness to risk assessment of community violence: taking stock at the turn of the century. *Journal of the American Academy of Psychiatry and the Law Online*, 28(3), 265–71.

Stein, P. (2005). *Roman Law in European History*. Cambridge: Cambridge University Press.

Stephen, S. J. F. (1883). *A History of the Criminal Law of England*. Vol. I. London: Macmillan and Co.

Thompson, E. P. (1975). *Whigs and Hunters: The Origin of the Black Act*. New York: Pantheon Books.

Toom, V. (2012). Bodies of science and law: forensic DNA profiling, biological bodies, and biopower. *Journal of Law and Society*, 39(1), 150–66.

Tuck, R. (1993). *Philosophy and Government, 1572–1651*. Cambridge: Cambridge University Press.

Wacquant, L. J. D. (2009). *Punishing the Poor: The Neoliberal Government of Social Insecurity*. Durham, NC: Duke University Press.

Whitman, J. Q. (2008). *The Origins of Reasonable Doubt: Theological Roots of the Criminal Trial*. New Haven, CT: Yale University Press.

Wiener, M. J. (1994). *Reconstructing the Criminal: Culture, Law, and Policy in England, 1830–1914*. Cambridge: Cambridge University Press.

Wood, J., & Shearing, C. D. (2007). *Imagining Security*. Cullompton: Willan.

Chapter 3

Avowal and criminal accusation

Introduction

Accusing someone of criminal wrongdoing occurs through a politics that recognizes distinctive identities: accuser, accused and legitimate overseers of situated accusatorial processes. Unfolding relations between these identities co-produces mutually sustaining accusatorial fields, calling selected subjects to account for actions that accusers somehow seek to define as criminally wrong. Through historically specific rituals, these identities jostle to define the truth of past events, the characters involved and the imputation of action or non-action. Their exchanges enable or deny entry to legal processes. While such relational complexes might change over time, they variously serve as gatekeepers to an immense crime-control industry (Christie, 2013). And as modern states marked in detail the spheres of life designated as 'criminal' wrongdoing, so centralized (state) criminal justice systems grew. Many commentators have noted the enormous costs – social, economic, political and cultural – of today's vast crime-control arrangements (Wacquant, 2010; Simon, 2014), but rather fewer have focused attention on the gatekeeping practices through which criminal accusations open pathways to swollen crime-control arenas (Pavlich, 2006a, 2006b).

Perhaps there is good reason for this. In social horizons defined so significantly by a cultural obsession with 'crime' and its 'punishment', where 'cultures of control' mark out spaces governing vast areas of society 'through crime', there is political expediency in obscuring processes that open gates to thriving and expanding criminal justice systems (Garland, 2002; Simon, 2007). After all, if points of entry to criminal justice operate in shadows, then fixed ideas of crime, and the consequent identification of 'criminals', might appear more a matter of discovering fixed identities than of their creation. Yet, those who have examined the opening moments that arrest ordinary everyday lives, might tell a different story (Ericson & Baranek, 1982; Pavlich, 2006a). From this vantage, processes of criminal accusation could be understood as socially situated gatekeeping mechanisms that decide on who to admit to remand spaces, thereby opening transitions to law's criminal justice. Those who are turned away from such gates usually face tarnished reputations and must frequently renegotiate identities in their everyday lives. By contrast, those for whom the gates to criminal justice are opened face various kinds of legal depersonalizations. However, from the accusatorial moments that arrest their everyday lives, accused persons face new forms of life as they negotiate legally framed contexts that decide their fates in juridical tribunals.

The following chapter analyses an element of such complex accusatorial processes; namely, the kind of truth-telling demanded of subjects involved in a criminal accusation, returning to Socrates' trial. To analyse theoretically what is at stake in such truth arenas, I refer to how this example reflects modes of avowal of Athenian accusatory entryways to legal wrongdoing, aspects of which have resounded through the ages. The framing theme here can be indicated by a question: what sort of truth-telling is expected, or required, of parties to an accusation of (criminal) wrongdoing, and how does that shape the subjective identities of each party?

With this question in mind, the chapter moves through four phases. The first examines Foucault's recently translated lectures on avowal as an approach to juridical forms of truth-telling, and specifically a dimension of accusation by which subjects constitute themselves as they make claims to truth deemed legible to specific juridical forms. The second traces Athenian accusatory rituals that called people to account for actions with the prospect of defining them as wrongdoing, alluding to transitional moments where specific actions were translated as wrong doing and made legible to legal authority. Third, it will explore how Socrates' accusers emerged as specific kinds of selves through their accusations. The fourth phase of the discussion probes aspects of Socrates' defence to indicate how someone accused of wrongdoing might avow and so shape a self-identity. The conclusion alludes to the technologies of self-formation that enabled the co-appearance of accusing and accused selves that – through a politics of legal recognition – validated the foundations for (albeit massively expanded) criminal justice horizons.

Modes of 'veridiction,' avowal and accusation

While the question of 'criminal' accusation's role in specific cases – including Socrates' defence against charges of impiety – has been noted (Pavlich, 2006b), this chapter attends to rituals of truth-telling associated with accusations of wrongdoing. Such accusations defer to complex forms of avowal, or required ways of speaking the truth in context. They also recursively rearrange the subject identities of those who utter such truths. In other words, required modes of truth-telling within accusatorial contexts in law directly imply subtle 'technologies of self-formation' through which self-identities and collective orders are mutually structured. When examining legal forms of avowal that shape subjects, one might recall Foucault's (2014) helpful distinction between two broad approaches.

The first is driven by an attempt to understand – *à la* Kant – the conditions under which a statement is taken to be true. By contrast the second – a 'critical philosophy' – is directed not to verifying claimed truths, but to examining contextual procedures/norms that subjects are required to follow if they are to speak the truth. He coins a neologism to refer to these as modes of '*veridiction*' (from *veri* – truth; *diction* – speaking). These context-specific modes require different things of those subjects deemed to offer truthful accusations. Foucault's concern is not with the ahistorical truth of particular avowals; rather, his approach examines contextually sanctioned ways of avowing, truth-telling, on the part of different subjects who make, oversee or respond to accusations of wrongdoing or crime. In other words, the focus here is on the practices and effects of avowal surrounding legally sanctioned accusations. What kind of political logic is at play, and what effects do technologies of avowal have on the creation of accusatorially produced subjects (accusers, accused and juridical agents)? What rituals are demanded of participants for them to be considered as speaking truths that conform to legal norms at the gates to (criminal) justice?

At this point it might be useful to note how Foucault approaches avowal, especially its use in juridical forms. He tells us:

> What separates an avowal from a declaration is not what separates the unknown from the known, the visible from the invisible, but what might be referred to as a certain cost of enunciation. Avowal consists of passing from the untold to the told, given that the untold has a precise meaning, a particular motive, a great value.
>
> (2014: 15)

Understanding an avowal is not then a matter of establishing its absolute truth value; in one sense an avowal must be regarded as true because, strictly speaking, 'if it is false, it is not an avowal' (Foucault, 2014: 19). Yet it always comes at a potential cost to the avower, and has value for those who hear the avowal. However, the significant bits here include why an enunciation appears as truthful in specific contexts, and how this specific way of speaking affects the very identity of the avower. In all instances, avowal 'implies that he who speaks promises to be what he affirms himself to be: precisely because he is just that' (2014: 16). For example, a subject who avows his/her love for another implies the assumption of an identity. In the very act of avowing something, that is, the subject passes from one state to another: s/he passes from 'the realm of the unspoken to the realm of the spoken by voluntarily constituting oneself as a lover through the affirmation that one loves' (2014: 16). Through such avowals, then, the avower implicitly constitutes him/herself as a specific kind of 'I' who loves another; that is, the avowal helps to bestow a sort of self-identity that falls within contextually understood boundaries.

Avowal is thus a kind of truth-telling; in contexts contoured by accusations of wrongdoing, legal rituals authoritatively sanction unique ways to speak the truth (e.g., following oaths in modern courts, countersigned documents, etc.). Following such rituals, through ordered acts of avowing in authoritatively sanctioned ways, accusers and the accused recursively come to assume self-identities. But here the idea of avowal runs a tricky course: on the one hand, from its earliest incarnations, law regarded accusatory avowals as something that must be 'freely' enunciated; on the other, the same authorities tended to require, demand or coerce certain avowals – even in some contexts to the extent of using torture to extract 'free confessions' (see Pavlich, 2006a). In so doing, a given power does what is common: it seeks 'to constrain those it forces to be free' (Foucault, 2014: 16).

The very act of legal avowal in relation to an accusation of wrongdoing thus subtly binds avowers to an authority through rituals of truth-telling that work through specific forms of *veridiction*. Selected representatives of that authority sanction rituals in context; and subjects who participate in these rituals thereby subjugate themselves to a regulatory ethos. But they do so in a rather subtle or oblique way: such avowals form part of the work done by subjects on themselves in efforts to shape their self-identities. That is, by providing the regulatory contexts within which subjects avow (in ways that recursively constitute themselves as circumscribed sorts of 'selves'); a sanctioned authority works remotely from the shadows of bounded freedom , enticing selves to form around specific identities. The liberty here involves choices between delimited identities; the option of eschewing a self-identity entirely is largely disabled (e.g. as in complete withdrawal), just as the possibilities for pursuing self-identifications beyond contextually permissible frames are limited.

As such, Foucault argues that

> one who avows a crime, in a sense, admits to being the author of the crime. By that I mean he not only accepts responsibility but also establishes this acceptance on the fact that he did commit the crime. In avowal, he who speaks obligates himself to being what he says he is.
>
> (2014: 16)

I interpret this somewhat cryptic statement to mean that avowal, more than simply an admission of a wrong (a crime) also involves a process of identification; in avowing or disavowing that a crime or wrong has been committed, accusers or accused thereby adopt forms of subjectivity, self-identities, tied to an authority that licenses specific processes of accusation. No doubt, accusation here governs through truth-telling (2014: 24); it enables technologies of the self where various subjects forge visions of selfhood decipherable to legal authority.

Technologies of self that are forged through these modes of *veridiction* are evident from ancient writings on Socrates' trial; the latter illustrate how from early legal forms different kinds of subjectivity and selfhood were generated through legal processes of accusing someone of wrongdoing. What juridical rituals of avowal are expected of an accusing or accused identity? And what is it to be the mediating party in an accusation? Let us explore further such questions.

Accusing subjects under Athenian law

How precisely subjects were called to account for actions through authoritatively sanctioned processes of accusation in ancient Athens is not always easy to discern from surviving texts (Carey, 2011; Dorjahn, 1941; Gagarin & Cohen, 2005). However, gatekeeping structures seemed to include various moments of decision that admitted disputes and disputants to legal processes, and ejected others (Johnstone, 1999). Socrates' accusation occurred at the threshold to ancient Greek law (399 BCE) where it was not state prosecutors who translated events into legal disputes. Rather, any citizen could accuse another of having done something wrong by a law attributed to Solon (Boegehold, 1995: 23). So, individuals might initiate specifically legal disputes by deciding on whether to pursue the 'case' as a private matter or in the 'public good' (Johnstone, 1999). In this context,

> [a] public case concerned an offence or dispute which was regarded as affecting the community as a whole and consequently, anyone who wished was entitled to prosecute. The volunteer could be any free adult male, except that some kinds of case could not be brought by a non-citizen and none could be brought by a disfranchised citizen. The offences for which public cases could be brought included those which obviously affected the whole community equally, such as treason or desertion from the army or embezzlement of public funds.
>
> (MacDowell, 1986: 57)

In all cases, though, accusers had successfully to navigate the entry points to legal fields, starting with the ratification of an accusation by a court official. The process went something like this:

> To initiate an action as prosecutor, a citizen notified a defendant formally and with witnesses. He did this by sending a crier along with friends who would act as witnesses, or, since he knew the notification would be in a public place, he could hope to involve casual bystanders as witnesses. This act of formal notification, once executed, required the defendant to appear before a magistrate. There he answered his prosecutor's charges. What magistrate to choose was the prosecutor's responsibility: it could be an archon, a general, or a committee such as the Eleven.
>
> (Boegehold, 1995: 23)

As is well known, the drama of Socrates' trial was initiated by three accusers followed by a pronouncement by the king archon as to whether the case should proceed to trial (see Brickhouse & Smith, 2002). The archon scheduled Socrates' case for a court heard by approximately 501 jury members (*diktats*). They listened to the water-timed arguments of prosecutors making the case followed by his 'apology' or defence (Brickhouse & Smith, 2002). It seems that a majority (about 280) of *diktats* found him guilty, occasioning further arguments about an appropriate sentence (Carey, 2011; Gagarin & Cohen, 2005; Johnstone, 1999; MacDowell, 1986). Socrates' arguments here might appear to be rather odd, amounting to a counter-claim that he ought really to be supported as a public figure for the services he had offered to the Athenian community. In many ways, his apology thumbs his nose at the jury, who in turn pass a death sentence (Stone, 1989). In consequence, we have him confined to a prison cell awaiting the execution of sentence – delayed a month due to the timing of a religious festival that prevented death penalties from being carried out. In Plato's accounts (*Crito, Phaedo, Symposium*) we are told of his continued dialogues with friends. In the end, his life abates as he drinks the hemlock without yielding his defence of a philosophy that he takes to be threatened by crass sophistry, bad poetry and the tyranny of wisdom attributed to craftsmen (Brickhouse & Smith, 2002).

Although there is much written on the details of Socrates' trial, rather less attention is paid to the initiating sequences where a translation of events as wrongdoing happened, not too distant from the way conflicts are translated into disputes (Felstiner, Abel, & Sarat, 1980/1981). The remainder of this chapter attends, therefore, to fragments of texts directed to the oft-eclipsed opening moments of accusation through which his accusers tried to cast several aspects of Socrates' past life as punishable wrongdoing. Though some may see in this an attempt to recount what really happened, or to engage in debate on whether the accusations against Socrates were motivated by religious or political disputes (Brickhouse & Smith, 2002: 190ff.), I shall instead focus on surviving discourses that address the authorized rituals for successful accusations (and associated avowals). Specifically, Plato's rich account in the *Apology* could be read as a theoretical reflection rather than blunt record (even though Plato was apparently present as a court reporter), but it does allow us to examine this key question: what legal rituals of accusation and truth-telling practices were Socrates' accusers required to enunciate to have these accepted as legally valid by authorized representatives of a given juridical order?

In response, one might ponder how criers initially accosted Socrates' everyday life, stating their oral accusations in the presence of two witnesses and summoning him to a meeting with the archon on a specified date. In the *Euthyphro*, Plato's brief statement affords glimpses of the procedure as Socrates stood at the portico of the Royal Stoa and engaged a friend Euthyphro who, we learn, is about to make an accusation against his father for homicide. Both made their appearances, one to accuse and Socrates to hear and contest a version of the accusations brought against him. At Socrates' preliminary hearing (*anakrisis*), Meletus would likely have read a version of the formal accusation that, according to Xenophon, went something like this: 'Socrates is guilty of the crime of not honouring the gods that the City honours, and of introducing other, new deities; and he is also guilty of corrupting young men' (Brickhouse & Smith, 2002: 87).

Past events were to be rhetorically re-assembled in narratives that pronounced them as wrongs against the public (rather than private wrongs), requiring wider legal intervention. For his part, the king archon was to, 'determine if the charges were in accordance with law and would then forward the case to a jury trial' (Brickhouse & Smith, 2002: 1).

His office derived from a Greek word meaning 'ruler', and emerged in a previous age of kingdoms, maintaining some of the old king's powers in matters relating to religion, including trials dealing with impiety (Waterfield, 2010: 8). By the time of Socrates' trial, however, the offices were held by some nine court officers appointed by lot to serve for a year: an *archon* with civic remit, the *polemarch* (who presided over war, foreign cases or those that involved metrics), the archon Basileus or the King ruler, and six juridical officers referred to as *Thesmothétai* (see Boegehold, 1995: xxii, 45, 84). The king archon, who once had wide powers, now oversaw reduced civic (e.g., homicide) and religious matters. Moreover, the rather infrequent charge of impiety would be sent to a court called the *Heliaea* (Miller & Platter, 2010: 5). In any case, the king archon was required to hear representations of accusers and accused to ascertain whether charges met the requirements of – or in more precise terms were legible to – what was contextually perceived to be legal wrongdoing.

This legal drama would have commenced with the accusers: Meletus was the principal one, a poet (to repeat, Socrates describes him as 'a hook-nosed man with long hair, and a scanty beard' in the *Euthyphro*); Anytus, a politician from a tanning family who had also been a general in the Peloponnesian wars; and, Lycon, a professional orator. They mounted their accusations as legitimate prosecutors in the eyes of Solon-derived law by couching their charges as safeguarding the general interests of the state, the polis. Critical to the success of accusations at these hearings, as Johnstone (1999) argues, lay rhetorical devices used to narrate disputes in ways amenable to legal interpretation. This crucial first step had the effect of summoning authorized people for decisions about whether to forward the case to juridical processes.

Even if little of the archive remains, one might envisage Socrates responding to Meletus' charges, whereupon both would have been required to swear oaths as to the veracity of their respective claims (Johnstone, 1999). Thereafter, the archon would possibly have asked specific questions about the claims and counterclaims, following which accuser and accused had an opportunity to question one another. The archon was, as noted, to evaluate the claims of accusers and accused to determine whether the accusation had merit and could proceed under the auspices of the Athenian law (Waterfield, 2010). At this stage, however, as Dorjahn (1941) argues, it is unlikely that detailed arguments of cases would have been made; this was not the opportunity to disclose one's strategy for defence or prosecution. Rather it provided a forum for assessing whether accusations could be considered lawful or not. If they were, as was the case in Socrates' situation, a court date was set for a public, jury trial.

From such rituals of accusation, one might distinguish three key factors in how gateways to the law in Athenian contexts operated at the time of Socrates' trial. First, the overarching figure of the king archon played a key role in opening or closing the gates to law, and did so by interrogating accuser and accused in efforts to determine which avowals were true from within a juridical context. Second, the archon received the accusation in ways that required narratives to be arranged in legally decipherable ways. This made narratives legible to law and demanded that an account followed strict tenets of how to construct what had happened and why it was legally problematic (Johnstone, 1999). Thus, in Socrates' case, the charges against him might well have had political or religious overtones, but for the purposes of the accusation it was precisely about a public matter of not following the city's gods, introducing new ones and corrupting the youth. The charges were thus phrased in such a way as to render Socrates' philosophical life as a kind of wrongdoing that worked against a public interest. Specifically, his constant questioning, and pushing the limits of what people considered to be acceptable at a given historical juncture, were translated as a legal wrong of being impious and sullying the minds of Athenian youth. Third, specific truth-telling practices required: accusers to swear to the truth of their allegations, and to face possible consequences for calumny; the accused to frame truthful counterclaims of the accused; and the king archon to provide a legally truthful evaluation of claim and counter-claim. The process here involved extracting avowals from all parties, demanding that they speak the truth in ways deemed acceptable to legal frameworks.

In such a relational complex, the identities of the key parties to the event were in some measure structured around legal demands for truth-telling, and so recursively constituted the identities. We are here dealing with a crucial technology of self-formation through performances within legitimate accusatory processes, where legal tropes demanded by the archon were calibrated to render sorts of subjectivity possible. In the next two sections, we shall turn to the subjectivities produced as accuser and accused avowed, in legally required ways, to negotiate the accusations of legal wrongdoing against Socrates.

Accusations of public wrongdoing: calling Socrates to account

What kind of truth-telling practices did Athenian juridical forms require for accusations of wrongdoing? Although speculative, one might extract theoretically significant elements of accusatory discourses that have through the ages operated in shadows. We have already noted Xenophon's description of the accusation, but Waterfield argues that a more detailed formulation has survived:

> This indictment and affidavit is sworn by Meletou of Pitthus, against Socrates Sophroniscou of Alopece. Socrates is guilty of not acknowledging the gods the city acknowledges, and introducing other new divinities. He is also guilty of subverting the young men of the city. The penalty demanded his death.
>
> (Waterfield, 2010: 5)

Meletus appeared as the chief accuser (see Nails, 2002). Seemingly a poet of no great repute, Meletus brought the first of the charges to the court. His accusations centred on impiety, declaring that Socrates' claims about science (as mocked in Aristophanes' *Clouds*) effectively eschewed the gods of Athens. As well, Meletus argued that Socrates' merciless challenge to poets indicates impiety, because – he alleged – poets were seers and teachers with divine authority. In this way, the truth of his accusations was not only divinely sanctioned, but in the public good.

On reflection, this accuser framed his claim as a higher truth formulated on behalf of gods and seers. He portrayed the unending, jarring iconoclasm of Socrates as the missteps of a gadfly so wrong as to require legal redress in courts. Whether Meletus meant this to bring about Socrates' death is an open question, but it was not uncommon for accusers to demand the death penalty to secure one of the lesser sanctions; e.g., fine, banishment, etc. (Carey, 2011). In any case, his avowals of purportedly divinely sanctioned truths could be read as an attempt to fuse legal and pious authority, for an accuser who by the very enunciation of these truths afforded a righteous and sanctimonious sense of self. Represented as rightly bringing a public accusation for the good of a particularly ordered community, this self aligned with accepted gods of the city.

A second accuser, Lycon, barely noted in Plato's *Apology*, is thought to have had knowledge of the law and its rhetorical dimensions (Creeden, 1994). Apparently, a rhetorician by trade, Plato's references to Lycon can be understood allegorically to emphasize the importance of language to law. Using rhetorical skills, Lycon appeared as the accuser whose rhetorical weapons were deployed to license an unleashing of law's force on the accused. Reflecting Constable's (2014) understanding of law as contested linguistic performance, Lycon described Socrates' acts as impiety – a relatively obscure charge. More than an action translated as a dispute through institutional processes, Socrates' philosophy was framed as a grave wrong that warranted the death penalty. Lycon appeared to have understood that rhetoric is critical to the generation of accepted legal truths, the substance of law and a means to select who law's force will target.

So, under his rhetorical direction, he pointed the jury to the legal precedents of Socrates' teacher, Anaxagoras, and the famous sophist, Protagoras, as cases where law tried similar charges. The former was accused of impiety for suggesting that the sun was a 'red-hot mass' rather than a god, and the latter for enunciating a form of deific agnosticism (Creeden, 1994: 175). Although condemned, Anaxagoras escaped into exile, Protagoras was banished and his books burned. With Lycon, then, we appear to have an accuser who avowed his truth in an efficacious juridical way by referring to precedent, and opening to the language of past law to authorize, and render the charges of impiety, as legible wrongdoing to an Athenian court.

What kind of self was recursively constituted by this accuser? One might speculate that the selves who accused were conversant with the intricacies of law's rhetoric; they called another to account in the name of the linguistically framed justice of a time and place. Lycon's voice seems to have been conversant with, and able rhetorically to enunciate, the truth of law's right from whence its might derives. That authorization in the name of a public law, for this poet, appeared as divinely ordained, and hence his explicit emphasis on the matter of impiety; of not following the gods that he deemed specific to Athens. These are no doubt lofty self-ascriptions, recursively positioning Lycon as a pious defender of the 'public' and Socrates as an 'other', as an enemy of the Athenian religious order. Yet, if Meletus was the chief accuser in this case, it might be that the third accuser to speak, Anytus (a well-known politician and past general of the Peloponnesian War), provided a behind-the-scenes driving force (see Creeden, 1994: 174ff.). He had previously escaped treason charges (for having lost Pylos to the Spartans), apparently by effectively bribing the jury – no mean feat given the size of Athenian juries (see Plutarch 1909: 378–379). Even so, Anytus secured a reputation for being one of the politicians who, in 403 BCE, helped to lead a democratic revolt against the Thirty Tyrants. Sparta had appointed the Thirty after the Peloponnesian war (1909: 431–434) with the aim of replacing the defeated democratic leaders with its selected heads. However, the successful uprising overthrew the tyrants and re-established a new democracy. Anytus claimed that Socrates' unyielding criticism of Athenian practices, and democratic institutions (he championed the need for an educated elite to lead Athens), had in effect corrupted the youth and threatened a future democracy. An amnesty had prevented charges being brought against those involved with the politics following the war, and perhaps Anytus thought this case provided a way of bringing Socrates to account for his criticism of Athenian democracy (even if he has also been critical of the tyrants).

However, there might have been other reasons too. In Plato's *Meno* we are told that Anytus offered this decisive and prophetic warning:

> Socrates, I think that you are too ready to speak evil of men: and, if you will take my advice, I would recommend you to be careful. Perhaps there is no city in which it is not easier to do men harm than to do them good, and this is certainly the case at Athens, as I believe that you know.
>
> (Plato, 1999: 132)

Even if taken out of context, Plato here referred to Anytus' worry about Socrates' critical politics. Equally, Socrates' response to Anytus' friend, Meno, reveals something about Socrates' underestimation of the rage that he had generated by his constant questioning of democratic politicians:

> Anytus is in a rage. And he may well be in a rage, for he thinks, in the first place, that I am defaming these gentlemen; and in the second place, he is of opinion that he is one of them himself. But some day he will know what is the meaning of defamation, and if he ever does, he will forgive me.
>
> (Plato, 1999: 133)

The envisaged forgiveness, as is well known, was never to be. Indeed, Anytus charged him with corrupting the youth of Athens by emboldening them to question the received wisdom of Athenian elders, and to challenge the accepted views of the day. As further evidence of his concerns, Anytus noted how Socrates' students turned out to be enemies of the city. Most notably, during the war, Alcibiades (for whom Anytus seems to have had a fondness – see Plutarch, 1909: 260) was said treasonously to have fled to Sparta; equally, Critias was one of the Thirty Tyrants (see Creeden, 1994: 176). But perhaps more than this, Anytus' seemingly unruly son was one of Socrates' followers. Anytus might well have blamed him in part for his son's non-conformist preclusions, and even for the latter's proclivity toward wine, which according to Xenophon, was not insignificant:

> The youth, taking pleasure in wine, did not stop drinking, day or night, and finally he became worthless to the city, his loved ones, and to himself. And Anytus, on account of the poor upbringing of his son and his own lack of good judgment, still, though he is dead, has a bad reputation.
>
> (Brickhouse & Smith, 2002: 87)

So, with Anytus, we have an accuser who claimed to tell a juridical truth that framed Socrates as a political nuisance; a man whose persistent criticism and followers undermined the Athenian political order. By encouraging people (the youth specifically) constantly to question received ideas, Socrates' genre of critical philosophy was portrayed as politically dangerous, corrupting, and a threat to the newly recouped democracy. The truth Anytus avowed was two-fold: a politically self-interested truth in support of a democracy with which he was associated as a leader; and a paternal disappointment with a son that was generalized to blame Socrates for corrupting the youth of Athens. His juridical avowals thus rendered a unique kind of subjectivity of a political leader in favour of a democratic order and against the violent tyranny of an immediate past, and a concerned father who viewed Socrates as one who had corrupted young minds by encouraging them to critically examine everything.

In concert, then, we can see the ways in which avowal, or more precisely juridical truth-telling, by Socrates' accusers generated diverse forms of subjectivity through the various accusations made in the name of a public order. Pondering such age-old rituals of accusation, one might note how accusers were recursively constituted as specific sorts of selves who negotiated contextually accepted discourses of morality and legality. They also claimed to be effective translators of selected actions as wrongdoing in the interests of a given order, requiring legal intervention. In rhetorical struggles that privileged legal truths, the accusers were at pains to translate actions of past social flows as decisive legal wrongs. Through accusations of wrongdoing, one finds keys to the gates that unlocked entryways to courts, exposing the accused to law's mighty force.

Socrates, the accused

Imagine a 70-year-old, impoverished Socrates in ragged clothes as he faced the court following an unsuccessful challenge to the accusations of his prosecutors before the king archon at the Royal Stoa. One might have expected a man facing death to comply with legal and rhetorical expectations. Instead, Socrates abjured the usual rhetorical strategies of the time (specifically written rhetorical defences in law, pleading for mercy, drawing on emotional ties), preferring, as he put it, to speak 'plainly' by offering logical challenges to the charges and accusers. The details of his arguments (Brickhouse & Smith, 2002; Carey, 2011; Miller & Platter, 2010), and possible reasons for his curious defence (Xenophon in Brickhouse & Smith, 2002: Chapter 3) have been canvassed in existing literatures (Stone, 1989). However, in what follows, one might consider Plato's *Apology* as signposting Socrates' unique avowals when called to account for actions that his accusers alleged as wrongdoing.

Returning to the initial accusation, we might consider how Socrates felt when the criers summoned him to face several accusations. Probably surprised, Socrates would likely have reflected on the self that was challenged. Why would these accusers now pronounce his actions and philosophical discussions – that had for many decades contoured his public life in Athens – as wrongdoing? Why these three accusers? Which factions of the city would they have mobilized to assure the success of their legal narrations of events? One might speculate further, but from Plato's *Apology*, three fundamental elements of the avowals deemed necessary to accuse another of wrongdoing surface.

First, Socrates' opening lines of the *Apology* reveal an important facet of criminal accusation, or accusations of legal wrongdoing: it arrests everyday life and signals different requirements for avowal and, correspondingly, new ways of working on the self to negotiate what it is to be an accused subject in context. Consider the significance of these words ascribed to Socrates:

> I don't know what effect my accusers have had on you, Athenians, but they were speaking so persuasively that I myself almost forgot who I am. And yet they said virtually nothing that's true. Of their many lies, one surprised me most of all: When they said you needed to be on your guard against getting tricked by me, because I'm a clever speaker. Their not being ashamed of that seems to me to be the worst thing they did, because I'm immediately going to refute them by what I do – as soon as I show that I'm not a clever speaker at all – unless they call a clever speaker one who tells the truth. If this is what they mean, I'd agree that I am an orator, though not the way they are.
>
> (Brickhouse & Smith, 2002: 42–43)

Various dimensions of these classic words have been explored elsewhere (see Chapter 1), but let us here focus on the sorts of avowal implied, and what this means for understanding key elements of accusation.

These opening lines, as indicated in chapter 1, reveal how Socrates experienced the call to account for his beliefs and actions. He listened to the convincing words of his accusers, and heard them articulate truth claims that rang entirely hollow for the kind of subject that he had in the past understood himself to be. Hence, while he comprehended the words that recast his past actions, they were for him false, lies, and calumnies. The accusing narratives stood in stark contrast to the philosophical sense of self that he had over the years, and with some hardship, sought to maintain. This was the 'truth' to which he addressed himself. While he accepted that, 'I must obey the law and make a defense' (Brickhouse & Smith, 2002: 44), his avowals would not be juridical, or cleverly rhetorical. As he put it, 'The truth is this: Now is the first time I've come before a court, although I'm seventy years old. I'm a complete stranger to the language used here' (Brickhouse & Smith, 2002: 43).

So, he elected to speak in a 'dialect and manner in which I had been brought up'. His truth-telling, so he alleged, would adhere to the plain speech of critical philosophy, not the caprices of sophistry or the flair of legal argument.

Socrates, therefore, did not follow what might be expected of a lawyer or sophist's argument. Instead, he opted for a way of telling the truth that explained – in a fashion that refuses to defer to the jury – why he has been accused of wrongdoing. He began by alleging that the reasons for the accusations lay not with the immediate claims made by the three accusers before him, but with a rather more significant proximate, unstated, prejudice against him and his philosophical way of life. Indeed, he claimed to be more concerned with the latter than the former since he recognized that, 'there's a great deal of hatred directed at me and by many people, you may be sure that's true' (Brickhouse & Smith, 2002: 53). His accusers probably tapped a rich vein of prejudgment against him for antagonizing all sectors of Athenian society by his relentless questioning. He might also have chosen this line of defence because, as Xenophon suggests, he was ready to face death.

Regardless, it seems that Socrates wished to preserve a sense of self as critical philosopher to which he had attached great importance throughout the course of his life (see Brickhouse & Smith, 2002: 81ff.). This is perhaps why he pursued a philosophical rather than 'legal' defence that begins rather obtusely by declaring utter surprise at having been informed that the Gods at Delphi saw him as the wisest person in Athens. In response, so Plato tells us, he questioned several politicians, craftsmen and poets that he considered wiser than himself. By his hardnosed grilling of each in turn, he seems to have offended many people. We are told that these examinations unexpectedly revealed that perhaps he was the wisest person, but only because he seemed at least aware of a basic human shortcoming; namely, 'I, just as I don't know, don't even think I know' (Brickhouse & Smith, 2002: 47). By coming to this conclusion via his interrogations of powerful people, he had aroused anger that made several people happy to move ahead with the accusations against him.

Socrates feared the 'background' accusations more than the immediate ones. The largely unspoken context was more difficult to confront than the specific accusations:

> I must make my defense, Athenians, and try to remove from your minds in such a short time the slander you accepted for a long time. I'd hope that this happens, if it's better for you and for me, and that in making my defense I do it successfully. But it's not lost on me that this sort of task I'm facing will be difficult.
>
> (Brickhouse & Smith, 2002: 44)

From this general difficulty, he challenged – via various syllogistic refutations – the claims of his accusers, focusing (given the time limits) on Meletus. Linking their accusations to Aristophanes' mocking play, *Clouds*, he declared how his accusers completely misread what he had always tried to do. In particular, his accusers more or less misrecognized him thus:

> 'Socrates does wrong and is too concerned with inquiring about what's in the heavens and below the earth and to make the weaker argument appear to be the stronger and to teach these same things to others' – something like this.
>
> (Brickhouse & Smith, 2002: 44)

Socrates rejected each of these allegations as false.

His defence might appear somewhat abstract, and at times seemed even to taunt the jury (Miller & Platter, 2010; Stone, 1989). Yet, there is another way to consider what he might have been doing; namely, avowing a truth in a juridical context, but in ways that remained within philosophical genres and which reinforced the practices of self-formation, and the creation of particular kinds of subjectivity, for which he was known. Socrates tells us he was not speaking cleverly, or presenting clever forms of truth-telling; rather he sought to – despite his being called to account for his actions and to respond in accepted juridical formats – tell the truth in ways that do 'not forget' who he was, and to do so in ways that were 'not the way' his critics spoke, nor in the 'way they are'. In short then, Socrates refused the self-identity required of him by either legal process, or the one enunciated by the rhetorical avowals of his accusers. He did so by recognizing that juridical lines of resistance would limit his refusals and require him to enunciate a defence of self in ways incapable of embracing the kind of (philosophical) subject he had enunciated himself to be. As such, he met the accusations with blunt refusals, and did so doggedly by relying on modes of philosophical avowal upon which he had always relied.

A second aspect of the calling another to account for actions that accusers defined as wrongdoing could be referenced. Calling someone to account in law demanded avowals that shaped participants' identities. In other words, accuser and accused (as well as the authority, no doubt) did not meet each other as immutable subjects with fixed identities: rather through different provocations and responses, accusations and counter accusations, challenges and refutations, aspects of the subjects in the case appear, or more precisely co-appear. Practices of accusation partly shaped the co-appearance of accuser and accused in specific contexts. So, for example, we have noted how avowals shaped the accusers, just as the legal calls for an accused to tell the truth might have expected Socrates to avow his innocence by disavowing his philosophical identity. However, in the event, Socrates refused legal expectations and narrated a truth of self that remained loyal to genres of philosophical avowal, thus shaping a specific sense of self against that offered by his accusers (especially Meletus). Here we detect an important dimension of accusations of wrongdoing – how they arrest everyday life and rely on legal techniques to produce forms of self in relation to given charges.

Finally, the very act of accusation encourages the accused to negotiate a new identity ascribed to him or her. In most instances, when contested, this takes the form of trying to comprehend the nature of the attributed identity before demonstrating how and why it is a fabricated, or false, one. Plato's Socrates seems to have accepted the general idea: 'It's right for me to make my defence, Athenians, against the first of the false accusations made against me and against my first accusers, and then against the later ones and the later accusers' (Brickhouse & Smith, 2002: 43). Such a defence would typically involve various elements: the accused would have alleged a calumny, a false accusation; the credibility and/or sincerity of accusers would be challenged; and a different way of conceptualizing the truth of the accused's identity might be proffered.

Thus Socrates' defence repeatedly framed his accusers' indictments as calumnies; he did so not only by portraying their claims as absurd, but also showing how logically the very basis of their claims was utterly incoherent. At the same time, he alleged that the three accusers laboured under false pretences in bringing the charges to court. For example, he claimed they were motivated by the previously noted general prejudices, and had brought their charges insincerely on behalf of others – Meletus for poets, Anytus for craftsmen and politicians and Lycon for orators (Brickhouse & Smith, 2002: 49). Through their deceptions, they were the wrongdoers. Socrates therefore alleged that Meletus was an insolent, uncaring and immature self-promoter:

> But I say, Athenians, that he does wrong. Because he is playing around in what's serious business, thoughtlessly putting people on trial, while pretending to be serious and troubled about matters which he has never cared about at all.
> (Brickhouse & Smith, 2002: 49)

Socrates' subsequent interrogation of Meletus further portrayed him as entirely indifferent to any of the 'public' concerns raised by the accusation. Indeed, as he put it,

> You're not to be believed, Meletus – and what's more not even to yourself! He seems to me, Athenians, to be completely insolent and out of control and this indictment is just the result of insolence, lack of self-restraint and immaturity.
> (Brickhouse & Smith, 2002: 52)

In short, Socrates' defence was here concerned with discrediting the honesty, sincerity, motives and credibility of his accusers. He directly contested the claims made by his accusers, and so opened a space in which to avow a truth about himself as a simple but sincere philosopher striving for honesty and truth and relentlessly questioning those who portrayed themselves in false lights. So foundational was his conception of self that he refused to avow in ways that might be expected of him in a legal context, or indeed to employ rhetorical flair to save his life. His avowals suggest a kind of self that was proud of a life devoted to philosophical truths, even at the cost of death:

> You're wrong, sir, if you think that a person who has any merit needs to consider the likelihood of life or of death and not to look only to this when he acts: is he acting justly or unjustly and performing the deeds of a good or a bad person?
>
> (Brickhouse & Smith, 2002: 53)

Defiantly, he then argued that whether or not the jury condemned him to death, he would not do anything else, 'even if I have to die many times' (55). This is the sort of self that Socrates strived for as a philosopher, refusing other forms of avowal, practices of truth-telling, and their attendant subjectivities – even in the face of imminent death.

Conclusion

In conclusion, the preceding discussion highlights several key elements of avowal that work with accusations of legal wrongdoing. It has referenced several technologies of self-formation imparted through complex accusatorial relations that require distinctive kinds of selves to avow truths in legally sanctioned ways. Of these gateways to law, one might glean that certain avowals are crucial to an accusatorial politics of recognition that either opens or closes figurative gates that allow law to face its accused persons.

Furthermore, the negotiations between accuser, accused and authorized legal agents are not the active work of fixed, or a priori, persons of law. Instead, co-appearing accusing, accused and authorized selves are fashioned through local rituals that call accused subjects to avow truths in relation to legally alleged wrongdoing. The co-appearance of accuser and accused might seem counter-intuitive, but these subjects surface out of the responses solicited through specific sorts of avowals. From that co-appearance one might detect the contours of locally framed versions of a politics that recognizes given subjects as potential wrongdoers in authorized (legal) ways. The gateways to legal judgments of wrongdoing are thus multifaceted and complex; but are also subtle and deeply bound to technologies of self-formation that, in turn, are tied to wider social hierarchies and orders. Indeed, it could even be that entryways of specific forms of accusation are inextricably tied to the orders in whose name they claim justly to serve. Such are the truth-telling dimensions of accusatory processes at gateways to criminal justice. By extension, they are perhaps foundational to the criminal justice expansions that have enabled such vast increases to the volume, number and type of subjects admitted to criminal law and its institutions nowadays. But that is a topic for another time.

References

Boegehold, A. L. (1995). The lawcourts at Athens: sites, buildings, equipment, procedure, and testimonia. *The Athenian Agora*, Vol. 28. Results of Excavation. Princeton, NJ: American School of Classical Studies at Athens.

Brickhouse, T. C., & Smith, N. D. (eds). (2002). *The Trial and Execution of Socrates: Sources and Controversies.* New York: Oxford University Press.

Carey, C. (2011). *Trials from Classical Athens.* New York: Routledge.

Christie, N. (2013). *Crime Control as Industry.* Abingdon: Routledge.

Constable, M. (2014). *Our Word Is Our Bond: How Legal Speech Acts.* Stanford, CA: Stanford Law Books.

Creeden, S. (1994). *Fair is Fair: World Folktales of Justice.* Little Rock, AR: August House.

Dorjahn, A. P. (1941). On the Athenian anakrisis. *Classical Philology*, 36(2), 182–5.

Ericson, R. V., & Baranek, P. M. (1982). *The Ordering of Justice: A Study of Accused Persons as Dependants in the Criminal Process.* Canadian Studies in Criminology 6. Toronto, ON: University of Toronto Press.

Felstiner, W. L. F., Abel, R. L., & Sarat, A. (1980/1981). The emergence and transformation of disputes: naming, blaming, claiming . . . . *Law & Society Review*, 15(3/4), 631–54.

Foucault, M. (2014). *Wrong-Doing, Truth-Telling: The Function of Avowal in Justice.* F. Brion & B. E. Harcourt (eds). Chicago, IL: The University Of Chicago Press.

Gagarin, M., and Cohen, D. (eds). (2005). *The Cambridge Companion to Ancient Greek Law.* New York: Cambridge University Press.

Garland, D. (2002). *The Culture of Control: Crime and Social Order in Contemporary Society.* Chicago, IL: The University of Chicago Press.

Johnstone, S. (1999). *Disputes and Democracy: The Consequences of Litigation in Ancient Athens.* Austin, TX: University of Texas Press.

MacDowell, D. M. (1986). *The Law in Classical Athens.* New York: Cornell University Press.

Miller, P. A., & Platter, C. (2010). *Plato's Apology of Socrates: A Commentary.* Norman, OK: University of Oklahoma Press.

Nails, D. (2002). *The People of Plato.* Indianapolis, IN: Hackett Publishing.

Pavlich, G. (2006a). The lore of criminal accusation. *Criminal Law & Philosophy*, 1(1), 79–97.

Pavlich, G. (2006b). 'Accusation: landscapes of exclusion', in W. Taylor (ed.), *Geography of Law: Landscape, Identity and Regulation.* Oxford: Hart Publishing, pp. 85–100.

Plato. (1999). *Meno.* Retrieved from: www.gutenberg.org/ebooks/1643 (access date: 5 March, 2015).

Plutarch. (1909). *Plutarch's Lives of Themistocles, Pericles, Aristides, Alcibiades, and Coriolanus, Demosthenes, and Cicero, C[ae]sar and Antony.* New York: P. F. Collier.

Simon, J. (2007). *Governing Through Crime: How the War on Crime Transformed American Democracy and Created a Culture of Fear*. Studies in Crime and Public Policy. New York: Oxford University Press.

——. (2014). *Mass Incarceration on Trial: A Remarkable Court Decision and the Future of Prisons in America*. New York: New Press.

Stone, I. F. (1989). *The Trial of Socrates*. New York: Anchor.

Wacquant, L. J. D. (2010). *Punishing the Poor: The Neoliberal Government of Social Insecurity*. Durham, NC: Duke University Press.

Waterfield, R. (2010). *Why Socrates Died: Dispelling the Myths*. Toronto, ON: Emblem Editions.

Chapter 4

The violent rhetoric of accusation

Cicero and the Marcus Ameleus Scaurus case

The accusation of Marcus Scaurus

On 6 July 54 BCE, Marcus Ameleus Scaurus was formally accused of extortion while serving as the *praetor pro consule* of Sardinia (Asconius, 2006; Cicero & Dyck, 2012; Henderson, 1958). An antagonist by the name of M. Valerius Triarius spearheaded the prosecution, with two brothers (M and Q. Pacuvius Caldus) and L. Marius serving as assistants or *subscriptiones* (Alexander, 2003: 100). This rather obscure group of accusers was probably seeking renown by accusing someone from a prominent family with political ambitions in that year's consular elections. And the family certainly was prominent: Scaurus' father had served as both consul and censor while his mother, Caecilia Metelus Diadematus, remarried none other than Sulla after Scaurus senior's death. A successful prosecution before the calendar elections would discredit Scaurus junior as a viable candidate for consul, and this promised his accusers political and pecuniary gain (Alexander, 2003: 105). Recognizing the stakes, Scaurus called upon six extremely well-known *patroni* (advocates) to mount his defence, including the famous Cicero.

From his analysis of remaining textual sources, Henderson (1958) reveals Scaurus' flamboyant life. Having accumulated substantial wealth from service for Pompey in Syria, he returned to Rome to erect a massive home on the Palatine (for which he bought an adjoining property) and, once elected as *aedile*, built an impressive temporary theatre for public games (decorated with no less than 360 massive columns and able to seat about 80,000 people!). Henderson also notes that Scaurus' exploits give the 'impression of rash scheming, ruthless ambition, and above all venality' (1958: 197). The profligacies for which he became known produced large debts, and his stint in Sardinia was to help defray these. While discontent with his actions as proconsul might have prompted the accusation, the actual trial played out in the context of consular politics at Rome (Alexander, 2003: 100). Indeed, his accusers sought a verdict before the calendar consular elections could take place, no doubt hoping to disqualify his run for office. They accused him of numerous offences over and above extorting local Sardinians, including the use of violence, sexual transgression and interfering with Rome's grain supply.

On one of the charges, Scaurus' accusers claimed he had a hand in the death of a Sardinian resident, Bostar, who had intended leaving the province before Scaurus' arrival. In the event, the man allegedly dined at Scaurus' home, but died before Scaurus' 'dinner was removed' (Cicero & Dyck, 2012: 101). The prosecutors blamed him for Bostar's death, arguing that he intended to gain personally from the man's family estate. In his defence, Cicero rejected this story, suggesting instead that Bostar's mother poisoned her son to secure the family estate. As well, the accusers blamed Scaurus for inciting the suicidal death of an unnamed woman. Seemingly her husband, Aris, had left for Rome without her and she had subsequently committed suicide. Scaurus' accusers alleged that she did so to avoid having to jeopardize her marital fidelity in the face of Scaurus' improper sexual advances. Again Cicero rejected the accusation, but this time relied on a prejudiced dismissal that the 'lady was not only supremely ugly but also in extreme old age' (Cicero & Dyck, 2012: 103). He suggested instead that she either killed herself because of her husband's treachery; or Aris had her killed, making it look like suicide, so that he could marry – as he had since done – Bostar's mother (a witness in the case). Also, the accusers indicted Scaurus for criminally speculating on the grain market and/or interfering with the grain supply. Cicero rejected this charge out of hand.

All in all, whatever the merits of the accusers' case, they seem neither to have investigated their indictments thoroughly, nor did they return to Sardinia for witness testimony, leading a commentator to this assessment: 'It seems clear that the accusation of Scaurus was a political manoeuvre, intensified by a number of personal considerations, and designed to prevent Scaurus from campaigning' (Henderson, 1958: 200). No doubt an unwanted intrusion into his election campaign for consul, Scaurus would stop at little to clear his family name.

Accusation, crime and standing courts in the late Roman Republic

As this case suggests, ideas and practices of accusation were basic to public law and 'crime' of the late Roman Republic. However, it is worth mentioning that, 'In republican Latin no words existed that can be literally translated as *murder, crime, criminal courts, or criminal law*' (Gaughan, 2010: 2). Even if what we call homicidal acts evoked communal disquiet, their general framing as 'crime' was indistinct (Gaughan, 2010). So, as Riggsby (1999) points out, in contrast to our emphasis on crime, Roman culture was indifferent to abstracted notions of criminality. It focused instead on individual instances of wrongdoing, the precise status of which was worked out via its 'public' law. That said, certain acts, such as extortion, were framed under the heading of '*crimen*' (that referred to accusation) and were defined publicly through accusatory processes (Riggsby, 1999).

In other words, accusation was integral to defining public or communal wrongdoing (Harries, 2007). The criminalization of events and subjects was legally initiated through specific accusations, and no crime or criminal was recorded without an accuser bringing the matter to light. If this underscored the significance of accusation to the appearance of crime in this society, it also highlighted the value of examining how accusers and the accused's defence initiated, structured, shaped and fed Roman patterns of public wrong. Such accusations did not simply operate through pre-trial procedures, for which there are scant extant sources; accusations and counter-accusations continued as integral elements of late republican court process. Throughout a jury trial, that is, criminal wrongdoing was claimed and countered, defined and redefined, just as specific accusations were made or displaced, and calumny asserted. Such accusatorial processes, which were considered to have a distinct nature, often also took place within a wider politics of the day (Gruen, 1968; Marshall, n.d.)

In his related analysis of Roman punishment over the course of the first century BCE, Bauman (1996) points to the changing organization of public (criminal) courts within which accusations of a crime-like nature could be enunciated. Compared with Roman society's elaborately formal civil law (Tellegen-Couperus, 1993: 53ff; Versteeg, 2009), or indeed its use of restitution through delict, public law was rather under-developed (Bauman, 1996; Powell & Paterson, 2004). Even so, actions considered as harmful to broader Roman society were gradually brought forward as 'public' legal measures in 'courts' of the *iudicium populi* ('judgment of the people' – see Harries, 2007: 14). Though varied, these 'courts' usually operated under the auspices of the 'tribune of the plebs' who summoned suspects to appear for an enquiry known as the *anquisitio* (Bauman, 1996: 7–10).[1]

In the changing political climate of the second century BCE, a species of 'courts' was established as special senate commissions (*quaestiones perpetuae*) to investigate particular circumstances. Governing as a dictator (which perhaps set the precedent for Caesar's later one), Sulla instituted multiple legal reforms including the introduction of standing courts:

> [W]ithin the framework of his political reforms Sulla reorganized the permanent courts and increased their number. Thereafter there were six courts: for murder and poisoning, for forgery of wills and other documents, for high treason, for bribery during elections, for extortion in the provinces and finally for embezzlement of public funds.
>
> (Tellegen-Couperus, 1993: 52)

These standing courts, *iudicia publica* ('public courts') became important sites for criminal accusation before authorized state agents, rendering them 'analogous' to criminal courts nowadays (Riggsby, 1999: i). They developed around specific crimes, identifying four as especially prominent during Cicero's time: '*ambitus* (electoral bribery), *de sicariis et veneficis* (murder), vis (assault, riot), and *repetundae* (extortion by provincial administrators)' (see Harries, 2007: 3; Riggsby, 2010: 198ff.; Riggsby, 1999: i). Headed by magistrates, including those who dealt with 'foreign' matters (e.g., *praetor peregrines*), the courts superseded the rituals of popular assemblies and targeted specific offences (Bauman, 1996: 17; Riggsby, 2010: 196ff.).

From an annually drafted list of jurors, the praetor chose between 50 to 75 jurors (*iudicum*) by lot; both accused and accuser were given an opportunity to reject a limited number of jurors. And it was in these courts that 'the public as a whole' could try to find amends for communal wrongs (Riggsby, 1999: xii).

Against this background, the accusations against Scaurus were made to a *quaestio de repetundis* [extortion court, or literally 'the court about [funds] to be recovered' (Cicero & Dyck, 2012: 2)], that was established in 149 BCE through Sulla's *Lex Culpurnia*: 'The court was to consist of a panel of assessors . . . presided over by a praetor charged with handling disputes between Romans and foreigners (*praetor peregrinis*)' (Cicero & Dyck, 2012: 2).

Caesar's later reforms allowed juries also to include non-senators, but the court's procedure was only overhauled by Augustus' Principate of 27 BC and later simplified as *cognitio extraordinaria* (Bauman, 1996; Versteeg, 2009: 126ff.). In any case, the drama of Scaurus' case unfolded where specific 'criminal accusations' were solicited, authorized and used as the basis for calibrating whether subjects could be considered guilty of crimes. The setting, the rules and the processes did not simply reflect pre-existing identities; rather they were active criminalization mechanisms, involved in creating criminals and leading toward coordinated (state) responses to wrongdoing.

Criminal accusation in action

Standing criminal courts of the late republic were accusatorial rather than inquisitional in the sense that, 'no action could be initiated unless the citizen laid a formal accusation (*accusatio*) against another and thereby undertook to prosecute at the trial' (Mousourakis, 2007: 80). To initiate an accusation, adult male citizens of 'good repute' (Bauman, 1996: 17) could lay an information (*nominis delatio*) before the praetor or magistrate of a relevant standing court, requesting permission to instigate charges (*postulatio* – Harries, 2007: 18ff.).

Once permission was granted, the accuser was required to present a written statement about the purported offence in front of the accused (Cicero & Dyck, 2012: 6ff.). The accuser and those supporting the claim (*subscriptores*) signed the document outlining the accusation (*inscriptio*), and the accuser then 'had to swear an oath that he did not issue a false accusation out of malice (*calumnia*)', or in collusion with the accused (Mousourakis, 2007: 80ff.). Magistrates were supposed to determine (*legibus interrogatio*) impartially whether the case was permissible under the laws relevant to the court (Alexander, 2003: 8). Here one might note that in so doing, the magistrates were, in effect, determining whether the accusation, as framed, was legible and understandable to an authorized legal authority. With such formalities out of the way, the accuser was then given time to prepare the case – usually ten days, but possibly more in extortion cases, to allow prosecutors time to visit provinces in search of evidence (Harries, 2007: 18). Accusers could also request that the court summon up to 48 witnesses (*testes*) – a number subsequently expanded to 120 (Cicero & Dyck, 2012: 6).

The actual criminal trial started with the accusers' opening speeches, the defence's reply and then an examination of witnesses (Powell & Paterson, 2004: 32). Harries describes the process thus:

> Speeches setting out the facts of the case and the lines of argument were made, first by the prosecution *patronus* (advocate) and then by the defence, both of whom were subject to time limits. Both sides then engaged in cross-questioning or interrogating the other (skill at which the quick-witted Cicero excelled) before moving to the calling of witnesses.
>
> (Harries, 2007: 19)

At Scaurus' trial one could expect a noisy court convened in an open forum where jurors, if bored, 'might walk about, chat with each other or in groups, send a slave to find out the time, or ask the president of the court for an adjournment' (Lintott, 2004: 63–64). The setting had 'something of a free-for-all' quality (Powell & Paterson, 2004: 36) since its rendition of justice was, 'both public and rowdy and there was little sense that the jurors might require a period of quiet reflection' (Harries, 2007: 19). Indeed, after witness examination, the jury members were expected to decide forthwith on ballots marked either '"A" for acquittal and "C" for condemnation' or could vote that there was insufficient evidence (op. cit.). There were no summary statements and no formal jury deliberation (indeed their votes were supposed to be independently cast).

Even so, justice here demanded that participants play recognized roles – accuser, accused, jury member, magistrate, witness, spectator, etc. Certain rhetorical rudiments were also viewed as fundamental to the very nature of accusation, and to rendering events intelligible to legal scrutiny. By implication, if accusers or defenders of the accused did not use appropriate rhetorical forms, the legitimacy of accusatorial forms of law was potentially undermined. But this, in turn, suggested that accusation was distinguishable from its perversions, and so could be said to harbour an essential nature. Rutledge frames the point in this way:

> There was something inherent in accusation, according to Roman rhetoricians, which was either violent by nature or which could easily lead to such an impression. Recognition of this fact led them to develop what was tantamount to a theory of accusation.
>
> (Rutledge, 1999: 562)

In other words, accusation could be discerned through a distinctive rhetorical practice; that this was a 'violent' nature underscored a recognition that of the damaging potential for participants' lives – their names, reputations and socio-economic standing. At the same time, there were differences in how this 'nature' played out in the rhetoric of accusers as opposed to the accused's defence. Let us then deal with each separately.

The accuser's 'violent' oratory

As noted, accusers in the late republic were neither government officials, nor public (state-sponsored) prosecutors. They were supposed to be men of 'good standing' within the general citizenry who, for various reasons, launched accusations. When initiating a charge, the accuser had to swear an oath before a magistrate indicating that the indictment was free from both: '*calumnia*, launching a prosecution that one knows to be unfounded; and *praevaricatio*, collusion with the defendant for the defendant's benefit' (Alexander, 2003: 7).

Since the very integrity of public law rested on 'truthful' accusations, severe punishments faced violators of either offence. As discussed, Foucault's (2014) helpful lectures on avowal – truth-telling across changing juridical forms – call attention to the importance of 'governing the truth' and how avowers were governed as accusatorially sanctioned truth tellers. This work also alerts us to the danger of assuming in advance that such identities as 'accuser' or the 'accused' exist a priori; on the contrary, it suggests that how law requires subjects to avow truths in juridical contexts is part of how they come to be constituted as subjects of that law. That is, the historically sanctioned requirements, processes and truthful narratives of accusation recursively shape the subjects at hand.

But what prompted people to avow truths as accusers? From Cicero's writings, as suggested, subjects tended to do so for various reasons: making a name for themselves; serving the public good; continuing a family feud; and representing people in the provinces in extortion cases (Alexander, 2003: 7). Also, accusers were often enticed by the prospect of economic enrichment as spoils could be directed to those most responsible for a conviction (Cowles, 1929). Others used legal processes to further political ambitions, such as in the Scaurus case where the prosecution seemingly levelled accusations (in part) to prevent him from running in the consular elections (Gruen, 1968).

Whatever the reason, accusing someone of a crime – especially in cases of extortion – involved considerable rhetorical and logistic aptitude: 'Extortion cases, involving as they did large – often huge – sums of money and witnesses from a foreign, often distant part of Rome's empire, required the greatest organizational effort from the prosecutor' (Alexander, 2003: 245).

Increasingly, with the development of standing courts, accusations were managed by practiced rhetoricians: 'the actual pleading of cases became a matter for professional orators' (Lintott, 2001: 105). That is, the courts offered new opportunities for occupations that today might be considered 'prosecutorial' in form. Indeed, Lintott (2001) describes the rise of the professional *accusator* as a product of such changes, and indeed this was accompanied by the rise of the index or informer who provided material for the former. Although not much survives about late republic informers, Rutledge surmises that they foreshadowed the Principate's prominent use of professional *delatores* (Rutledge, 2001). But, during Cicero's time, it would seem that the informer's status was generally considered as less than salutatory: 'Accuser (*accusator*) is the neutral term; informer (index) implies somebody on the fringes of the crime he denounces. Hence our earliest references to accusers who were not themselves victims are already pejorative' (Robinson, 2007: 207). Even if held in negative regard, informers did serve as key aids to accusers, helping to stock and sharpen their rhetorical arsenals — 'digging up dirt' as it were in efforts to persuade juries of an accusers' denunciations (Lintott, 2001; Robinson, 2000, 2007).

Yet, it was not only the index whose morality was questioned. Robinson points out that the moral status of accusers, who prosecuted others of crime, required justification: 'Criminal prosecution, even apart from the rewards, and the temptation of calumny, was thus morally dubious, rather than neutral. It could be justified, but it needed justification' (Robinson, 2007: 211).

Cicero largely agreed with this assessment (Dillon & Garland, 2015: 87), and even wrote a kind of apology for participating in an earlier prosecution of *Veres* (Cowles, 1929). At the same time, however, he thought that, like the geese and dogs that stood guard at the Emperor's palace, criminal accusation served to deter crime by offering a persistent threat:

> It is a useful thing that there should be a number of accusers in the state, so that audacity may be held in check by fear . . . This is the reason why we are all ready to allow that there should be as many accusers as possible, because an innocent man, if he is accused, can be acquitted, but one who is guilty, unless he is accused, cannot be condemned. For it is more expedient that an innocent man should be acquitted, than that a guilty man should not be brought to trial.
> (quoted in Robinson, 2007: 209).

Cicero and other rhetoricians such as Quintilian and the unknown author of *Rhetorica ad Herennium* thus described accusation as having a distinctive rhetorical style: there was a proper way to accuse another person of crime. In his analysis of effective orators who admirably accused others, Cicero (2006) construed oratory properly suited to successful accusations (Dillon & Garland, 2015: 88). Rutledge's review of surviving texts that describe how to accuse or prosecute effectively, leads him to the view that making an accusation was premised on a priori knowledge of proper ways to accuse. Specifically, he argues that 'Terror, treachery, and singularity of purpose were the foundation blocks of the *accusor*, whose task was to excite . . . [hatred, anger and envy] . . . in his audience by drawing a caricature of the accused based on innuendo and probability' (Rutledge, 1999: 563). As a result, he argues that the rhetoric of accusation appeared as innately 'vehement', acerbic, emotive, hard-hitting and even 'violent' in its attempts to annihilate the accused's character and reputation. Additionally, for Quintillian, the nature of the accusation was premised on a basic objective:

> By the accuser nothing more is to be kept in view than that he must prove that something was done; that a particular thing was done; that it was done wrongfully; and that he brings his action according to law.
> (Quintilian, 2010: Book 3, Chapter 6: 85)

To achieve this (see Book 3, Chapter 6), the accuser had to take full advantage of the element of surprise available to him as the first to speak – whether at initial indictments or at trial. This advantage, which he thought made accusing easier than defending, afforded accusers unique opportunities to prepare and plan a rhetorical strategy to reach a clearly defined end (whereas the accused is always left in a position of reacting to charges). So, the accuser might use this advantage slyly by putting gentle, even irrelevant questions to the accused before suddenly shifting to very direct accusations designed to throw the accused onto the back foot (Book 3, Chapter 5: 717–718). This opening perfidy provided a way for accusers to disarm the accused, and clear the way to a full-frontal attack on character.

The rhetorical use of caricature and character assassination as techniques was especially important to the rhetoric of both accuser and accused. Accusers, however, as Rutledge (1999) indicates, were expected to caricature the accused in the worst possible light, trying to assign a character that contemporary Romans would have expected to commit the alleged crimes – thus the murderer might be cast as rash, the thief as greedy, and so on. If they could not pin such character traits on the accused, then a 'fall back' position was to allege that there must always be a first time (Quintilian, 2010: Book 7, Chapter 2: 33). Such rhetorical techniques seemed to tap a pervasive sense that people's characters are more or less 'fixed' throughout adult life, and that a close, but incomplete, link exists between character and action (Riggsby, 2004: 169–170). Sometimes people acted 'out of character', or concealed their true characters, but in general they acted in line with past 'character'; as a result, Riggsby notes that 'Accounts of a person's character (most commonly but not necessarily that of the defendant) clearly count as evidence of guilt or innocence in a Roman court' (2004: 177). The aim of referencing character was thus, in part, to amplify the savageness of the person able to commit an atrocious crime, and doing so in as emotive a way as possible (Quintilian, 2010: Book 6, Chapter 2: 27–28). The able accuser was also expected to direct attention to the motives anticipated of the caricature ascribed to the accused; and if no such motives could be found, he was to declare the crime even more atrocious for not having one (Book 7, Chapter 2: 35–36).

Reflecting on the wider significance of strategic character battles, one might note that a successful accusation constituted the very basis for declaring wrongdoing in context:

> Whether the orator will prevail or not depends not on the crime itself, but on how the prosecution represents it. The character of the accused must be represented in such a way that it corresponds to the type of crime that the defendant is accused of having committed.
>
> (Rutledge, 1999: 563)

Even with limited sources indicating the precise *modes operandi* of Scaurus' accusers (but see Alexander, 2003; Asconius, 2006), one might infer that they sought to impugn his character by alluding to recurring accusations against his father (this is perhaps why Cicero opened and closed with a defence of the father and the family's contributions to Rome). Here, 'facts' could be considered as secondary to effective argument. Indeed, a proper accusation demanded well-developed rhetorical strategies to convince jurors that: a 'crime' had taken place; it was committed by the accused whose character either motivated the offence, or did not disqualify him from so doing; and that all the accusations were made in accord with law and the nature of accusation. Accusers were encouraged to speak indirectly, casting 'facts' in a suspicious light and making copious use of innuendo to appeal to jurors' emotions, and even flattering them with charms about their age and social status (Quintilian, 2010: Book 4, Chapter 2: 81). A basic aim was to incite feelings of anger, hatred, outrage and fury toward the accused. And in that quest, the accuser was to be 'remorseless and unrelenting, driving away all sympathy from the accused'; he 'must, in short, make the defendant's crime appear as savage as possible' (Rutledge, 1999: 564). We can then see why accusing could be cast as a 'violent' affair, for successful prosecutions made use of rhetoric for 'aggressive parody of the defendant's character' and to incite, 'anger or hatred to manipulate the audience' (Rutledge, 1999: 566). It is not hard to see why prosecutors created 'antagonism' since their trade was plied on anyone, and could bring about 'total ruin for a convicted defendant' (Alexander, 2003: 14).

Accusations also often fed and could affect the politics of the day. From the timing of the accusation, and the accusers' eagerness to prosecute him as expeditiously as possible – even declining to visit Sardinia in search of witnesses (Cicero & Dyck, 2012) – one could infer political overtones behind Scaurus' prosecution. Indeed, Alexander argues that

> Scaurus' prosecutors clearly wanted to finish their trial before the calendar elections, in the hope that they would be able to convict Scaurus by then and that, therefore, he would not be able to stand for office as a matter of law, he would not be a viable candidate as a matter of practical politics, or both.
>
> (Alexander, 2003: 105)

From this, one might note that the rhetorical nature of accusation was not simply a legal matter; it formed part of wider Roman politics (Gruen, 1968, 1974; Stein, 1999). It was especially influential in a politics of recognition where statuses were made and broken, and where vehement rhetorical practices sought to liquidate political characters through allegations of criminal activity. Regardless, it is worth pausing for a moment on the sorts of accusing subjects that such practices generated; namely, to be successful, accusers had to be unflinching in their ruthless, violent rhetoric designed to destroy the characters and past lives of those they accused. Behind this lies a bordering and ordering politics that generated accusers as subjects who rendered events legible as crimes to legal authority, force and framing political (sovereign) contexts.

The accused and the 'nature' of accusation

Extending Rutledge's important insights about the nature of accusation generally, one might argue that Cicero's rhetorical strategies followed what he believed to be essential elements of an effective defence for the accused. This was especially pertinent when considering that the law had already cast the accused as an increasingly silent witness to legal procedures, delegating 'representation' to specialist orators with knowledge of how to defend those accused of wrongdoing. In the Scaurus case, esteemed defence orators were hired to speak on his behalf; this platform was used to define his identity. Their orations rejected the accusers' accounts (often by alleging calumny) in attempts to convince juries of his innocence. They drew on accepted knowledge that detailed the multifaceted nature of accusation, and specifically how to defend an accused party. Cicero's counsel, for instance, followed his enunciations of effective defence oratory; he had written about the topic by examining the styles and techniques of successful orators such as Crassus, Antonius, etc. (Cicero & Watson, 1986). In effect, Cicero here enunciated knowledge of how to defend against accusations, and so added a dimension to the overall 'nature' of accusation. He argued that defensive rhetoric certainly operated in realms of opinion, but viewed it as founded on an art of how to persuade people; knowledge of this art was to be discovered by carefully studying past successes (Solmsen, 1938). By extrapolation, Cicero's defence of Scaurus tapped what he considered to be essential to defending an accusation.

In the fragmentary remains of his defence, Cicero referenced Roman versions of an ancient Greek tradition of practising 'forensic oratory' (Powell & Paterson, 2004), and so opened with an exordium. The aim of this opening was to secure the jury's and other listeners' attention, and to curry their good will (Lintott, 2008; Powell & Paterson, 2004). In the rhetoric of the defence he offered, Cicero framed himself as an impartial truth-teller, one who avowed entirely in accord with the law, as might be expected of a great Roman leader. His exordium respectfully but frankly engaged the jury, recursively marking him as a fair peer among equals – someone who could be trusted as an insider. Although courteous, his tone was unapologetic, pleading that Scaurus hoped – as any juror might – to 'without giving offence or causing distress, hold on to the standing of his line, his family, and his name, which is what he was always particularly eager to do' (Cicero & Dyck, 2012: 101). Here, as elsewhere, he tried to take the jury into his confidence, enabling him to claim to have a secret truth that he was prepared to share with peers.

He portrayed Scaurus as having an unassailably good character from a good family, before showing the duplicitous and devious motives of the accusers' bad characters. So, he took time to share the Scaurus family's longstanding contributions to Rome. Acknowledging – to prove his commitment to truth – that Scaurus senior had over the years been accused of various things, Cicero was quick to point out that none stuck and all were products of devious accusers seeking to feather their own nests. He thus confronted the prosecutors' negative attacks on the Scaurus family, while simultaneously contrasting the family's communal standing with a history of false accusations. This allowed him to mount a brief attack on the current accusers, framing their prosecution as disorganized and based on dubious assertions of scoundrel witnesses wishing only to benefit from, and thereby reduce, the fortunes of that family.

He then summarized the main arguments that would comprise his defence: they would contest the very kind of accusation presented, challenge the character of Sardinian witnesses upon which the persecution rested, and contrast this with the debt Sardinians owed Scaurus who – it had to be said – never disrupted the grain supply. Through his plea, Cicero seamlessly cast the accused in a favourable light, using structured assertions, digressions and arguments to present a character faithful to Roman law, and to portray Scaurus as entirely deserving of the social standing that he currently enjoyed. Magnifying a view of the accused as an undeserving victim of calumny from ungrateful and greedy accusers, Cicero emphasized his impartiality on the matter. He claimed to be happy to yield to the prosecution case were it based on reliable and truthful claims that could be backed by unassailable evidence:

> The argument appropriate to the matter – nothing else can truly be called an argument – is the voice of the facts, the footprint of nature, the mark of truth; whatever it is, it must remain immutable; it is not invented but taken by the speaker. Therefore if I am bested in a prosecution of this kind, I would yield and give way; for I would be defeated by the facts, by the case, by the truth.
>
> (Cicero & Dyck, 2012: 104)

His defence engaged a specific idea of truth as descending from the 'voice of facts'. In context, this would require accusers to back all claims with unimpeachable witness testimony that immutably declared the truth. This rhetorical move allowed Cicero to reject the strategy of refuting specific accusations; he argued instead that all their accusations were so vague and amorphously construed as to render them impossible to support.

Cicero's implication here was no doubt clear to his contemporaries: the accusers had violated the proper or inherent nature of accusation. They had inexcusably misrepresented the 'facts'. For example, as already referenced, he challenged the accusers' account of the events surrounding Aris' wife's death. She did not commit suicide, according to him, because of Scaurus' supposed advances, but because she had to face the shame of her husband's adulterous relations with Bostar's mother in Rome. In his version, Aris' wife was

> upset by the disgrace of adultery; when she heard that Aris had gone to Rome with his beloved pretending to flee in fear – so not only had there previously been a relationship between them but they would even be joined in matrimony – she flared up with a woman's rage and preferred to die rather than endure it.
>
> (Cicero & Dyck, 2012: 103)

Cicero here presented an evocative, emotive and patriarchal interpretation of 'facts' in a lexicon designed to tap jurors' prejudices to portray Scaurus as a maligned victim of false accusations.

Moreover, he contested the actual 'type' (nature) of the accusation levelled against Scaurus in two ways. First, he claimed that the accusations were scandalously slapdash and disorganized; they were so blatantly political that the accusers did not even bother to visit Sardinia to investigate the charges, or to produce reliable witnesses to support their allegations. Because of this complete lack of expected diligence, Cicero called on jurors to

> resist the entire type of prosecution in which you see nothing has been undertaken in the customary way, moderately, with deliberation, with integrity, on the contrary everything has been undertaken in a base, disorderly, hasty, rapid way by collusion, command, authority, hope, and threats.
>
> (Cicero & Dyck, 2012: 108)

In other words, the prosecutors had mounted an improper kind of accusation that neither reflected integrity nor followed 'customary' ways of doing things. Corrupt accusers masked their political motives and indeed coerced, threatened and cajoled witnesses to support their vague accusations. The overall implication was that the case presented fell short of the customary thresholds that would have allowed it to be described as a proper accusation.

Second, he noted that the accusers had failed to investigate their claims in Sardinia, and so could not provide reliable witness testimony. This allowed him to cast their claims as 'savage' because they could have crushing effects on Scaurus and his family. Consequently, Cicero rhetorically asked of Triarius the chief prosecutor: 'What manner of accusation is this, Triarius, that, in the first place, you have not gone to investigate? What was the basis of that confidence? So savage, so assured, that you could crush my client?' (Cicero & Dyck, 2012: 105).

Cicero framed the 'type' of accusation at hand as so disorganized, incompetent and without merit that one might ponder why it was presented at all. This astute rhetorical move allowed him to attribute devious political and pecuniary motives to Triarius. His accusations were not driven, as they should have been, by a public concern for truth; they were political attempts to gain an advantage in the race for consul. Indeed, Cicero pointed out, had he actually visited Sardinia, he would have discovered the true, positive 'state of opinion' about Scaurus.

Having thus discredited the general type of accusation presented, and the character of a main accuser, Cicero's defence circled back to a previous claim; that the prosecution's case rested ultimately on the credibility of witness testimony that it could not supply. Here he challenged the very foundations of the case, eliminating the need for detailed refutations of more specific claims. A considerable portion of his speech sought to discredit Sardinian witnesses by prejudicially ascribing to them a 'general type' of character; namely, as descendants of 'nations' whose 'vices' were, as enemies of the Punic wars, at odds with Roman interest. From here, he imputed an even more bigoted version of character:

> When I speak of a people's vices, I certainly make exceptions. But I have to discuss the general type; within it, by their character and culture, some may have conquered the vices of their line itself and their people. The facts themselves show clearly that the majority is without credibility, without partnership and bond with our nation.
>
> (Cicero & Dyck, 2012: 109)

This paved the way for another extraordinary claim; namely, that Sardinians 'not only lack all credibility and authority but do not even have the appearance or semblance of witness', and that their 'credibility is destroyed by their very unanimity' which amounts to a 'conspiratorial pact' (Cicero & Dyck, 2012: 108). As if such imperial bigotry were not enough, he went on to allege that their participation was prompted by 'well-known greed' and the 'hope and promise of rewards', implying a mendacious people who claimed a 'licence to tell lies'. However astonishing such assertions might now appear, Cicero imputed these character traits on the assumption that they were widely held, and to collapse the prosecution's case around the testimony of its discredited witnesses.

Cicero then moved to his conclusion, or peroration, leaving the jurors with a positive account of the Scaurus family's achievements: their tangible contributions to Rome were abundantly evident in many buildings in striking distance of the court (for example, the Senate house, the Temple of Castor and Pollux, etc.). He described the accused as a humble representative of a great family who wished no more than to continue the family line, a reasonable desire threatened by the accusers' avarice and false accusations. As Dyck notes, this appeal to pity was invited by 'a standard part of Roman judicial "theatre" for the defendant and family to dress in squalid clothing in order to appeal to the jurors' pity in the peroration' (Cicero & Dyck, 2012: 161).

Cicero concluded his defence with a basic question: 'By now, jurors, surely no residue of suspicion lingers in these charges does it?' (Cicero & Dyck, 2012: 104). Based on this and the other five defence orations, the jury acquitted Scaurus of the accusations, and several members even moved a motion to pursue calumny charges against the accusers. In the event, this motion was rejected, but from the above we get a sense of how an accused's identity was shaped by defence arguments, and how these might have been weighed by the jury to render a verdict with considerable consequences. Scaurus did eventually run for the consulship, which appears to have led to all the candidates, including him, being accused of bribery. Confirming the political tenor of the charges, this time he was convicted, even with Cicero's defence. It is perhaps not irrelevant that he no longer enjoyed Pompey's favour after marrying Pompey's ex-wife Mucia. In any case, Scaurus was seemingly exiled from Rome (Cicero and Dyck, 2012).

Concluding musings

From the above analysis, one gleans that the late Roman Republic framed images of wrongdoing from communal strictures about perceived threats to its well-being. It developed legal rituals to deal with 'crime' that descended from public law institutions – more or less organized peoples' assemblies, leading to standing courts headed by magistrates (often *praetors*) with large juries (Harries, 2007; Riggsby, 1999) and directed to individual offences. The latter were dependent upon initiating accusatorial processes, the course of which determined how to define and then deal with given circumstances thought to challenge community order (Riggsby, 1999: see Chapter 6). If this cemented the importance of accusation to an emerging criminal law, and consequent conceptions of crime, it also shows how late republican thinking understood rituals of accusation as constituting a distinctive rhetorical field, necessary to the very possibility of regulating crime, and framing persons as 'criminals'. This realization has several important implications for understanding criminal justice then, and potentially today too.

First, as we have seen, accusation was presented as having a distinct and intrinsic rhetorical nature that could be detected on its own terms. Although recognized as an art dealing with opinions, the field of accusation was also deemed capable of yielding knowledge of how properly to accuse someone of wrongdoing (crime), and how to mount an apposite defence against such accusations. In many ways, Roman thinking suggested that its rhetorical essence could be discovered by studying examples of successful orators, and the technologies they employed either to accuse people of crime, or defend those so accused. Accusation could then be designated as a discrete rhetorical field with an intrinsic set of qualities to further the authority of emerging legal structures. It was thereby tied to the foundation, even constitution, of public law and the development of ideas around crime as an offence against the entire community that required initiating public responses. Accusation became, in short, the starting point for criminalizing processes that might produce a criminal identity.

Second, the rhetoric of 'proper' accusations depended on accepted techniques of persuasion, even though their format depended on whether one was accusing, or being accused. We have isolated and analysed several techniques in relation to the specifics of the Scaurus case. To begin with we saw how accusers and the accused, through the process deemed proper to accusation, tried to contest the facts as presented by opponents. Accusers had the advantage of offering their narratives of events and participants first, while defenders of the accused were left to react and respond to what was alleged to have happened. An accuser was expected to use cunning methods to catch the accused off guard, and to use any rhetorical advantage to maximal effect. The accused might have been left to react to accusers, but their defence was expected to be equally unremitting in its challenges and attempts to attribute dubious or deliberately misleading intentions to accusers, or using emotive devices to make the accusations appear to be false, or worse, deliberate calumnies.

Another technique concerned the use of terror and treachery to destabilize the assurance with which accusations were declared or denied. One of the more enduring techniques in this respect, used by both accusers and accused, revolved around the ascription of character, or the promulgation of pithy caricatures. As noted, the close relationship between character and action was generally upheld in the courts and allowed accusers to evoke past indications of character to explain why one might have expected the accused to commit the criminal actions in question. Similarly, the accused was to discredit the character of the accusers, or witnesses supporting the accusers' case, to question the credibility of the people responsible for enunciating and solidifying criminalizing narratives. So, as we have seen, allegations of calumny might be attributed to politically ambitious characters, just as extraordinary extravagance might be attributed to someone accused of extortion. Such characterizations and counter-characterizations were to become critical features of a tango between accusers and the accused, accusation and counter-accusation. We also referenced the technique of repudiating witness testimony, especially by the accused, which, in the Scaurus case, had Cicero claiming that the prosecution's case rested entirely on the presentation of witnesses whose character he impugned via a prejudiced attack on an entire 'nation' – the Sardinians – as being incapable of reliable testimony.

Third, accusation was deemed to involve an essentially violent rhetorical nature, for it involved the decimation of people's everyday lives; the designation of criminal or false accuser stood as potential effects of its socially destructive force. Either way, people's lives and reputations were shattered through single-minded and intentional rhetorical attempts to cast people as worthy of being stripped of their social standing. Its violent rhetoric lay at the heart of legal designations that would later be called crime. Accusation provided a way of bringing matters to the court that pitted accusers against the accused, with state authorities (*praetors*) as mere arbiters for accepted court procedures. In this respect, Roman formulations of accusation provided us with a helpful way to understanding the roots of an adjudicative justice approach that called upon accusers and the accused. Local identities were mutually constituted out of criminal accusation processes, and so too the overseeing authorities and the sovereign orders in whose name prosecutions proceeded. One might say that the rhetorical form of accusation was then more than simply a way to accuse pre-existing subjects; its 'nature' was also to mould the identities of participants to its processes, and at the same time buttress the orders in whose name the accusations and their consequences proceeded.

Fourth, it is important to note that accusation was very much involved in what eventually materialized as a 'crime' and who was designated as 'criminal'. As Harries points out, what was then taken to be criminal in the later republic was not a function of previously established criminal codes. Rather there was a decidedly 'after the fact' quality to what appeared as criminality, starting with specific accusations that might eventually be identified as 'criminal', or 'an offence against the public good' for, as Harries suggests, because 'it was up to the community to decide not only on guilt but also on the nature of criminality itself, it was not necessary that a statute should be in place to outlaw wrongdoing' (Harries, 2007: 15).

The courts did not then work off general laws, beyond a magistrate deciding whether a given accusation could be tried in the court to which application was made. Instead, as reflected in the concept *crimen* (meaning 'reproach', 'charge', or the manner of 'calling subjects to account' for wrongdoing through accusation (Ayto, 1991)), procedures of accusation did not so much claim to 'discover' crime as formulate its presence in given instances. Its role lay in fashioning narratives on the legal facts of events, and framing particular acts as wrongs against the public with specific individuals as criminals. This placed accusation at the heart of emerging criminalization processes. It is worth quoting Harries at length on this:

> The law on 'crime' was defined in terms not of a hierarchy of offences but of the nature of the accusations that could be brought and the procedural and penal consequences of so doing for both accuser and accused. The Romans therefore did have a vocabulary for what might be termed 'crime' in a moral sense but there was no one word for 'crime' in Roman law. Instead, the procedure, through public accusation, served as a signal as to the nature of the offence. The 'accuser' asked the public, through its courts, to hold the accused to account.
>
> (Harries, 2007: 5)

From this passage, we might note that the rhetorical nature ascribed to accusation served as a foundation for defining crime, criminal wrongdoing and criminal persons through criminal trials.

Finally, aside from an internal politics of recognizing specific participants as accusers, the accused and so on, criminal accusation also contributed to the political life of the republic. It was framed around specific offences defined as threats to the Roman public; the actions that could be enunciated as criminal were bound to the political consolidations of a sovereign order, and were largely defined by the court decisions made in its name. But one might here echo the observation that:

> Roman criminal trials were political not because they were co-opted by politicians; politics is in a strong sense at the very heart of the definition of offences tried in the *iudicia publica*. At Rome there were no crimes that were not political crimes. The courts existed not for the sake of justice in the abstract . . . But for the good of the Roman people as a whole . . . The public courts are those where the community protects itself, its property and its rights. This idea, if not always in the front of the minds of the jurors is one they could be led to accept. Hence a higher political good may on occasion be used to preempt the issue of guilt or innocence.
>
> (Riggsby, 1999: 157–158)

Gruen reiterates the point by showing how the rise of standing courts provided a venue for various sorts of political struggle, from 'personal rivalries' to important constitutional matters that hinged on 'the outcome of a prosecution'; in short, criminal trials provided a mechanism 'for struggles within the governing class, or indeed a means whereby to attack that class itself' (Gruen, 1968: 6–7). In various ways, then, criminal accusation was used as 'political weapon', so much so that 'the business of politics' was frequently conducted in courts (Gruen, 1968: 6). For example, the 'governing class' often took accusations in criminal trials as offering the prospect of permanently neutralizing political opponents, affirming as with the Scaurus case, a means to wage 'political warfare' decisively (Gruen, 1974: 260). Indeed, 'electoral defeat was only temporary embarrassment' whereas 'conviction on a criminal charge might entail permanent exclusion from the public scene' (ibid.).

From the above, one glimpses the constitutive role accusation, understood as having an intrinsic if vehement rhetorical nature, played in the development of crime as an idea of general public wrong, and criminals as wrongdoers against a wider 'public'. Although much more can be said about this, the previous discussion highlights the misdirection of criminology's big mistake: its decision to study crime *sui generis* when its etymology suggests that it should have examined the idea of *crimen* as a calling to account through accusation. This recognition might surely have turned its gaze away from abstracted notions of crime and its causes to the accusations that gave rise to concepts of legal wrongdoing in the first place.

Note

1 This early enquiry process played out over three different days where the guilt of the accused was affirmed and suitable penalties devised (Bauman, 1996: 7–10). In these contexts, spectators shouted out comments, allowing the Tribune to gauge public opinion; but the decision rested with the Tribune unless the accused did not confess. In the latter instance, the matter would be referred to a formal assembly, usually of the *Commitia Centuriata*, for a vote without discussion (Mousourakis, 2007: 37ff.). Another version of this early court dealt with market-related offences under the auspices of specific *aediles* (Bauman, 1974).

References

Alexander, M. C. (2003). *The Case for the Prosecution in the Ciceronian Era*. Ann Arbor, MI: University of Michigan Press.

Asconius, P. Q. (2006). *Commentaries on Speeches of Cicero*. A. C. Clark, J. Harries, & R. G. Lewis (eds). Oxford: Oxford University Press.

Ayto, J. (1991). *Dictionary of Word Origins*. New York: Arcade Publishing.

Bauman, R. A. (1974). Criminal prosecutions by the aediles. *Latomus*, 33(2), 245–64.

——. (1996). *Crime and Punishment in Ancient Rome*. London: Routledge.

Cicero, M. T. (2006). *Cicero's Brutus or History of Famous Orators*. Retrieved from: www.gutenberg.org/ebooks/9776 (access date: August 10, 2016).

Cicero, M. T., & Dyck, A. R. (2012). *Marcus Tullius Cicero: Speeches on Behalf of Marcus Fonteius and Marcus Aemilius Scaurus: Translated with Introduction and Commentary.* Oxford: Oxford University Press.

Cicero, M. T., & Watson, J. S. (1986). *Cicero on Oratory and Orators.* Carbondale, IL: Southern Illinois University Press.

Cowles, F. H. (1929). Cicero's debut as a prosecutor. *The Classical Journal*, 24(6), 429–48.

Dillon, M., & Garland, L. (eds). (2015). *Ancient Rome: Social and Historical Documents from the Early Republics to the Death of Augustus* (2nd edn). New York: Routledge.

Foucault, M. (2014). *Wrong-Doing, Truth-Telling: The Function of Avowal in Justice.* Chicago, IL: The University of Chicago Press.

Gaughan, J. E. (2010). *Murder Was Not a Crime: Homicide and Power in the Roman Republic.* Austin, TX: University of Texas Press.

Gruen, E. S. (1968). *Roman Politics and the Criminal Courts, 149–78 B.C.*: Cambridge, MA: Harvard University Press.

——. (1974). *The Last Generation of the Roman Republic.* Berkeley, CA: University of California Press.

Harries, J. (2007). *Law and Crime in the Roman World* (1st edn). New York: Cambridge University Press.

Henderson, C. (1958). The career of the younger M. Aemilius Scaurus. *The Classical Association of the Middle West and South*, 53(5), 194–206.

Lintott, A. (2001). Delator and index: informers and accusers from the republic to the early principate. *Accordia Research Papers*, 9(3), 105–22.

——. (2004). 'Legal procedure in Cicero's time', in J. Powell & J. Paterson (eds), *Cicero the Advocate.* Oxford: Oxford University Press, pp. 61–78.

——. (2008). *Cicero as Evidence: A Historian's Companion.* New York: Oxford University Press.

Marshall, B. (n.d.). Two court cases in the late second century B.C. *American Journal of Philology*, 98(4), 417–23.

Mousourakis, G. (2007). *A Legal History of Rome* (1st edn). Abingdon: Routledge.

Powell, J., & Paterson, J. (eds). (2004). *Cicero the Advocate.* Oxford: Oxford University Press.

Quintilian. (2010). *Institutes of Oratory.* L. Honeycutt, & A. M. Riggsby (eds). Austin, TX: University of Texas Press.

Riggsby, A. M. (1999). *Crime and Community in Ciceronian Rome.* Austin, TX: University of Texas Press.

——. (2004). 'The rhetoric of character in the roman courts', in J. Powell & J. Paterson (eds), *Cicero the Advocate.* Oxford: Oxford University Press, pp. 165–86.

——. (2010). *Roman Law and the Legal World of the Romans* (1st edn). Cambridge: Cambridge University Press.

Robinson, O. F. (2000). *The Criminal Law of Ancient Rome.* Baltimore, MD: Johns Hopkins University Press.

——. (2007). 'The role of delators', in J. W. Cairns & P. J. du Plessis (eds), *Beyond Dogmatics: Law and Society in the Roman World.* Edinburgh: Edinburgh University Press, pp. 206–21.

Rutledge, S. H. (1999). Delatores and the tradition of violence in Roman oratory. *The American Journal of Philology*, 120(4), 555–73.

——. (2001). *Imperial Inquisitions: Prosecutors and Informants from Tiberius to Domitian* (1st edn). New York: Routledge.

Solmsen, F. (1938). Cicero's first speeches: a rhetorical analysis. *Transactions and Proceedings of the American Philological Association*, 69, 542–56.

Stein, P. (1999). *Roman Law in European History* (1st edn). New York: Cambridge University Press.

Tellegen-Couperus, O. (1993). *A Short History of Roman Law* (1st edn). New York: Routledge.

Versteeg, R. (2009). *Essentials of Greek and Roman Law*. Durham, NC: Carolina Academic Press.

Chapter 5

Cultural grammars of accusation

Thomas of Monmouth's blood libel accusations

As is evident from the previous chapters, accusations of illegal wrongdoing surface from settings that somehow confuse and disrupt taken-for-granted meanings. Though invariably a contingent matter, subjects who make sense of such circumstances through accusation typically do so by vocalizing their suspicions and pointing fingers of blame. This chapter explores, through an early twelfth-century example of a blood libel accusation, selected meaning-forming processes at the heart of what it is to accuse others of doing wrong. It does so by charting what might be termed a 'cultural grammar' that delimits idioms of accusation in context. This grammar specifies basic and contextually emergent ideas about: how to distinguish a true accusation from a calumny; what rituals must be followed to accuse another of wrongdoing correctly; what counts as evidence for a valid accusation; what makes an effective accuser; what to do as an accused; and so on.

The approach here musters a fluid sense of the word 'grammar' rather than a fixed, discoverable and metaphysical essence. Allied with Wittgenstein's (1980: 371, 373) sense of grammar noted in the introduction as expressing essence, emerging from 'forms of life', and specifying locally appropriate uses of words in 'language games' that yields meaning, my use of this term is itself rooted in convention – perhaps of socio-legal thinking influenced by the uncertainties that previously might have sought discoverable structures and certainties. In this sense, I work off the idea of grammar as no more than a conceptual placeholder, a nominal idea that becomes contingently through local ideas, rationales, rules, rituals and procedures that (covertly or otherwise) define valid accusations. Collectively, accusatory processes emerge locally through a grammar that enables a local lore – as opposed to law – of accusation to surface, and this broad terrain forms the topic to be discussed here.

Even though interpreting an accusation launched several centuries ago, this chapter recognizes the continuing relevance of its cultural grammar. To be sure, it parsed different sorts of denunciations from those that open or close gates to today's criminal justice systems, but its foundational imprints still shadow criminal jurisdiction and juridical claims over selective wrongs. Yet my chosen example is also foundational in another sense, being perhaps the 'first in the centuries-long series of ritual murder charges' (McCulloh, 1997: 701), and possibly the earliest in Britain (Rose, 2015; Bennett, 2005a; Holmes, 1981). Authored by a Benedictine monk, Thomas of Monmouth, *The Life and Passion of Saint William of Norwich*[1] consolidated what he took to be 'common knowledge' to launch a broad accusation; namely, that a 12-year-old boy was ritually murdered by Norwich's Jewish community – 'I accuse the Jews . . . as guilty in this matter, spillers of blood' (Book 1: XVI). Making such accusations stick promised to enhance Thomas's standing in the church hierarchy as champion of William's martyrdom. In the event, one of the far-reaching bequests of his accusatory exploits was to encourage religiously inspired, anti-Semitic prejudices whose future would resonate through horrifying atrocities, pogroms, exiles, genocides, and a catastrophic holocaust (Rees, 2017; Smith, 2003; Bauman, 2000; Chazan, 1997).

My aim, however, is to focus on how Thomas's document implicitly embraces a local grammar upon which his accusatory sense-making practices rested. The *Life and Passions*, that is, relied on a syntax to guide appropriate uses of words in the symbolic struggles that followed the confusions of finding a corpse in the woods. Reacting to ruptures in ordinary meaning horizons, several discursive pivots were enunciated; they, in turn, facilitated meaning-forging practices that flowed around culturally framed notions of suspicion and blame. Underscoring ideas and rituals of how to realign disconcerting circumstances, this cultural grammar guided contingently accepted ways to spin chains of signification from truth-based avowals that named distrust and culpability. Such pre-trial, meaning-creating, idioms seldom attract explicit scrutiny, and this might have something to do with regulatory efficiencies proportionate to their invisibility; that is, to accusation's ability to operate in unsighted shadows as imperceptible mantles of necessity.

Approaching Thomas's text

Highlighting the cultural grammar of a mid-twelfth-century instance of blood accusation in Norwich might seem an arbitrary choice. To be sure it is; but such aleatory in research is unavoidable and the promise is to envision forms of accusation at some distance from, with genealogical links to, our present practices. In this example, that is, we glimpse how rationales and rituals of accusation were integrated into canonical juridical administrations, standing alongside age-old private accusations and the reforming preliminary criminal procedures of the King's justice (Pollock & Maitland, 2012; Langmuir, 1984). In addition, Thomas's accusations were enunciated through hagiographical justifications which – viewed from different interpretative horizons – highlight the unpredictability, culturally situated character and socially consequential effects of accusatory struggles over meaning. As well, they show how a culturally authorized grammar of accusation flowed from discursive pivots and avowals of 'truth'. Even if penned six years after the symbolic confusions generated around the discovery of William's corpse in March 1144, Thomas's text affords a glimpse of the cultural ideas and rituals that enabled his accusation. It underscores in spades that accusations do not simply emerge from timeless bodies of customary evidence; they surface out of local symbolic struggles that draw on surrounding cultural prejudices and follow conventionally decreed grammars (see Chapter 7). Although the outcome of such meaning contests is never sure, Thomas's discriminatory claim that a ritual murder was committed by Norwich's Jewish community supported local battles for William's beatification – even if it did not rouse the violent force of the King's justice (Rose, 2015; Bennett, 2005a).

Over the years, commentators have dissected the *Life and Passions* in different ways, carefully sifting through its unbridled claims and assertions (Johnson, 2016, 2012; Bennett, 2005a; Langmuir, 1984; McCulloh, 1997). Some hone in on the psychodynamic disarray behind Thomas's (and his cast of accusers') selective use of symbols, rhetoric and hagiography in phrasing prejudicial accusations (Johnson, 2016; Langmuir, 1993; Helmholtz, 1983a). Blood libel accusations are taken here to signal stunted psychodynamic forces, especially 'repression, projection and a vision of an internal insecurity regarding boundaries' (Johnson, 2016: 23). Langmuir (1993), for instance, carefully points to darkly psychic rewards that such accusations yield to accusers, and Johnson (2012, 2016) looks to problematic normative cultures and their psychological effects. Seeing value in linking psychology and history, she recognizes that cultural practices inform psychic displacements or resolutions. Her work adds to studies of 'the psychology of antisemitism in history' an active quest for 'other stories' beyond those anchored to the 'persecuting mind', moralizing legal judgment or Freudian psychodynamics (2016: 13), on the understanding that: 'It is not only the anti-Semite who is broken, in other words, but the culture that produces him' (Johnson, 2016: 15). Such cultural fractures, I will suggest, enable grammars of the sort that guide accusation.

Rose (2015), for her part, points to underlying structures and associated ambitions. She highlights the changing cultural, economic, social and political context of mid-twelfth-century Norwich against which Thomas's ambitions within the church hierarchy were silhouetted. For example, Thomas's dogged accusations seemed to be motivated by a quest for the fame bestowed on a person fronting a successful beatification: 'Brother Thomas perhaps hoped to make William a posthumous success on the scale of St. Thomas Becket. He completed his book on William within a few years of the archbishop's death in 1170' (Rose, 2015: 28). Or, perhaps, a pecuniary opportunity for the church presented itself in the form of a saint from the congregation. This would have helped with funds for the priory and could attract pilgrims. So, Thomas's unceasing efforts to accuse the Jewish community simultaneously drew on, shaped and amplified a symbolic division between religious groups, with personal benefits accruing to his churchly investiture; now he could potentially secure a position within the hierarchy assigning him care over William's relics.

As important as these approaches certainly are, they tend not to focus on the cultural grammar that inspired a lore of blood accusation in context. Focusing on that grammar, as this chapter does, has much to gain from Foucault's (1980,

2000, 2002, 2007, 2014) concepts that show how changing 'regimes of truth' accompany relational practices and specify what is to count as a truthful juridical avowal. I will, however, adapt his insights to emphasize a fluid, culturally formed grammar of accusation that is forged through local power relations and surrounding juridical 'regimes of truth'. That grammar guides discourse around truthful avowals authorized by juridical meanings and patterns of subjection. Again, one finds that Foucault's (2014) analysis of avowal is particularly useful when exploring how cultural grammars govern the ways accusations reorder shattered familiarities through specific forms of subjection.

I will also heed Langmuir's important, if largely forgotten, call to attend to Thomas's description of the accusations *per se*, rather than to focus on the proverbial 'who done it?' question: 'The most significant question to be put to the *Life*, therefore, and one that is not directly answered by it, is not who killed William but who first accused Jews and why that accusation was made' (Langmuir, 1984: 822).

To Langmuir's 'who' and 'why' questions regarding the accusation, I will add a focus on the overlooked 'how' question – thus directing my interpretative gaze to the cultural grammar guiding how accusations could be presented as ecclesiastic and juridical truths. This addition should alert readers to the meaning struggles that spawn accusations in local truth regimes (Foucault, 1980). If accusation sequences settle disordering experiences, they do so by reordering frayed meanings, creating discursive pivots for unfolding chains of signification that point fingers of suspicion and blame. Cultural meaning is restored through authorized rhetorical practices, as well as juridical rituals and technologies that order through the symbolic borders they erect.

Thomas's accusations in context

By way of the broader background to this tack, I rely mostly on Rose's comprehensive discussion that opens with this understated, if pertinent caution:

> The origin of the blood libel, or the ritual murder charge – the accusation that Jews killed Christian children in order to use their blood for medicinal or ritual purposes and in mockery or hatred of Christ – has never been determined. Such accusations appear in accounts from mediaeval, Reformation, and modern Europe, and in England, France, Spain, Italy, Germany, Poland, Hungary, Greece, and Russia . . . Ritual murder has become a quintessential 'mediaeval' accusation, one that for many people seems to sum up all that is darkest about the Middle Ages.
>
> (2015: 1)

She also points out that such accusations were made in the face of strict Hebrew prohibitions on the consumption of blood, and without what might today count as legal, scientific, or even common sense evidence (see also Johnson, 2012: 2).

The social context within which Thomas launched his accusations assumed importance in 'the High Middle Ages' which could be cast as

> a period of rapid social, political, and economic change. The so-called 'renaissance' of the twelfth century witnessed significant population growth, expanded trade, promotion of the Crusades, the revival of Greek science and Roman law, and the bureaucratic development of the European nation-state. (Rose, 2015: 4)

Accompanying these socio-economic and political alterations were cultural reforms in the arts and 'the development of chivalric ideals' that placed an 'emphasis on affective piety and emotional engagement in religious devotion' (2015: 4). Following upheavals of the earlier Norman conquest and its unsettling clashes and compromise, Norwich emerged as the second largest city in medieval England, forming the 'governmental, ecclesiastical, and economic centre of eastern England (East Anglia)' with a 'thriving market', a 'massive fortified castle', and a Romanesque 'cathedral complex' (Rose, 2015: 5).

It is not insignificant that the cultural horizons framing Thomas's accusations were forged after Henry I's death, which in 1135 precipitated a civil war between followers of his feuding children, Mathilda and Stephen. Norwich was one of Stephen's strongholds, and felt the brunt of a protracted conflict, ending only in 1154 when another Henry, the first Plantagenet, succeeded to the English throne (Rose, 2015: 17). Thomas's views were possible because of additional instabilities promoted by a second – none too successful – Crusade (1147–1149) that had a considerable impact on everyday life in Norwich. Aside from the long absences of its participants, this crusade drained resources and created an acute demand to fund crusaders and the families they left behind.

Although little is known about Norwich's Jewish community around this time, Rose (2015: 5) indicates that they numbered around 200 residents of a city with some 5,000 residents by 1200. She notes too that Norwich became 'a place of refuge for Jews later in the century' (2015: 6), and they were well integrated into the city, working in diverse occupations in trades, commerce, medicine, moneylending and precious metals crafts. Despite significant contributions, riots in 1189 fuelled anti-Semitic sentiments that simmered with varying intensity until Jewish people were expelled from Britain in 1290 (Rose, 2015: 6; Bennett, 2005b). Within that fluid context, Thomas' accusation of ritual murder directed to the community set up a prejudicial and consequential 'turning point in the history of the Jews in mediaeval England' (Rose, 2015: 6). In many ways, his text could be approached as forging accusatory pivots that allowed William to be defined as a saintly martyr; they also enabled an 'enduring myth of Jewish ritual murder' (McCulloh, 1997: 701; see also Holmes, 1981). Suffice here perhaps to note the depth of the socio-cultural changes from which discursive pivots were forged and accusations of ritual murder narrated. The divisive social effects would resound historically with life-destroying effect. But let us here turn back to Thomas's narratives of accusation.

Death, confusion and guided accusations

As noted, Thomas began writing the *Life and Passions* six years after the boy's body was found at Easter in 1144 (only completing it several decades later), yet it revived a flagging case without much political momentum. Rhetorically, Thomas set himself the task of recounting how William was killed for his faith and so, 'deserved to be hailed as a saint' (Rose, 2015: 13). But his narratives, as Langmuir (1984: 822) argues, are much 'too unreliable or insufficient' to determine who killed William. Indeed, he offers a strong caution about the author's assumptive universe: 'Thomas was a monk of the twelfth century, concerned with his status on earth and in heaven, and convinced that loyal service to William would benefit him in both realms' (Langmuir, 1984: 829). As such, Thomas tapped into contemporary religious discourses to retrieve cultural pivots around which his bald accusations of blood libel could turn. Even if not a witness to the immediate events, he claimed to offer evidential and faith-based truths (Johnston, 2015: 33; Langmuir, 1984: 829).

In Books 1 and 2 of the *Life and Passion*, Thomas tells us that William was an apprenticed leatherworker from humble roots, even though it seems that he hailed from a notable Norwich family with close ties to the church (Rose, 2015; Resnick, 2015; Helmholtz, 1983a). His mother, Elviva was the daughter of Wlward, and his father Wenstan (about whom little is said) was a relatively well-off farmer. Elviva's sister, Leviva, married a priest named Godwin Sturt and their son Alexander was a deacon. Her other son, Robert, William's cousin, became a monk at Norwich. By Thomas's account, on 20 March before his death, a stranger claiming to be the archdeacon's cook sought Elviva's consent for William to work in his employer's kitchen. Assuming the man to be a Christian, and after receiving some money, she consented. Thomas alleged that William was instead taken to the home of a leading Jewish banker where he was closeted and subjected to tortures resembling those inflicted on Christ, and 'in mockery of the Passion of the Cross, sentenced him to be crucified'. He claimed further that they tied a knotted rope around his head, and 'having shaven his head, they wounded it with an infinite number of thorn pricks and made him bleed miserably' and finally 'they inflicted a grievous wound to his left side' (Book 1, V).

The story continues: William's corpse was initially found on Easter Saturday (25 March) by a young 'peasant' who noticed it underneath a tree in Thorpe Wood (now known as Mousehold Heath), just outside of Norwich (Bennett, 2005a; Langmuir, 1984). Neither he, nor an aristocratic nun who later also stumbled over the body, reported anything to authorities (Book 1: X; see also Rose, 2015: 12–13). The young man who first discovered the body had a change of heart and told a local forester. The latter, Henry of Sprowston, who patrolled the woods on behalf of Norwich's bishops and monks, was granted the right to cut lumber in return for duties that included juridical matters (Book 1: XI). He and the 'young peasant' did not recognize the body, and decided to postpone further investigations until after the Easter weekend. The forester's later inquiries led him to consult a priest about unspecified suspicions, but this came to nothing; and on Monday he buried the body where it was found. Some of William's friends recognized the body and reported to Godwin Sturt what they had seen. He returned to the scene with his two sons on Tuesday, whereupon they dug up the body and instead of pursuing justice, or indeed burying William in consecrated ground, they simply reburied him on the same spot (Langmuir, 1984: 830).

Afterwards they reported their discoveries to Leviva who, we are told, reminded Godwin of her dream some two weeks before. In the dream, she imagined that members of the Jewish community encircled her in the marketplace and attacked her (Book 1: XIV). Godwin interpreted this dream as a sign that the Jewish community would take something dear from her. He repeated this interpretation to Elviva, the boy's mother, and she reacted in a way that one might imagine as deep shock and grief, expressed through idioms of suspicion and blame. In so turning, we are told, she tapped meaning horizons of a prejudiced local culture and apparently 'accosted everyone with horrible cries and asserted that her son had been seduced by fraud, kidnapped from her by cunning, and killed by the Jews' (Book I: XV; see also Langmuir, 1984: 831).

This dramatic sequence indicates a foundational, if often disregarded, element within the grammar of an accusation. It highlights the forging of a discernible discursive pivot that at once signalled and responded to perplexing events, and set the stage for new sequences of meaning that produced accusations of ritual murder. In his recollection thereof, Thomas evoked gendered preconceptions of the day to insist that Elviva's discursive pivot was both credible and truthfully avowed:

> Nevertheless, out of many and credible conjectural arguments she was able to conclude that it was not Christians, but Jews, who had dared to commit the crime in that way. She accepted these speculations with a women's credulity; and she at once broke out in public with abuse of the Jews in word, noisy clamour and formal accusation.
>
> (Book 1: XV)

Without underplaying the misogynist overtones, one could note too his attempt to signal the truth of Elviva's spontaneous reaction: it created a meaningful pivot that simultaneously defined mysterious circumstances and made sense thereof. Moreover, according to Thomas, she settled on this pivot not as a matter of 'maternal instinct', but as a 'woman carried away by feminine and reckless daring' (Book 1: XV). Regardless, and whatever emotions she was experiencing, Elviva's accusation pivoted out of a dream that responded to confounding discovery.

Despite the commotion of her accusing a group of people in public, the matter did not precipitate official juridical procedures – either through canon law or the King's justice (Langmuir, 1984: 831). Indeed, the inquiry by the king's local representative, Sheriff John de Chesney, found no reason to pursue the accusation, and he advised the Jewish community not to participate in the church's ordeals

(Book 1: XVI). Even within the church, the accusation's validity was slow to be recognized, contrasting markedly with the rapid veneration of the murdered Thomas Becket of Canterbury roughly 25 years later (in 1170). Since William and Becket occupied quite different levels of the church hierarchy, it might not be surprising that William's death passed 'without a second thought'; but Thomas's text helped to change all that by successfully agitating for his martyrdom (Rose, 2015: 15). In any case, only in mid-April did the priest Godwin first accuse the Jewish community of the crime before a synod under Bishop Eborard (Book 1: XVI).

Thomas noted that the bishop was initially not convinced; yet he later summoned the Jewish community to answer the charge, a request, as noted, they refused on the advice of the sheriff (op. cit.). He relayed that they did attend the bishop's next summons, but left without 'submitting to judgment' or agreeing to have Godwin submit to an ordeal to prove the truth of his accusation (Book 1: XVI; see also Langmuir, 1984: 831). Thomas's narrative wove itself through the warp and weft of widely diverse avowals of truth, including: the 'confirmations' of circumstantial evidence, miracles of many different kinds, Leviva's 'very remarkable warning vision', Elviva's spontaneous accusations, 'the crafty frauds of the cunning messenger of the Jews' (Book 1: XVI), the purported practices that they are supposedly bound to carry out on specific days (Book 5: 1), and so on. However absurd the evidence might appear from historical truth regimes still confronting the holocaust, Thomas's accusations eventually led to William's body being moved from an unholy grave in the wood to the monks' cemetery (Langmuir, 1984: 832). The political tides at the cathedral had come to embrace Thomas's concerted and dogged interventions:

> [A]fter five years of neglect, William of Norwich suddenly received the kind of attention merited by a saint. He appeared in numerous visions, was promptly moved inside a monastic building, and the following year was raised first to the high altar of the cathedral and then to a special chapel.
>
> (Rose, 2015: 67)

One might note, too, that Thomas's enunciations were not made at usual openings to juridical proceedings in either ecclesial or King's legal processes of the day, but were directed more generally (Rose, 2015: 19). As discussed in Chapter 2, these were changing significantly – juridical frameworks added new, official and more centralized (church or king) processes for launching accusations as complements to private accusations (Pollock & Maitland, 2012; Helmholtz, 1983a; Pollock, 1898, 1899). Furthermore, there was probably a lack of political will to pursue this breach because of the raging civil war: 'A thorough investigation of William's death might have exacerbated bitter divisions in the community, and no good was likely to come of it' (Rose, 2015: 18). Even so, the creation of a saintly martyr was in process, and that change of fortune rested on discursive pivots that supported the family's, a bishop's and Thomas's accusations against the Jewish community.

Cultural grammar, discursive pivots and accusation

But which symbolic struggles following the finding of a dead body proved influential in creating accusations of ritual murder? As indicated, the *Life and Passions* appears to hinge its accusations on a cultural grammar that worked off discursive pivots; the latter arrested the disquieting confusions of a perplexing encounter and set chains of meaning on a course that would end up pointing fingers of blame at a whole group of people. Other participants' familiar chains of signification were arrested by perceptions of a suspicious happening, which shifted their understandings in the direction of culpability. Such accusatory processes reached for wider cultural meanings, enabling subjects to make sense of what had challenged their ordinary meaning horizons; no doubt seeking to tame the confusions of disrupted life worlds. At its foundation, then, the accusation pivoted out of mundane everyday understandings, such as the previously discussed leap to conclusions by William's family, and Elviva's subsequent public accusation.

However, the *Life and Passion* (Book 2) described another unlikely pivot erected some six years later, and this revived political momentum for William's hibernating case (Bennett, 2005a; Langmuir, 1984). It recounted a courtroom trial of a quite unrelated case in 1150 involving Bishop William Turbe of Norwich who appeared in King Stephen's court to defend and exonerate his destitute knight (a Norman nobleman, Sir Simon de Novers). The latter was prosecuted for murdering a man (Deulesalt), apparently, a Jewish moneylender in Norwich. The knight, Thomas told us through a 'fictional' account of the trial, had participated in the unsuccessful second crusade (in 1147). Few knights and nobles returned from this endeavour, and those who did, failed to obtain the usual bounty (Rose, 2015: 64). Since participation in crusades required many knights to take out loans from monasteries or moneylenders; failed crusades often translated into debt (Rose, 2015: 52).

Such was the fate of Sir de Novers. Representatives of the Jewish community accused him formally of getting rid of his debt by having his creditor murdered. Preliminary court hearings took place in both Norwich and London before the king. Prosecutors alleged that the knight probably thought he would get off lightly because most returning crusaders faced similar predicaments. Their case rested on the knight's strong motivations to kill the banker (who apparently armed himself with a sword in anticipation of trouble). As Rose comments, 'The case seemed open-and-shut, and the outcome appeared obvious' (Rose, 2015: 77), but it placed the king in a difficult predicament. It put him between knights (upon whom he depended militarily), Jewish creditors ('who provided cash to pay soldiers') and religious leaders who had supported his claims to the throne (Rose, 2015: 71). At the same time, he had tangibly to uphold the peace that his throne claimed over the war-struck realm. Confronting this proverbial rock and a hard place, the king might have welcomed the exit provided by Bishop Turbe's defence.

Thomas told how, at trial in London, the bishop astutely summed up his audience as including a 'group of aristocrats and churchmen who were predisposed not to believe his excuses for the indented knight' (Rose, 2015: 80). Consequently, he adopted a novel rhetorical approach to the defence. Praising the accused knight's character, he glossed over his apparently criminal actions and rhetorically blamed the victim. Instead of launching into a rhetorical defence of his knight, as might have been expected, he abruptly called for an adjournment. To 'turn the accusation around' (Book 2: XIII), the bishop conveyed this blunt counter-accusation:

> We think that we Christians should not have to answer in this manner to the accusations of the Jews, unless they are first cleared of the death of our Christian boy, of which they themselves are known to have been previously accused and have not been purged.
>
> (Book II: XIII)

Even though Turbe had not brought the Jewish community to face such charges in the previous four years, since being appointed, he recalled an accusation to support his idea that the murdered man had kidnapped and tortured William for three days (emulating Christ's torture). In this way, he set the accusation of his knight on a radically different course, suggesting that the crime at hand could legitimately be considered a revenge execution.

Evincing how accusatorial meanings were negotiated in this context, the bishop referred to the testimony of Theobald – 'a person who was once a Jew and later one of our monks' (Book 2: XI). This shadowy figure claimed that cities were drawn by lot and so selected for ritual murders – Norwich being selected for the year of the boy's death. Incredibly, Thomas accepted this second-hand assertion and reported that, 'all the communities of the Jews of England offered their consent by letters or by messengers for the crime to be performed at Norwich'. In any event, as Resnick (2015) notes, the bishop's smoke and mirrors tactic worked and led the case to a pragmatic stalemate with enormous consequences: 'Neither de Novers nor the Jews were ultimately prosecuted, leaving questions of guilt and innocence unresolved. But Turbe's strategy produced, as a side effect, the blood libel' (Resnick, 2015: 4–5).

One might say, then, that the defence strategy of a different case yielded cultural meanings that forged another discursive pivot. Now, retold accusations of blood libel – however prejudiced, absurd and wrongheaded they might seem from a different meaning horizon – appeared to have bolstered Thomas's bid for William's sainthood.

From this vantage, we see how Thomas's accusations flowed out of a cultural grammar that sanctioned multiple discursive pivots – including the interpretations of William's family, Elviva's stark public accusation, Theobald's assertions, the bishop's concluding defence strategy. These interspersed pivots, that is, enabled a reordering of confused everyday meanings through a direct, and socially divisive, accusation. It is worth noting too that by accusing the Jewish community of ritually murdering William in this way, Thomas's story etched religious partitions between communities of Norwich, thus foreshadowing an egregious template for future social brutality.

Local meanings and accusation: ordering, avowing and subjecting

Though complex, we have seen how a blood libel accusation – whether framed by Thomas or the characters to which he refers – was forged through local discursive pivots that responded to the symbolic ruptures following shocking events. A grammar guided participants' meanings and actions through processes that governed how to realign everyday meanings around suspicion and blame. In the process, it helped to forge contingent subject identities – accusers, the accused and multiple authorities who mediate symbolic and/or social reorderings. One might here allude to three mechanisms behind a cultural grammar that governed Thomas's remarkable accusation:

- reordering confused chains of meaning around accusatory pivots;
- employing rhetorical devices that cast 'true' accusations;
- forging subjects as vehicles and targets for accusatory rituals.

1 Ordering disorder: working off divisive accusatory pivots

We have already seen how Thomas's accusations sprang off symbolic negotiations following confusions encircling William's death. Experiencing the mystery of this finding jolted the lifeworlds of 'peasant', 'aristocratic nun' and forester alike. Even if encounters with corpses might be expected in contexts of civil war, these actors were sufficiently disoriented not to know precisely what to do about their unhappy findings. Framed by religious and hierarchical meaning horizons, their respective discoveries of the corpse redirected familiar, ordinary experiences of the world, occasioning reflexive questions that confronted commonplace flows of meaning. Though of a different world view, I hazard that their unfamiliarity with the setting would have transformed unreflective into reflexive experiences of the world, throwing ordinary understandings into disarray and raising questions of how best to 'make sense' of the situation.

Similarly, Godwin and his sons at first conceived the event in ways that led them simply to rebury the body. As we have seen, a later recollection of Leviva's dream about Jewish people encircling her at the market changed the terms of their discourse, and yielded Elviva's public accusation. The latter pivot was taken as one foundation for Thomas's subsequent narrative, channelling meanings through the assumptive grids of his 'proofs'. In addition, the young man described by Thomas as a 'peasant' initially turned away for fear of involvement, just as the nun initially had done. For instance, we are told that the nun, Legarda, returned to the scene and this time made sense of the situation by claiming to see a bright light, and two ravens 'attempting with a frenzy of raven-like voracity to dismember him zealously with the beak' (Book 1: X). Seemingly, she took the raven's failure to break the body as a sign that William had 'many merits' and consequently she 'said a prayer and commended him to her saviour' (op. cit.). Having thus made sense of the situation she felt she could 'return home with her associates full of thanks' (Book 1: X).

Equally, we are told that Sprowston did not recognize William, but on examination he 'noticed that the boy was wounded and saw in his mouth a wooden instrument of torture'; from this he detected 'unusual kinds of torment' and started making sense of the situation by beginning, 'already to suspect' the Jewish community (Book 1: XII). Sprowston is said to have reported this to the priest, but in the end his suspicions did not amount to much and the body was buried where it was found. Thomas's account of these meaning struggles, scant though they might be, suggest how such experiences produced different reactions and channelled flows of meaning into the blood libel accusations that he described, endorsed and used to frame his own accusations of ritual murder.

But it is important to offer a caveat here – contested meanings simultaneously drew on multiple pivots and narratives to make sense of the events, and some rejected the blood libel accusation. Representatives of the King's peace (e.g. the Sheriff Chesney), for example, disavowed the accusations in William's case, dismissing them and preventing them from moving along juridical paths – an action that Thomas claims led to the sheriff's death 'caused by the fitting wrath of God' (Book 2: XV). The sheriff's views might have carried the juridical day, but Thomas's socially divisive accusations proved, deplorably, more enduring over centuries (e.g., Rees, 2017; Smith, 2003). They also surrounded subsequent portrayals of William as a saintly martyr deserving of beatification. Even so, the grammar of such accusations gained traction out of local discursive pivots with humble beginnings: the experiences of key actors who made sense of perplexing circumstances by appealing to surrounding cultures, and reordering social meanings.

2 Rhetoric, evidence, and truthful avowals

Thomas's blood libel accusations (recursively?) followed the pivots he helped create, and drew on a wider politics of truth contoured by destructive prejudices. As McCulloh notes:

> Europeans of the twelfth century were already prepared to believe that the Jews as a people were capable of extraordinary inhumanity. Thomas of Monmouth accepted that view, and he offers us a unique window onto a specific manifestation of it – the spreading myth of ritual murder.
>
> (1997: 740)

Endorsing such cultural bigotry, Thomas carved a narrative and presented his accusations as unequivocally true. Anticipating possible criticism, Thomas asserted his 'zeal for truth' against critics who 'exhaust the air with tedious barking and with whipping lashes of the tongue, and with the dog-like bites are in the habit of attacking honesty, and disdainful of heavenly gifts' (Book 2: I).

Signalling again the cultural grammar enabling this accusation – i.e., claiming fidelity to 'the truth' – he evoked hagiographic rhetorical techniques for constructing what were then taken to be truthful avowals. Following Foucault (2002), we could say that Thomas's 'modalities of enunciation' claimed to provide privileged access to truth from Christian epistemological regimes of the day.

Regardless, by privileging certain rhetorical techniques for enunciating the truth, he framed an accusation as true by 'the nature of the torments', 'sure signs of the wounds', and 'truthful' witnesses (Book 2: VIII). The 'truth' of his accusation also rested on the revelation and 'proofs' that were documented as testimony or argument. For Thomas:

> Since it is agreed, both by signs of revelations and by many documents as proof, that the most placid boy and monitor William was killed by the Jews, we believe it happened by God's just judgement that justice so struck those guilty of so horrible crime, for the perpetration of the disgraceful act, and that divine vengeance exterminated or dispersed them within a short period of time.
>
> (Book 2: XII)

Considering this, what rhetorical techniques did the *Life and Passion* employ to avow the 'truth' of blood accusation in William's case?

His hagiography 'revealed' several seemingly unconnected signs and 'miracles' as 'proofs' of the 'truth' of his accusations. Expressing contempt for sceptics, Thomas insisted that those who mistrust miraculous revelations simultaneously 'destroyed the mighty works of piety or diminish or even corrupt them all together under the pretence of religion' (Book 2: I).

Miracles had, according to him, to be taken as deific signs that William's martyrdom was real; and if so, that reality implied a blood sacrifice that challenged Christianity. Such miraculous signs, we gather, included: a perfumed fragrance that attended William's second burial (Book 1: XII); a rose that grew mysteriously on his grave (Book 2: V); a person who came back from the dead and saw a vision that also appeared in a similar form to 'a certain virgin' (Book 2: V); a pregnant woman who was 'miraculously freed from pain' (Book 2: VI); a 'youth who vomited live serpents' (Book 5: III); and so on. Indeed, scattered throughout Books 3–7 one finds other such revelations presented as signs of William's saintly status, and by inverse (even perverse) logic of his ritual murder at the hands of the Jewish community. Thomas's unfamiliar logic here evinces something else: a discursive regime that sanctioned and privileged selected revelations as 'signs of truth' that today's truth regimes would likely dismiss as at best irrelevant, and at worst, entirely preposterous.

At the same time, his emphasis on hearsay and circumstantial evidence as 'proofs' suggests a specific epistemological ethos (Johnson, 2012: 41). His opening 'proof', for example, recalled that the boy was seen by witnesses in the presence of a Jewish group prior to his death. Key among these was a young girl who reportedly watched him enter the banker's house before the door was closed.

This report of hearsay appears in the *Life and Passion* as a third-hand account of a child witness who came forward long after the event (Book 1: V; Book 2: IX). To this 'proof' of his accusation, Thomas adds a second. Another witness, a 'Christian woman' who worked in the kitchen of the Jewish house, is reported to have glimpsed William being tortured and ridiculed 'to the shame of Christ' that 'she happened to see through the open door – with one eye since she could not with both – the boy fixed to a post. Having seen this, she was horrified; she closed her eye and they shut the door.' (Book 2: IX). Off the flimsy recollection of 'one eye', Thomas created and inferred detailed descriptions of what happened behind the closing door. And he added that the woman clammed up in silence because she was fearful of her safety as a 'Christian'. At the time, we are told, she decided simply to go around doing the work, but 'noted definite clues to what had happened'. What were these clues? Well, 'She showed us the belt with these objects and pointed out the signs of martyrdom on the doorposts of the house' (Book 2: IX).

A 'third proof' asserted that when the Jewish community realized that they might be 'charged by law of his killing, they tried in many ways to quell the accusation they had incurred or to invade it for the time being' – including a 'peacemaking bribe' (Book 2: X). These speculations were offered alongside a 'fourth proof' that alleged an attempt to bribe the bishop in the previously noted case. The upshot of these unsupported claims (they are merely asserted) was to underscore a view that, 'the Jews would not have acted in this way or promised such things if they had felt themselves to be innocent of the charge brought against them' (Book 2: X).

A fifth 'proof' referenced Theobald's extraordinary assertions, and presented them as a further 'efficacious sign of truth' (Book 2: XI). We are also told that King Stephen, with the support of the local sheriff, allowed the Jewish community to become more confident and might even have suggested that there would be a governmental benefit to killing a martyr (see Rose, 2015: 15; Bennett, 2005a; McCulloh, 1997). Whether an 'efficacious sign' or not, this 'proof' suggests an eccentric conspiratorial claim whose origin seems to me as elusive as is its evidentiary status. Regardless, Thomas's final 'proof' involved further reports of hearsay, suggesting that gossip about overheard arguments between Jewish folks somehow too could qualify as demonstrating the truth of his accusation. Hearsay of overheard gossip in the heat of an argument appears then as a further 'proof' of his accusation.

One might read these various assertions as rhetorical strategies enabled by their historical epistemic regimes. A cultural grammar guided how accusation might work out of initial pivots and so respond to meaning-disrupting events. It permitted Thomas to declare, on the strength of revelations, circumstantial (and hearsay) evidence and argument, a blunt conclusion: 'And so, after so many and such [great] proofs have been put forward to manifest the truth, there can be no longer any doubt in my opinion that the holy motto William was killed by the Jews' (Book 2: XII, Conclusion).

3 Transcription, public fame and fluid subjects of accusation

The negotiation of cultural pivots behind this blood libel accusation took place as juridical rituals and techniques for avowing accusations were in flux. Facing the uncertainties of civil war, juridical processes for legitimately launching accusations in both church and King's justice remained fluid; they were later addressed by Glanville after the death of Henry II, several decades after Thomas's text (Pollock, 1899). The dual influences of inquisitorial and rising accusatory rituals required truthful avowals as the basis of accusations. The legacies and development of private, monarchic and ecclesiastic accusations coexisted, as did blurred jurisdictional ideas about criminal matters (Helmholtz, 1983 a, 1983b; Pollock, 1898). In context, rituals for initiating accusations of criminal wrongdoing continued to rely on private accusers (e.g., the family), just as tensions between ecclesial and secular jurisdiction over criminal matters played out. For instance, Sheriff Chesney's refusal to do anything in the name of the King's peace (Book 2: XV), contrasted with Thomas's stark accusation (for more on the clash of secular and ecclesial justice, see Pollock & Maitland, 2012; Pollock, 1898).

Indeed Thomas's accusations revealed emerging entrances to church courts and its contests with the King's peace, as well as the rise of new sorts of presentments, prior to trial – what Maitland (1889: xxxi) portrayed as a gradual, and contested, shift from private to more centralized kinds of criminal accusation in both secular and church settings. Regardless, rituals for dealing with accusations prior to trials (by ordeal or court) were increasingly organized through new technologies (Helmholtz, 1983a, 1983b; Pollock, 1898). By way of illustration, two key technologies contoured Thomas's account: championing written transcriptions as privileged evidence, and relying on 'public fame' to determine the validity of an accusation.

Apropos the first, his text's rhetorical quest for truth was tied in with claims to remain close to his various sources. Thomas attempted to overcome the transitory character of spoken words by handwritten documentation, preserving oral claims as records for the enduring archive that his *Life and Passions* had become. Echoing a rising emphasis on 'documentality' in juridical administration, he placed considerable emphasis on hand-scripted transcriptions of evidence (Ferraris, 2012). Thomas's aim here was to write down for future generations the immediacy and integrity of the 'proofs' behind his accusation:

> If . . . someone considers that we have included in this little book anything that appears to be untrue, let that person not, indeed, impute the sin of lying to us, because we have taken care to write down nothing but what we have seen or what we have learned as carried by common knowledge in order to inform the devotion of those alive and generations to come.
>
> (Prologue)

This led him to a grandiose declaration: 'I, Thomas, Thomas of Monmouth, with God's will, have undertaken to commit them to writing, lest the memory of them be lost for posterity and in order to preserve it for future times' (Book 1: II).

One might here note his transposition of complex symbolic clashes framed in spoken words. These words were rendered in written idioms decipherable to juridical processes centred on truthful avowals. To be sure the idioms, privilege and rituals of truthful juridical accusations might have changed, but a grammar that works off culturally formed pivots and legally authorized ways of enunciating remain. It was also precisely this element of that grammar that allowed Thomas to declare a schismatic accusation – with a chilling genocidal future – as truth:

> We claim that he was surely slain by the Jews, both because it is the custom of *dierum penalium*, and also because of the nature of the torments, and by the sure signs of the wounds, too, as well as by the most truthful of humans we have from witnesses.
>
> (Book 2: VIII)

Second, implied by the 'common knowledge' mentioned in his 'prologue' (see quote above), and as Helmholtz's (1983b) study of Church Act Books suggests, public (or common) fame was an influential contemporary basis for launching a credible accusation. One might here emphasize a subtle, but detectable, aspect of accusation's grammar – the unseen sway of 'public' or 'common' fame. Used to determine the fate of accusations in both secular and canonical settings, Helmholtz notes how cases following the route of public fame required that, 'there be pre-existing fame that the accused had committed a crime' (1983b: 13). Such fame, that is, had to 'rise to the level of openly disseminated rumour', and required accusers to swear oaths 'to the existence of public fame' (1983b: 14). The crucial point here is that fame was considered quite apart from the 'truth of the underlying matter' – it also afforded the accused a chance to 'show the lack of public fame' (Helmholtz, 1983b: 14). In other words, accusations investigated in this way did not proceed by evaluating evidence of 'actual' wrongdoing; rather, they were exclusively concerned with establishing whether there was a communally held suspicion that someone had committed an offence. In this way, public fame was used to determine the fate of an accusation and served as a 'preliminary question, the answer to which decided whether further action was necessary' (Helmholtz, 1983a: 619–20).

This juridical technology was important enough to be included among Henry II's ordinances in the 1166 Assize of Clarendon, where 'the sworn men of the inquest were asked not to accuse anyone, still less to evaluate evidence set before them, but to give voice to a common fame. Who is publicly suspected? That is the question they answered' (Helmholtz, 1983a: 616–17).

In both secular and church settings, such fame had to be 'held by good and substantial persons'; that is, public fame could not be asserted by the accused's 'enemies, or by untrustworthy men and habitual perjurers' (Helmholtz, 1983b: 14). In turn, those accused by public fame rumours might refer to juridical tests (e.g., ordeals) to prove their innocence (Thayer, 1892: 263). They could also look to processes of compurgation to clear common fame suspicions:

> Similar to a wager in law in the secular courts, canonical purgation required the accused to take a formal oath that he was innocent of the crime and to find a number of commutators who would support his oath by swearing that they believed he had sworn truly. The compurgators swore not to the truth of the underlying facts, but to their belief in the trustworthiness of the oath of the accused.
>
> (Helmholtz, 1983: 13)

The political rationale behind this technique also supported the development of oath-taking technologies, such as grand juries (Helmholtz, 1983a; Maitland, 1889; Thayer, 1892).

Given the prominence accorded to public fame in juridical assessments of valid accusations at the time of Thomas's writing, one might read the *Life and Passion*, in part, as his attempt to capture and spread public suspicions regarding Norwich's accused Jewish community. As we have seen, he tapped local cultures to assert the existence of public fame, and thus to support blood libel accusations against a whole community. However, his use of public fame was somewhat oblique. As noted, he insisted that his text truthfully described a 'common knowledge' about William's death (Prologue). He also claimed that 'the fame of the holy martyr was spread far and wide' (Book 3: XXXI), as was the 'fame of miracles' variously described (Book 3: XVII). So, from Thomas's account, William's martyrdom was widely held by common or public fame; this knowledge was in turn premised on a belief that he was ritually murdered for religious reasons. By this knotted logic, public fame for William's martyrdom implied that he was ritually murdered for religious reasons. Thomas accused the Jewish community of the murder and further claimed – by putting words in the mouth of an imagined Jewish person, supposedly involved in William's murder: 'Therefore, what remains to become common knowledge, if not the truth of the events, and the discovery of the truth to the detriment and danger of us all' (Book 1: VI). Thomas's dreamt up character, in other words, expressed great fear not simply of the 'truth of events', but also 'the truth' reflected by suspicions of wrongdoing. Were the latter to become 'common knowledge', juridical accusations would be deemed valid. As further evidence of truthful public fame, he claimed that having summoned the Jewish community to face the accusation against them, the bishop 'consulted with wise men and a common opinion was reached to suggest to John that he should not support the Jews against God' (Book 1: XVI).

Alarmingly, the bishop also warned that if the Jewish community 'did not purge themselves very soon, they should know that they would without doubt be destroyed' (Book 1: XVI). Indicating vividly the public stakes of the accusation, Thomas in these oblique passages referenced a background technology that evaluated accusations against publicly held suspicions and perceptions of who to blame. He saw his role as spreader of a 'common knowledge', as a vehicle for directing public suspicion toward the Jewish community, and thereby validating his own blood libel accusations. At the very least, Thomas's quest to cast aspersions might be interpreted as a bald attempt to mobilize widespread public suspicion and fame. One might note here, in passing, how ideas of public fame resonate with risk-based, actuarially framed, accusations that claim legitimacy by declaring 'known' profiles as legitimate foundations for suspicion and blame.

Regardless, pausing briefly to reflect on the idea that a whole group (and not simply an individual) could be accused of committing a wrong, one might allude to the subjections that Thomas's accusations imply. The previous chapters refer in more detail to fluid rituals and techniques of accusation that produce contingent subjections and concomitant subject identities – loosely formed around accuser, the accused and mediating authorities. But in context, Thomas – through his accusations – became a specific sort of accuser; one who articulated and justified specific claims by rhetorically describing, reframing or referring to accusations made by others (the boy's family, this of the bishop, etc.). If this ritualized sort of accusation added to Thomas's identity a monk, it also supported the authority of the church's juridical hierarchy as a legitimate institutional receptacle for accepting and mediating such accusations. Moreover, it implicitly questioned the kings' juridical representative – the sheriff – as such a legitimate authority, indicating the preferred juridical authority (Helmholtz, 1983a; Maitland, 1889). Here, it is relevant that Thomas should have dedicated his *Life and Passions* to Bishop Turbe of Norwich. Equally, one might note the way he pointed to a collectively framed Jewish community – rather than to specific persons – as the target of his blood libel accusation.

Suggesting also how this collectively identified accused was generated out of local accusatorial processes, Thomas noted that the community, or representatives thereof, assembled at the synod by the dean of Norwich at the bishop's behest; they were to face the priest Godwin's challenge to prove his accusation under oath by ordeal: 'On the sheriff's advice the Jews denied the crime imputed to them, but asked that the issue of proof by ordeal be granted some short respite'; supposedly they 'feared greatly the proof by ordeal' (Book 1: XVI). The jurisdictional clash between sheriff and church may be evident here, with the former described as the 'protector of the Jews' (Book 2: XV); but we also see that culpability is directed to a collective target, highlighting the unsettled form of the identities that it is possible, historically, to accuse.

Of course, much more could be said here, but suffice to observe that rituals and technologies of accusation do not simply work with pre-established subjects who make sense of problem events; rather such rituals and technologies are actively involved in shaping, and subjecting, those who recursively serve as vehicles for accusation. A cultural grammar of accusation enabled ideas and procedural rules regulating these subjects. Thomas was, for instance, able to accuse an entire community of ritual murder because of the different rationales, rituals and juridical processes through which he could launch his accusations. Such collectively directed accusations might be disallowed in contexts where grammars require free will as a basis for juridical wrongdoing, and where responsibility for actions is assigned to individual persons. But this observation merely underscores a basic point: those subjected to grammars of accusation are both creatures and creators of the very powers that forge their historical emergence.

Conclusion

The foregoing analysis has referred to a mid-twelfth-century case in English archives, charting elements within a grammar that regulated its accusations of wrongdoing. Thomas issued an early blood libel accusation within changing socio-political and legal contexts, and from a cultural grammar whose epistemic horizons sanctioned hagiographic revelation and circumstantial/hearsay 'proofs' as granting access to truth. That grammar enabled Thomas's religious meanings to flow along channels that commenced their tortuous journey from mundane pivots that reacted to unsettled frameworks of everyday meaning upon finding a boy's dead body. Thereafter, they enunciated suspicions through sanctioned truth-telling practices, landing up sharply accusing an entire community. The grammar of his blood libel accusation, that is, worked off pivots spawned by confused perceptions on finding a young boy's corpse; they made sense of the circumstances through narratives of culpability and blame. The latter were consolidated in a hagiography that simultaneously accused Norwich's Jewish community and pitched William's beatification. It also revealed that his accusations were both forged out of, and enabled by, epistemological contexts that provided ecclesial rituals and juridical institutions within which Thomas's truths could be avowed. Here one senses his appeals to modalities of enunciation deemed capable of providing 'proofs', buttressed by such political technologies as reordering pivots, transcription and ordeal-determined public fame. These technologies, born to the grammar at hand, forged ritualized subjects and subjections around the accusations.

The contingent character of Thomas's accusation might appear distant, but it suggests accusatory auspices and rituals whose traces still contour how we accuse subjects of 'criminal' wrongdoing today. Without by any means claiming a universal presence, traces of the cultural grammar that enabled Thomas's accusation endure in shadows cast by what we do today when we preliminarily decide on whether particular accusations are valid, and whether thereby to admit selected subjects to various criminalization processes. If nothing else, perhaps, Thomas's text alerts us to threshold struggles, to subtle, frequently invisible and largely overlooked ways that cultures of accusation regulate symbolic battles at moments that arrest everyday life and initiate new meanings around perceptions of suspicion and blame. That the vagaries of these struggles have such massive social effects on the lives of all participants serves to highlight the significance of naming the fluid grammars that unleash accusations and their attendant bordering, ordering and social division.

Note

1 Thomas of Monmouth (2015); hereafter *Life and Passions*, or Book/Section references alone.

References

Bauman, Z. (2000). *Modernity and the Holocaust.* Ithaca, NY: Cornell University Press.

Bennett, G. (2005a). Towards a revaluation of the legend of 'Saint' William of Norwich and its place in the blood libel legend. *Folklore*, 116(2), 119–39.

——. (2005b). William of Norwich and the explosion of the Jew. *Folklore*, 116(3), 311–14.

Chazan, R. (1997). *Medieval Stereotypes and Modern Antisemitism.* Berkeley, CA: University of California Press.

Ferraris, M. (2012). *Documentality: Why It Is Necessary to Leave Traces.* New York: Fordham University Press.

Foucault, M. (1980). *Power/Knowledge: Selected Interviews and Other Writings, 1972–1977.* New York: Vintage Books.

——. (2000). *Power.* New York: The New Press.

——. (2002). *Archaeology of Knowledge.* Routledge Classics. London: Routledge.

——. (2007). *The Politics of Truth.* Semiotext(e) Foreign Agents Series. Los Angeles, CA: Semiotext(e):

——. (2014). *Wrong-Doing, Truth-Telling: The Function of Avowal in Justice.* Chicago, IL: The University of Chicago Press.

Helmholtz, R. (1983a). The early history of the grand jury and the canon law. *University of Chicago Law Review*, 50(2), 613–27.

——. (1983b). Crime, compurgation and the courts of the medieval church. *Law and History Review*, 1(1), 1–26.

Holmes, C. (1981). The ritual murder accusation in Britain. *Ethnic and Racial Studies*, 4(3), 265–88.

Johnson, H. (2012). *Blood Libel: The Ritual Murder Accusation at the Limit of Jewish History.* Ann Arbor, MI: The University of Michigan Press.

——. (2016). Stories people tell: the blood libel and the history of antisemitism. *Law & Literature*, 28(1), 11–26.

Langmuir, G. I. (1984). Thomas of Monmouth: detector of ritual murder. *Speculum*, 59(4), 820–46.

——. (1993). *History, Religion, and Antisemitism* (rev. edn). Berkeley, CA: University of California Press.

Maitland, F. W. (1889). *Select Pleas in Manorial and Other Seignorial Courts*, Vol. I, Reigns of Henry III and Edward I. University of Michigan. Retrieved from: https://archive.org/details/selectpleasinma01maitgoog (access date: September 28, 2016).

McCulloh, J. M. (1997). Jewish ritual murder: William of Norwich, Thomas of Monmouth, and the early dissemination of the myth. *Speculum*, 72(3), 698–740.

Monmouth, T. of (2015). *The Life and Passion of William of Norwich.* M. Rubin (ed.). London: Penguin Classics.

Pollock, F. (1898). The King's justice in the early middle ages. *Harvard Law Review*, 12(4), 227–42.

——. (1899). The King's peace in the middle ages. *Harvard Law Review*, 13(3), 177–89.

Pollock, F., & Maitland, F. W. (2012). *The History of English Law before the Time of Edward I*, 2 Vol. London: Liberty Fund Inc.

Rees, L. (2017). *The Holocaust: A New History.* New York: Public Affairs.

Resnick, I. (2015). The mundane origins of a historical drama. Review of *The Murder of William of Norwich: The Origins of the Blood Libel in Medieval Europe*, by E. M. Rose.

Oxford University Press, 2015. *Los Angeles Review of Books*. Retrieved from: https://lareviewofbooks.org/contributor/irven-m-resnick/ (accessed: December 15, 2016).

Rose, E. M. (2015). *The Murder of William of Norwich: The Origins of the Blood Libel in Medieval Europe*. Oxford: Oxford University Press.

Smith, H. W. (2003). *The Butcher's Tale: Murder and Anti-Semitism in a German Town*. New York: W. W. Norton & Company.

Thayer, J. B. (1892). The jury and its development. *Harvard Law Review*, 5(6), 249–73.

Wittgenstein, L. (1980). *Philosophical Investigations*. Oxford: Blackwell.

Chapter 6

Creating crime

Accusatory entryways to criminal justice

Introduction

While critical attention is often directed, and rightly so, to the various stages of criminal justice – from policing to prisons – rather less is paid to the moments that launch criminalizing rituals. How, for example, do local subjects come to recognize particular events as 'criminal'? Which contextual procedures are deemed legally appropriate for receiving and processing information that a crime has taken place? In what ways does law establish the identities of accuser, accused and authorized agent at entrances to criminal justice? And how do legal processes regulate truth-telling practices at entrances to criminal justice? Such questions take seriously critical approaches that showed crime to be a historical creation of underlying socio-political, cultural and economic structures (e.g., Foucault, 2014; Christie, 1994; Taylor, Walton, & Young, 1973; Reiman, 1990). Crime emerges in societies, that is, from the partisan decisions of legislators, deponents, police and prosecutors, justices of the peace, juries and judges. However, at the start of criminalization processes, one finds momentary suspensions of everyday life. Though often overlooked, these suspensions enable criminalizing law's sanctioned authorities to step in as gatekeepers in order to judge whether specific acts and persons should be considered as 'criminal'. Focusing specifically on such inaugural instants of decision at entryways to criminalization, the following discussion examines two late nineteenth-century Western Canadian cases – one in 1888 at Edmonton (North West Territories, now Alberta) and the other in 1890 at Nanaimo, British Columbia. Surviving archival records in both instances narrate how colonial law opened preliminary legal gates, exposing two accused subjects to the prospect of criminalization.

Clearly, with two arbitrarily selected cases, my aim is not to reveal a colonial past in which Canada's 1867 confederation looked westwards, explicitly seeking to impose dominion law and order over a vast territory occupied by indigenous peoples and some settlers (Foster, 1994; Strange & Loo, 1997; Harring, 1998; Loo, 1990, 1994a), many somehow associated with the fur trade (Innis, 2015; Komar, 2015; Loo, 1994b). For more on this complex background, readers are referred to texts of a different order – focused histories. These include studies of how dominion law was enforced by the quasi-military North West Mounted Police's march west

(Macleod, 1976; Macleod, 1978; Stonier-Newman, 2006; Wilkins, 2012; Beahen, 1998), alongside the deployment of the British Columbia Provincial Police over the Vancouver Island Colony (Foster, Buck, & Berger, 2008; Foster, 1994; Parker, 2015; Loo, 1994b; Stonier-Newman, 1991), or the emerging Province of British Columbia (Barman, 2007, 2008; Ferguson, 2009) and the expansion of court configurations (Gavigan, 2012; Farr, 1944, 1967). My rather different aim is to chart and interpret the official records of two archived files that afford unique glimpses into how the dominion's criminal law met local contexts, and how legal narratives and practices lodged themselves at opening moments of criminalization (Foster, 1990, 1992). These moments were consequential because they imposed dominion criminal law over local contexts, and in so doing literally created 'crime' in context. Indeed, the acts and subjects (persons) that an unfolding legal force elected to criminalize had the effect of defining the jurisdiction of criminal law (Dorsett & McVeigh, 2012). That law's jurisdictional expansion was thus tied to the growth of entryways by which definitions of crime could be enforced over a vast terrain. The following is a limited tale of that unspoken legacy which tenaciously endures in the shadows of today's vast criminal justice networks.

Entry narrative 1: information and accusations of a break and enter

Consider these reported events. On 9 March 1888, Thomas Rees a miner and resident of the east side of Edmonton (North West Territories (NWT), today the Province of Alberta) presented information and a complaint to a Police Inspector Casey, who simultaneously served in the capacity of a justice of the peace (see Chiste, 2005). Rees informed him that a crime had taken place; he accused John Sunday of breaking and entering his house near Fraser's Mill, and intending to steal his watch. One day later, on 10 March, Casey transcribed the accuser's sworn 'information and complaint' using the appropriate legalese of the day: 'That John Sunday did on the ninth day of March in the year above mentioned feloniously break and enter my dwelling contrary to the statutes in such cases made and provided.'[1]

One might imagine the described events playing out in a 'dwelling' that a newspaper report described as a 'shanty' (*The Edmonton Bulletin* of 18 March 1888).[2] Its fire offered, at that time of the year, life-preserving warmth and shelter from a disabling winter cold that would also have been familiar to those, some 14 years prior, who at the command of the dominion of Canada were to 'bring law' to an imperially defined 'West' (Macleod, 1976: Chapter 3).

Once a fort in the Hudson's Bay Company's fur trading network (Hesketh & Swyripa, 1995; Palmer & Palmer, 1990), the larger settlement of Edmonton now offered no witnesses to confirm or deny Rees's account. As such, the justice of the peace was tasked with deciding, on the strength of the information provided, whether the first of several figurative gates should be opened so that the accused John Sunday might stand before the dominion's colonial criminal justice.

Casey apparently thought so and signed a 'Warrant to Apprehend' him, addressed to all constables and peace officers of the NWT. Two days later, on 12 February, a magistrate's court (with him and J. A. Macdougal presiding) was convened

> upon a charge laid upon the information of William Thompson Rees of Edmonton – miner who saith that John Sunday an Indian did feloniously break and enter his dwelling house with the intent to commit a felony therein contrary to the statutes in such cases made and provided.

Whatever might have been said in the earlier confrontation between the neighbours, they now faced each other as accuser and accused in a legally organized 'magistrate's court' (*The Edmonton Bulletin* of 18 March 1888). This court was to decide whether to open its figurative gates to the 'due courses of law' and a criminal trial. In 'evidence' sworn before this court, Rees is said to have stated these words before the magistrates and the accused:

> I was away from my house working, on my return I found the door ajar and some strange keys in the locks which was opened on entering I saw the prisoner John Sunday standing opposite the wall directly in front and close to where my vest hung with my watch in the pocket – the chain had been detached from the Button hole and was hanging down the watch remaining in the pocket – I asked the prisoner what he was doing there he said to see what time it was. I recognize the keys produced in court as the ones that were in the lock when I found Sunday in the house. My dwelling is in the east end of Edmonton the prisoner lives in the next house to me about 2000 yards away . . . The door was locked in the morning by me before I went to work.

In Casey's handwritten 'Statement of the Accused', Sunday was seemingly issued this caution:

> Having heard the evidence do you wish to say anything in answer to the charge. You are not obliged to say anything unless you desire to do so but whatever you say will be taken down in writing and may be given in evidence against you at your trial.

In response, the accused 'says as follows':

> I tried my key in the lock of course I opened it I did not think it would open it I was hungry I saw a pot on the stove. I took off the lid I took not quite half a plate full of beans after I had eaten the beans I took the watch in my hand and took the chain out of the button hole I opened the watch to see what time it was I shut the watch and put it back in the pocket and I was just going to leave when the prosecutor came and caught me in the house.

Even with the imposition of the justice of the peace's legalese, one senses differently arranged horizons behind such phrases as 'of course I opened it' and 'I was hungry . . . I took not quite half a plate full of beans'. Sunday seemed thus to regard his actions as ordinary, even mundane. An indigenous man, and a neighbour of the accuser, Sunday's perception of the situation did not appear to include that a 'break and enter' was at issue, or that eating some beans and holding the watch warranted any further comment.

Regardless, the magistrates sided with Rees's account and a 'Warrant of Commitment' propelled Sunday's journey further into criminal justice networks. He was taken into custody in anticipation of being 'delivered by Due courses of law' at the next Supreme Court. Reflecting tangibly the contact between local social context and imposed law (Gavigan, 2012), his sense of the world was subjugated to the advancing dominion's 'law and order' as he found himself in legal custody answering made charges against him (see Harring, 1998). That journey was temporarily interrupted by a 'Recognizance of Bail' for $200 dollars – $100 from Sunday ($100), and $50 each from Charles Stewart (a 'merchant' at Edmonton) and Bella Croaknose (a 'widow'). Sunday's bail condition required him to plead to

> such indictment as may be prepared against him for and in respect to the charge aforesaid and takes his trial upon the same and does not defeat the said court without leave then the said recognizance to be void otherwise to stand in full force and virtue.

The Edmonton Bulletin (Saturday 12 May 1888, 1) reported that this case was to be heard the following Monday before Judge Rouleau of the NWT Supreme Court who had travelled up from Calgary to Edmonton to hold court. The following week, it followed up with a report that in the case 'Queen vs John Sunday, housebreaking, with felonious intent' a certain R. Strachan appeared for the crown, and Shaw and Prince for the defence before a jury of six men – who as it turned out, 'rendered a verdict of acquittal' (*The Edmonton Bulletin*, 19 May 1888, 3).

Entry narrative 2: accusations of attempted self-murder

A second case with scattered texts filed in a state-funded archive recounts an attempted suicide as a 'crime'. The narratives take us to William Boyle's house in Nanaimo on Vancouver Island at approximately 7:10 am on 28 October 1890. In witness depositions, recorded on 2 December (Form (M) Sec s. 29 for 'Indictable Offences'), we are told that a Joseph MacDonald, the local 'milkman' did as he usually did at Boyle's house – he called out 'milk'.[3] But something struck him as odd that morning: 'the door was open for about an inch and a half. The can for his milk was usually set on the railing of the Veranda, but this morning it was not there'.

His curiosity raised, he again called 'milk' and this time, 'Boyle came to the door his face, neck and hands up to his elbow were covered with blood'. MacDonald also noticed a pool of blood on the floor and immediately enquired as to what was happening. Boyle apparently responded by saying that, 'I cut my throat yesterday' and pointed to the blood saying that a hog had been killed there. Strangely, MacDonald continued with his milk delivery round and 'served four or five of my customers' before thinking that he had 'better inform' the city constable O'Connell, whose house was not far away. At about half past seven, he found that the constable was asleep following the previous night's duty and so left his 'information with Mrs. O'Connell'. A note in the archived documents indicates that the 'prisoner' had no questions to ask, suggesting that the accused was present when the witness testified.

From his sworn deposition, Constable Thomas O'Connell received the information at roughly 7:40 am and saw a man walking to the nearby hospital *en route* to Boyle's house. He found the door 'wide open'.

> I went into the house and saw blood all about the floor and a large dish pan of water was coloured with blood – and close such as pants, socks and a coat, were lying on the floor soaked with blood – I found a razor upon the floor . . . the razor was covered with blood.

He then proceeded to the hospital and encountered Boyle who had 'an ugly gash in his throat'; when asked how that happened, Boyle confessed to doing it. O'Connell escorted Boyle to the police station. His testimony also indicates that Boyle had being drinking to excess 'for some weeks previously – he had neglected his work and given himself to drink', seemingly in the wake of his wife and two children leaving him.

Peter Joseph Rice, a registered medical practitioner, examined Boyle in the Nanaimo gaol at about 9 o'clock on 28 November with a Dr Davis attending. Rice noted the blood and 'some cloths around his neck, also saturated with blood'. When he removed these cloths, he found an 'incised wound at the throat' with a cut

> extending from 3 inches to the right of the middle line of the body to 2 inches to the left of the middle line . . . It was 4 inches in depth – the windpipe and gullet were not injured but only a severed membrane was left between the back part of the wound and the base of the tongue . . . A number of the muscles the throat was severed . . . But bleeding had arrested before I saw him.

He dressed the slash with a temporary antiseptic dressing and sent him back to the hospital, where later that afternoon 'Dr. Davis and myself stitched up the wound' which had since 'progressed most favourably.'

These complex relations were reduced to a standard form stating, 'The information and complaint of Thomas O'Connell of Nanaimo, Constable . . . before the undersigned . . . Her Majesty's Justices of the Peace in and for the said district or county of Nanaimo'. The information was recorded thus:

> On the 28th day of October in the year 1890 aforesaid one William Boyle of Nanaimo in the said district, at the city of Nanaimo in the said district, did unlawfully cut and worked himself in the throat with a certain razor with intent, thereby then and there feloniously wilfully and of his malice aforethought to kill and murder himself against the peace of Our Lady, the Queen, Her Crown and Dignity.

A form for indictable offences entitled *Statement of the Accused* repeated the indictment in the presence of 'prosecution witnesses' and asked whether Boyle had any response – to which he replied 'I make no statement'.

Boyle was indicted but granted bail on condition that he appeared before the 'next court of competent Criminal Jurisdiction to answer any indictments that may be found against him by the Grand Jury in respect of the charges aforesaid'.

A grand jury was convened and concluded with these presentments:

> And the jurors aforesaid upon their oath aforesaid do further present that the said William Boyle afterwards to wit on the day and your aforesaid did unlawfully attempt feloniously wilfully and of his malice aforethought himself to kill and murder against the peace of Our Lady the Queen Her Crown and Dignity.

To hedge their bets, since it was two years before the introduction of the criminal code in Canada (see Brown, 1989), this jury decided too that he 'did unlawfully cut and wound himself in the throat with a razor with intent thereby to commit suicide against the peace of our Lady the Queen.' Such a decision set the course of Boyle's life down the road of a criminal trial, the outcome of which I have yet to determine.

Interpretative orientations: approaching the 'lowly beginnings' of crime

How might one interpret these cases? We have already noted that crime is born out of contextual legal negotiations that decide on whether to criminalize specific acts or subjects. Echoing the point in his analysis of the 'long march' of the North West Mounted Police (NWMP) westwards, expressly to enforce dominion law, Macleod astutely observes that:

> Every society in every age works out its own definition of antisocial and therefore proscribed behaviour. . . . In theory the police are merely the agents of society in identifying and apprehending offenders to whom the courts then apply the appropriate punishment. In fact the police play a mediating role in determining which offences will be taken most seriously . . . This kind of selective perception and enforcement of the law is apparent in the history of the North-West Mounted Police.
>
> (Macleod, 1976: 114)

That 'selective perception and enforcement of the law' followed on from dominant perceptions of crime,[4] and how to enforce dominion law and order in local contexts. The attempt to forge a monopoly over the use of legal violence, and to define materially what its order required, is nicely framed by Nietzsche's scattered – yet iconoclastic – references to crime (see Pavlich, 2009).

Whatever its liabilities, the value of Nietzsche's thinking on criminal law lies in his call to understand the 'lowly beginnings' of Western (imperial) morality, politics and law (Sedgwick, 2013). That is, his approach helps us to grapple with a far flung 'will to power' behind the imposition of dominion law and its creation of crime. Nietzsche insists that:

> More strictly: one must admit nothing that has being – because then Becoming would lose its value and actually appear meaningless and superfluous. Consequently one must ask how the illusion of being could have arisen (was bound to arise).
>
> (Nietzsche, 1968: 708)

In this sense, we should not consider crime and criminal subjects as ontologically distinct beings but as elements of historical processes (the 'becoming') whose 'being' is enforced by, and in the name of, an overriding social order. Furthermore, he indicates that the 'most decisive act' performed by a 'supreme power' as soon as it is 'strong enough to do so – is the institution of the *law*'. Such impositions of law involved

> the imperative declaration of what in general counts as permitted, as just, in its eyes, and what counts as forbidden, as unjust: once it has instituted the law, it treats violence and capricious acts on the part of individuals or entire groups as offences against the law, as rebellion against the supreme power itself.
>
> (Nietzsche, 1997, II, #11: 75–6)

For our purposes, then, the often violent expansion of dominion law defined the forbidden, appropriated disputes from subjects, and disallowed injured parties from pursuing private revenge. It also denigrated any other claims to law, and vilified the idea that indigenous law might rival its 'progressive' jurisprudence (Borrows, 2002; Harring, 1998; Foster, 1981).

In short, from this vantage, the 'lowly beginnings' of dominion crime, and the forces that carried it into being, have much to do with initial moments that successfully defined specific actions and persons as potentially criminal. Often, the starting point involved an accusation that the sovereign order had been criminally violated – such accusations were crucial to the selective 'perception and enforcement of the law' visited upon local subjects and situations. But there is a caveat here – the *lore* of criminal accusation should be distinguished from the *law* of accusatorial procedures through which dominion justice networks initiated criminalization (Chapter 7). As I see it, the lore of criminal accusation is basic since it defers to everyday horizons of meaning used to calibrate specific acts and people as potentially criminal. That is, through rituals seeking to make sense of specific events as criminal, accusation plays a formative role and opens local relations to the imposition of dominant criminalizing processes – in our two cases, the latter involved expanding the Dominion's networks of criminal justice.

Initiating criminal pathways: accusation and the lore of ordinary lives

With this general approach in mind, the above cases reveal much about initiating moments that mobilized the force of dominion law. In Sunday's case, one might imagine a walk home that detoured past his neighbour's dwelling. He had a key that opened the door and decided to feed his hunger with the beans on the stove. A watch chain caught his eye and he removed it from the coat for closer inspection. Soon after, Rees returned home, his suspicions raised by the strange key in his door. Similarly, a door left ajar interrupted the milk delivery person's ordinary routines, and the absence of a milk bottle that typically rested on the veranda rail. Though not emphasized in the documents, it was precisely through these slight, almost humdrum, perceptions of the strange that everyday familiar comfort zones were momentarily arrested, challenged and suspended. At such moments, suspicions disrupted ordinary meaning horizons; familiar ways of thinking about the world dissolved into disordering disquiet. The secure comforts of taken-for-granted meanings were interrupted by events that challenged expectations of ordinarily arranged lattices of understanding and called out for some resolution.

In both contexts, something considered out of place touched off reflective attitudes of suspicion and blame, instigated by a sense that all was not quite right. Living through such moments, Rees's and MacDonald's immediate responses made sense of the situation by repairing – reordering – disrupted meaning horizons by evoking notions of crime. Seemingly inconsequential experiences became pivotal for initiating new chains of signification that alleged a crime had occurred. For instance, Rees's reaction to the surprise of waylaying Sunday with the watch in hand was first to ask questions, then to alight on the idea that a crime had transpired. This set him on a course of action that culminated with an accusation that Sunday had 'unlawfully' entered his home (seemingly to steal his watch); offending not only against Rees, but also contrary to the Queen's law (which he likely perceived via the presence of NWMP agents and symbols). Under different perceptions, Sunday and Rees might have engaged one another directly, negotiating their differently aligned meaning horizons and social understandings of what had just taken place. In the event though, Rees elected to lay an information and complaint before the local justice of the peace, leading to Sunday's apprehension and eventual acquittal.

Such sequences suggest how startling disruptions to familiar meaning patterns serve as precursors to criminal accusations. With Boyle's attempted suicide, one might ponder the social context in which a milk deliverer encounters a man in medical distress, offers no immediate assistance and then decides to move on to his next customers. Perhaps it was the shock of seeing Boyle's bloodied state that confused MacDonald; but that upset again indicates precisely a disruption that jolted his ordinary meaning horizons, leading to disordered voids where blaming, accusation and allegations of crime emerged as viable ways to rearrange scattered experiences. Why would MacDonald's compassion not have spurred him to seek medical assistance? Of course, one cannot answer that question definitively, but the archived texts relate chains of signification that led MacDonald to restore meaning to his world by informing the constable of the matter. He came to view the injured Boyle not as someone facing a medical emergency, but as a person whose acts merited police intervention. In other words, his response to a situation that had jumbled his ordinary lattices of understanding had him turning to law to recalibrate the unsettling events as criminal. It is, of course, revealing that the constable – even as he accosted an injured Boyle – should also take him to the police station rather than hospital.

To reiterate, these surviving narratives suggest how turns to criminal justice repaired ordinary socio-cultural meanings upset by events. In Edmonton, tangled meanings were reframed by expressing the events as a break and enter (theft) without entertaining the possibility that different sense horizons might have led Sunday to act as he did. In Nanaimo, we have a distraught man whose life had led to family breakdown, misuse of alcohol and perhaps a cry for help by the attempted suicide; somehow these tragic actions were cast as criminal, as an offence against the Queen's order. That either situation should be cast as criminal reveals something of the successful attempts to enforce dominion law as the only legitimate definer of transgressing acts and persons (see also Foster, 1994). Legal control over how the chaos of disrupted social meanings was legally managed in local moments speaks directly to the lowly beginnings that initiated the creation of crime.

Criminal subjections: accusers and the accused

As seen then, disrupted socio-cultural meaning horizons sometimes enabled criminal accusations to surface and spurred contacts between local events and dominion law. Those points of contact initiated entryways to criminalization as authorized subjects played various roles in legal rituals that selected who were to become accused criminals in context. No doubt, the imposition of dominion law had followed, with modification, English models of justice (Farr, 1967), and the latter come to frame criminal acts as injuring victims, but in addition as violating a sovereign's order (Foucault, 2015).[5] Indeed, the two cases at hand suggest that dominion law embraced these wider developments by recasting private accusers as witnesses or deponents who merely provided information to state-sanctioned accusers, now authorized to control entry into an expanding criminal justice system. The growth of the dominion's capacity to criminalize selected subjects relied on locally formed – and fluid – identities of accuser, accused and mediating authority. As the two cases indicate, these identities were negotiated through power relations seeking to impose dominion versions of 'crime' and 'criminals'. They emerged out of rituals that legally authorized selected criminal accusers to hear information and complaints from informants before deciding on whether to unleash criminally accused identities. Such fluid identities proved to be vital to local law enforcement.

In the dramas that comprised entryways to criminalization in the two cases then, each participant was recognized as performing stipulated legal roles. Those who stood before its law with information that a crime had taken place were required to adopt legally legible identities. So, for instance, Rees was described as a miner with fixed abode and thus presented two credentials decipherable to law, enabling him to adopt what was imagined as a credible accuser identity. His role as informer became possible once the NWMP had established enough of a presence for authorities to receive, record and manage information at entrances to a criminal justice system. His very participation in these entryway procedures had the recursive effect of shaping his identity as a victim and informant who swore to the truth of his criminal complaint. In Boyle's case, the milk deliverer would likely have been aware of the expansion of dominion law across Vancouver Island (Loo, 1994b; Parker, 2015) and the rise of the British Columbia Provincial Police (Stonier-Newman, 1991). That might have affected his decision to portray the events as potentially criminal, and to recognize an obligation to inform the local constable. However, it also subjected him to adopting a specific identity; namely, one that eschewed an empathetic focus in favour of a legal one.

These various informant identities signal moments where direct contact was made between everyday life and the authorities of an unfolding dominion law seeking to expand its jurisdiction over more areas of society (Loo, 1990; Foster, 1994; Strange & Loo, 1997). Whatever their precise motivations, these identities were crucial to opening moments, the lowly beginnings, that comprised a first step in creating crime – where law and society intermingled. They also formed an initiating element of the various crown identities that offered or refused entry to criminal justice networks. To begin with, the constables were authorized to countersign that credible information about an indictable offence had been lodged. In such documents, the police often cast themselves as bearers of sworn witness testimonies, and were thus authorized to act on sworn information that a crime 'against the peace of Our Lady the Queen Her Crown and Dignity' had potentially occurred.

Other actors occupied roles that decided whether to admit accused criminals to face charges in criminal courts. For example, in the Edmonton case, where grand juries were not integrated into criminal entryways (Parker, 2015), the matter of deciding whether to proceed with the accusers' information was passed along decision-making paths. The police constable who later laid the information – without regard for potential conflicts of interest – assumed the role of justice of the peace and decided to subject the matter to a magistrate's hearing. As if that were an insufficiently conflicted course to adopt, Casey then assumed the identity of one of two magistrates who decided to channel the matter further into the criminal justice system. If this indicates a conflation of gatekeeper identities at entryways of dominion criminal justice, it also suggests that law's requirements fashioned various subjects at entryways to criminal justice. In the Vancouver Island case, signalling somewhat different entryway processes, a grand jury was convened to evaluate the information and complaint that Boyle's suicide amounted to a criminal form of self-mutilation or murder. With the jury's indictments, a command was issued for the accused to 'answer' the charges as 'prisoner' at the next convened court competent to hear criminal matters. Again, such responses demanded subjects whose identities (e.g., as a grand jury member) were negotiated through legal rituals and assemblies that led them to decide whether criminal charges were to be answered in court.

One glimpses here how the imposition of dominion law enabled local political arenas with legally decipherable identities in relation to allegations of a crime. What then of the accused? Their identities were also negotiated out of the unfolding situations at hand, out of a politics that recognized limited 'legal persons' from much more complex social beings. We have seen that in his 'statement of the accused', Sunday seems to have viewed his actions as quite ordinary. Equally, it is doubtful whether Boyle would have described his desperate act at the end of a protracted alcoholic binge to have been criminal – worthy of empathy and consideration perhaps, but certainly not a criminal violation of the Queen's peace. Yet, in its quest to secure an exclusive criminal jurisdiction, dominion law silenced rival ideas about these subjects and their actions; it could not recognize a competing, indigenous sense of social order, or that a desperately unhappy man who injured himself might not be criminally violating the Queen's order (Harring, 1998; Foster, 1981). Instead, it shaped the 'accused criminal' identities at entryways by allowing limited responses to allegations. In their statements, neither accepted law's imposed identities – Sunday by refusing to view his acts as criminal, and Boyle by electing to say nothing. However, accused criminal identities (a break-and-enter thief, an attempted self-murderer) were enforced through ritualized entrances to criminalization. Even though negotiable, these identities were hard to shake off once imposed by law's requirements at entrances to criminalization. Regardless, we see here how accused identities were fashioned through unfolding fields of law.

In sum, one might glean from our interpretation of the narratives that complex social and political relations contoured the gateways to criminal justice; multiple agents were required to negotiate legal identities around putatively criminal matters. However, these identities were not fixed in advance: they emerged out of sociopolitical relations that constituted criminalizing entryways. Witnesses, accusers, accused and authorities were required to enunciate truths about themselves in relation to given sets of circumstances, and so specific legal persons and identities emerged within legally enforced limits. Stated differently, fluid identities surfaced out of relational complexes at entryways by the kinds of responses required of differently conceived legal subjects and processes – from laying of information and complaints, justice of the peace decisions, to grand jury presentments and to managed statements from the accused. All played their changing and negotiated parts in unfolding dramas of local legal context.

Avowal at law's gates: 'telling the truth, the whole truth and nothing but the truth'

Recognizing modifications and differences in the way law developed in the background to our two cases, the previous sections have indicated how broader socio-cultural and political auspices, together with accusation-based subjections, shaped entryways to dominion justice. As points of contact between everyday life and criminal law, these entryways also deployed spaces within which law could manage avowals of truths by participants. Again, Foucault's (2014) lectures on forms of avowal specific to shifting juridical formats help us to conceptualize what is at stake here. That is, legal spaces required subjects to enunciate truths about themselves in ways (e.g., swearing oaths, referencing science, etc.) that echoed changing juridical processes. So, the imposition of dominion law was accomplished in part by creating entryways with clear ideas of what legal avowal, or truth-telling, was to involve; that is, how participating subjects were to meet the requirement of telling – under oath and with God's help – 'the truth, the whole truth and nothing but the truth' in relation to the events at hand. As indicated previously, such truth-telling requirements produced kinds of subject identities that were shaped by, and yet served as conduits for, opening moments of possible entry to criminalizing processes.

However, one might note three important aspects of avowal and truth-telling practices elucidated by the two records examined: a reliance upon uniform idioms to indicate legal truth; the use of lexicons of fact-based truth-telling; and, using practices of transcription to render legal truths available to judicial assessment. First, as indicated above, all testimony in the archived cases was 'sworn' under oath, signed by witnesses and countersigned by law's local authorities – justices of the peace, magistrates, etc. Statements had to follow idiomatic customs to count as legally valid. Specifically, witness avowals were taken down in writing and represented as legitimate to the extent that they emerged from structured spaces under the directed purview of authorized legal agents. The latter rendered legal narratives in relatively uniform formats that were considered decipherable to law, and bounded by the threat of perjury charges if deemed 'false'. In efforts to ensure that avowed statements were legally decipherable, this law often utilized standardized word patterns set out on forms. These were used to record information, complaints, witness depositions, indictments, specific bail conditions, statements from the accused, and so on.

For example, a 'Statement of Accused' form could be handwritten (the Edmonton case) or uniformly printed (the Nanaimo case). In the latter case, stock phases and performative statements signalled a domain in which particular forms of avowal were demanded:

> And the said charges being read to the said ________ and the witnesses for the prosecution___________, bring severally examined in his presence, the said _______ is now addressed by me as follows: 'Having heard the evidence, do you wish to say anything in answer to the charge? You are not obliged to say anything, unless you desire to do so; but whatever you say will be taken down in writing, and may be given in evidence against you at your trial.

One might read here prescribed ways of receiving statements of truth from an accused subject. The form indicates what sort of avowal is required from the accused: it must be voluntarily asserted after hearing, and been given an opportunity to question, the evidence presented against him or her. In addition, the form specifies that the justice of the peace countersign that the following statement 'is read to the accused':

> You have nothing to hope from any promise of favour, and nothing to fear from any threat, which may have been holden out to you to induce you to make any admission or confession of your guilt, but whatever you shall now say may be given in evidence against you upon your trial, notwithstanding such promise or threat.

From such forms, we glimpse this law's attempt to standardize truth-telling practices at entrances to criminalizing rituals. With the guiding injunctions of uniform language, completed and countersigned forms alleged that avowals conformed to procedural requirements and so counted potentially as legal truths. No doubt, comparative assessments of such truths had significant, sometimes violent, effects on people's lives; they were also used to decide on journeys through law – both Sunday and Boyle had to answer charges before competent criminal courts on the strength of the legally avowed truths.

Second, the legal genres used in both cases relied heavily on lexicons where avowals were recorded via a factual, staccato-like style. The countersigned records presented witness testimony using flattened rhetorical formats: 'I was away from my house working', 'on my return I found the door ajar and some strange keys in the locks which was opened', 'I called at the house of William Boyle', 'I called out "Milk" as usual', 'his face, neck and hands up to his elbows were covered with blood', and so on. The rhetoric of juridical depositions at entryways did not allow for complicated argument, proof, rhetorical flair, convincing prose or stylistic flair – in law, truth was to state only bald facts. The composite of sworn, validated, one-idea statements was accrued as 'evidence' relating to specified events. This writing style created records that subsequent juridical reasoning would use to decide on whether to proceed with a criminal indictment. If so, the evidence was distilled further into the legally framed indictments noted above, to be 'answered' by the accused at 'competent' criminal courts. One senses here a progressive reduction, a filtering, from the sheer complexity of discourses at an event to the simple documents *ex post facto* framed as legal records – all now reduced to factual lexicons presented as sworn truths decipherable to law, and so amenable to its reasoning and decisions about who to select for potential criminalization.

Third, sworn legal truths and the reductions of fact-based legal lexicons relied on how statements of truth were both captured and represented; hence the juridical importance of writing oral evidence down, or *transcription*. An exemplar here might be where a subject – Rees or MacDonald – orally avowed truths about putative criminal events. Their spoken words were translated into legal lexicons by authorized identities; sworn under oath, juridical protocol required that they be signed by the avower, and countersigned by the transcribing authority. Such transcribed documents not only initiated criminalizing entryways but also became the currency of subsequent juridical governance. It is thus not surprising that attempts should have been made to standardize juridical lexicons through forms and sanctioned traces of putatively criminal events. That is, witness testimonies, depositions, indictments and judgments enabled a form of legal regulation centred around the creation, control, archiving and recording of legal documents (Ferraris, 2012: 247ff.). Coupled with a political capacity to declare these as the privileged (even singular) truths, colonial law's agents could then define particular narratives of events as *the* final truth that was used to govern entryways to criminal justice.

Moreover, legal avowals 'captured' or 'represented' in written documents left documentary traces for subsequent juridical scrutiny and argument. These narrative traces reduced extremely complex events to 'factual' legal lexicons, and forged hierarchies of truth among written traces, elevating the power effects of certain statements over others (e.g., grand jury presentments over depositions). As the cases suggest, complaints that triggered criminalizing rituals began by filtering compound social relations into narrow legal traces. One might, for instance, imagine the complexity of the interactions between, say, Rees, Sunday and the justice of the peace, or between Boyle, MacDonald, O'Connell, the doctors, justices of the peace and the grand jury. Yet the legally transcribed narratives eschewed any reference to relational intricacy, leaving increasingly condensed traces in the form of staccato-like statements of fact in hierarchically arranged documents, from sworn witness testimony, information and complaints, statements from the accused, indictments, to magistrate decisions and grand jury presentments. The 'case' was often reduced from pages of testimony to sentence-long indictments that claimed to summarize key facts, culminating with decisions made at criminal justice entryways.

From the previous section, one glimpses how entryways to criminal justice distilled legal traces in the wake of complicated events: idiomatic signatures attesting to sworn oaths reduced the nuances of everyday events into transcribed witness statements of fact, avowed truths taken down as staccato-like phrases rendered its lexicons decipherable to juridical reasoning of the day. Transposing relational complexity into the reduced and narrow language of law compressed pulsing corporeality into muted indictments that alleged clear-cut transgressions of criminal law and the Queen's peace/order. The heterogeneous meaning horizons surrounding Sunday's excursion into Rees's shanty in search of food and the ambiguous holding of the watch could then be framed as immutable evidence of a simple case of break and enter with the intent to steal. Such juridical reductions of everyday life were also evident in the legal silence about the desperation behind weeks of drinking that surrounded Boyle's suicide attempt. The archived documents, that is, left legally created and ordered traces of reductive stories leading to a simple indictment – a man who committed a crime by cutting and trying to murder himself. The compressions required to render intricacies of social context into indictments betray a subtle insertion of that law as it claimed to offer a privileged, definitive, fact-based and truthful account of past events. As gatekeepers to criminal justice, dominion law and its representatives privileged their archived traces in a constrained language of indictment and accusation that crimes had been committed against the Queen's order, in whose name it operated.

Conclusion

The preceding discussion has interpreted surviving records of two cases in late nineteenth-century Western Canada with an eye to understanding the imposition of criminal law, and specifically the entryways that decided on which acts and persons to criminalize in given circumstances. Having orientated my interpretations around selected comments by Nietzsche on crime, law and opening moments of criminalization, it highlighted three themes.

To begin with, the significance of seemingly inconsequential events and perceptions was highlighted – an unfamiliar key in a door, or an open door and an empty bottle not left in a usual spot. Encounters that dislocated socially familiar ways of making sense of the world generated comparable disorder and chaos, leaving subjects open to criminalizing tales by which to reorder meaning horizons. In the examples examined here, such ordering occurred by alleging or accusing someone of committing a crime, and taking the matter to legal authorities. These moments proved consequential, for it was here that the law and society interweaved; it was also where attempts to impose dominion law over the west came to material fruition. In other words, law inserted itself into local social relations as a privileged, ordering force. But such points of contact were also significant in that they initiated the local generation of entryways into criminal justice, enabling us to locate the foundations of potential crime creation, and the relational hubs from whence criminalization derives.

Second, these entryways brought several subjects into contact with one another; they shaped identities that performed the roles of informer, accuser, authorized agent and the accused. Through the limited responses demanded by subjects at entryways, legally legible identities were negotiated, thus restricting the subjects that could be legally recognized. This allowed specific sorts of identities to serve as vehicles for entryways to criminal justice. Expanding criminalizing entryways could then insert law's recognition rituals into local social relations.

Third, the contact between society and law involved a matter fundamental to law: what it meant to tell the truth, to avow, in unambiguously legal ways in context. Dominion law licensed limited ways of telling the truth so that informers, accusers and the accused were required to perform specific rituals to speak 'the truth, the whole truth and nothing but the truth'. Such juridical truth-telling in the Canadian west at the end of the nineteenth century revolved around specific rituals of swearing oaths, testifying truthfully, signing statements and countersigning documents. As well, the lexicons for truth-telling practices in law were radically circumscribed by the use of a language that claimed to record the facts in a staccato-like, abbreviated and reduced fashion. Forms too demanded a 'proper' and common language. All in all, oral accounts were transcribed, and indeed translated, into legally decipherable linguistic codes that became the currency for subsequent juridical governance.

By way of conclusion, one might say that my interpretations point to moments that initiate an imposed creation of crime through locally generated entryways to criminalization in context; they also show how law and its criminal justice was expanded over further jurisdictions. But I also wish to return to a point raised in the introduction; namely, the tenacious legacy of such imposed criminalizing entryways on vast criminal justice networks today. To be sure, my interpretations emerge from current meaning horizons and signal attempts to confront the costly and exclusionary effects of ever-expanding criminal justice networks. Indeed, crime is a product of prior criminalizing processes, of legally arranged rituals and practices that constitute entryways used to define specific acts and persons as criminal. As one surveys the enormous criminal justice institutions of our time, overwhelmed perhaps by their sheer dominance, the difficulty of engaging their socially damaging effects might return us to the 'lowly beginnings' of crime at the entryways to its control networks. Such beginnings have been sidelined – even silenced – by the now dominant sense that crime has a being of its own, and that disciplines such as criminology can determine the etiology of that fixed entity. But we should recall that the '*crimen*' of this discipline has etymological links to accusation, suggesting the basic importance of the logic by which persons come to be accused as criminal (Pavlich, 2000). In this sense, the legal creation of crime at entryways could be understood as a pivot for sustaining or perhaps stemming the ongoing population flows into criminal justice arenas. The previous interpretations intimate the prospect of stalling the seemingly limitless criminalizing pathways by confronting the governmental logic that sustains such vast, unequal and socially damaging criminal segregations.

Notes

1 All references to the Edmonton case file are to be found in: *The Queen v. John Sunday (break and enter)*, 1888, GR1983.0001 Box 1/4, Provincial Archives of Alberta.

2 Newspaper references can be found at the University of Alberta Peel Library, http://peel.library.ualberta.ca/newspapers/.

3 All references to the Nanaimo case file may be found at *Queen vs. Boyle (Attempted Suicide)*, 1890, GR-2840.2.16, British Columbia Archives and Museum.

4 He also notes that

> Crime, like other human activities, tends to reflect the predominant social ideas of the era in which it occurs. In the case of the 19th century Canadian West, crime was very closely tied to class and to popular concepts of class. Respectability was the dominant virtue of the middle and upper classes, which meant that criminal activities were associated in the public mind with lower classes. A middle-class individual who was discovered in some serious violation of the law became almost automatically a social outcast. Everyone expected that the lower orders would break the law. It was one measure of their inferiority.
>
> (Macleod, 1976: 127).

5 As Farr puts it:

> The judicial system of England was used as a model for the administration of justice in the colonies, but the conditions of rough and pioneer territories modified and re-shaped that institution in innumerable ways. The modified system that resulted from these influences was of a different nature in British Columbia than in Vancouver Island, and appeared in a different form in the United colony than in the independent colonies.
>
> (Farr, 1944: 127).

References

Barman, J. (2007). *The West Beyond the West: A History of British Columbia* (3rd edn). Toronto, ON; Buffalo, NY: University of Toronto Press, Scholarly Publishing Division.

——. (2008). *British Columbia: Spirit of the People*. Madeira Park: Harbour.

Beahen, W. (1998). *Red Coats on the Prairies: The North-West Mounted Police, 1886–1900*. Regina, SK: Centax Books.

Borrows, J. (2002). *Recovering Canada: The Resurgence of Indigenous Law*. Toronto, ON: University of Toronto Press, Scholarly Publishing Division.

Brown, D. H. (1989). *The Genesis of the Canadian Criminal Code of 1892*. Toronto, ON: Osgoode Society.

Chiste, K. B. (2005). The justice of the peace in history: community and restorative justice. *Saskatchewan Law Review*, 68(January), 153.

Christie, N. (1994). *Crime Control as Industry: Towards Gulags, Western Style* (2nd edn). London: Routledge.

Dorsett, S., & McVeigh, S. (2012). *Jurisdiction*. Oxon: Routledge-Cavendish.

Farr, D. M. L. (1944). *The Organization of the Judicial System of the Colonies of Vancouver Island and British Columbia, 1849–1871*. Vancouver: University of British Columbia Press.

——. (1967). The organization of the judicial system in the colonies of Vancouver Island and British Columbia, 1849–1871. *University of British Columbia Law Review*, 3(March), 1–35.

Ferguson, J. H. (2009). *James Douglas: Father of British Columbia*. Toronto, ON; Tonawanda, NY: Dundurn.

Ferraris, M. (2012). *Documentality: Why It Is Necessary to Leave Traces*. New York: Fordham University Press.

Foster, H. (1981). 'The queen's law is better than yours', in J. Phillips, T. Loo, & S. Lewthwaite (eds), *Essays in the History of Canadian Law: Crime and Criminal Justice*. Toronto, ON: The Osgoode Society for Canadian Legal History, pp. 41–111.

——. (1990). Long-distance justice: the criminal jurisdiction of Canadian courts west of the Canadas, 1763–1859. *The American Journal of Legal History*, 34(1), 1–48.

——. (1992). *The White Man's Law in the Far West: Establishing Legal Institutions in British Columbia*. Working Paper Series, University of Manitoba. Canadian Legal History Project: CLIP-WPS-92-12. Winnipeg: Canadian Legal History Project, Faculty of Law, University of Manitoba.

——. (1994). 'The queen's law is better than yours': international homicide in early British Columbia', in J. Phillips, T. Loo, & S. Lewthwaite (eds), *Essays in the History of Canadian Law: Crime and Criminal Justice*. Toronto, ON: University of Toronto Press, pp. 41–111.

Foster, H., Buck, A. R., & Berger, B. L. (2008). *The Grand Experiment: Law and Legal Culture in British Settler Societies*. Law and Society. Vancouver, BC: University of British Columbia Press.

Foucault, M. (2014). *Wrong-Doing, Truth-Telling: The Function of Avowal in Justice*. Chicago, IL: The University of Chicago Press.

——. (2015). *On the Punitive Society: Lectures at the Collège de France, 1972–1973*. London: Palgrave Macmillan.

Gavigan, S. A. M. (2012). *Hunger, Horses, and Government Men: Criminal Law on the Aboriginal Plains, 1870–1905*. Vancouver, BC: University of British Columbia Press.

Harring, S. L. (1998). *White Man's Law: Native People in Nineteenth-Century Canadian Jurisprudence* (1st edn). Toronto, ON: University of Toronto Press.

Hesketh, B., & Swyripa, F. (1995). *Edmonton: The Life of a City*. Edmonton, AB: NeWest Publishers.

Innis, H. A. (2015). *The Fur Trade in Canada: An Introduction to Canadian Economic History*. Toronto, ON: University of Toronto Press.

Komar, D. (2015). *The Bastard of Fort Stikine: The Hudson's Bay Company and the Murder of John McLoughlin Jr*. Fredericton, NB: Goose Lane Editions.

Loo, T. (1994a). *Making Law, Order, and Authority in British Columbia, 1821–1871*. Toronto, ON: University of Toronto Press.

——. (1994b). 'The road from Bute Inlet: crime and colonial identity in British Columbia', in J. Phillips, T. Loo, & S. Lewthwaite (eds), *Essays in the History of Canadian Law: Crime and Criminal Justice*. Toronto, ON: University of Toronto Press, pp. 112–42.

——. (1990). "Law and Authority in British Columbia, 1821–1871." Ph.D. thesis, Vancouver, BC: The University of British Columbia.

Macleod, R. C. (1976). *The North West Mounted Police and Law Enforcement, 1873–1905* (1st edn). Toronto, ON: University of Toronto Press.

——. (1978). The shaping of Canadian criminal law, 1892 to 1902. *Historical Papers*, 13(1), 64.

Nietzsche, F. (1968). *The Will to Power*. New York: Knopf Doubleday Publishing Group.

——. (1997). *On the Genealogy of Morals: A Polemic*. Oxford: Oxford University Press.

Palmer, H., & Palmer, T. J. (1990). *Alberta: A New History*. Edmonton, AB: Hurtig.

Parker, N. (2015). 'Swift justice and the decline of the criminal jury trial', in H. Foster & J McLaren (eds), *Essays in the History of Canadian Law Volume VI: The Legal History of British Columbia and the Yukon*. Toronto, ON: University of Toronto Press, pp. 171–203.

Pavlich, G. (2000). Forget crime: accusation, governance and criminology. *Australian and New Zealand Journal of Criminology*, 33(2), 136–52.

——. (2006). The lore of criminal accusation. *Criminal Law & Philosophy*, 1(1), 79–97.

——. (2009). 'Being accused, becoming criminal', in D. Crewe & R. Lippens (eds), *Existentialist Criminology*. Abingdon: Routledge, pp. 53–69.

Reiman, J. (1990). *The Rich Get Richer and the Poor Get Prison*. New York: MacMillan Publishing.

Sedgwick, P. R. (2013). *Nietzsche's Justice: Naturalism in Search of an Ethics*. Montreal, QC: McGill-Queen's University Press.

Stonier-Newman, L. (1991). *Policing a Pioneer Province: The BC Provincial Police 1858–1950*. Madeira Park, BC: Harbour.

——. (2006). *The Lawman: Adventures of a Frontier Diplomat*. Canadian Electronic Library: Books Collection. Victoria, BC: TouchWood.

Strange, C., & Loo, T. (1997). *Making Good: Law and Moral Regulation in Canada, 1867–1939*. Themes in Canadian Social History. Toronto, ON: University of Toronto Press.

Taylor, I., Walton, P., & Young, J. (1973). *The New Criminology: For a Social Theory of Deviance*. London: Routledge.

Wilkins, C. (2012). *The Wild Ride: A History of the North West Mounted Police, 1873–1904*. Vancouver, BC: Stanton Atkins & Dosil Publishers.

Chapter 7

The lore of criminal accusation

And yet, if you arrest me,
You are the judge and executioner
Of that which is the life of life: the breath
Of accusation kills an innocent name,
And leaves for lame acquittal the poor life
Which is a mask without it.

(Shelley, *The Cenci*, Act iv, iv: 140–45)

By way of introduction

Degrees of collective amnesia are commonplace in contexts preoccupied with 'crime' as an a priori being, a reality of fixed proportion. The rigid impression masks rituals involved in producing a 'criminal', allowing reifications of crime to command vast criminal justice terrains. One effect of this condition is to reframe complex ethical matters as technical problems, and to solve many of these through exclusionary impulses. Crime then appears as something amenable to resolution in much the same way as an engineer might approach a wobbly bridge. If this ethically bereft approach approximates a Sisyphusian satire of tragic proportions, it also signals what is silenced by cultural milieus fixated on crime; namely, how crime is relationally constituted from the moment of allegation to a guilty judgment with attendant crime reports and records. Especially conspicuous by its absence is an emphasis on the founding moments of accusation where suspicion first arrests everyday life and clears a path for subsequent criminalizing processes. In what follows I address that absence by focusing on the ethical import of a lore that for centuries has traced meanings of criminal accusation.

Examining the lore, rather than, say, the law, of criminal accusation involves – if one defers to a dictionary definition – 'a body of traditions and knowledge on a subject or held by a particular group' and that is 'typically passed from person to person by word of mouth' (*New Oxford American Dictionaries*, 2nd edn).[1] When articulated to 'criminal accusation', the concept intimates a productive ambiguity. The Lore as traditional knowledge of 'criminal accusation' therefore stands apart from everyday lore that enables and facilitates the accusation of crime in a specific case: the Lore of criminal accusation versus, let us say, the lore of what it takes to successfully accuse somebody of a crime. This bifurcation coalesces around two sorts of questions: *what does it mean to accuse someone of committing a crime?*; and, *what in a given (socio, historical, political, cultural) context enables a successful accusation of criminality?* Although both senses and questions find expression in what follows, I focus on the first: the Lore of criminal accusation.

An immediate issue surfaces regarding how to address the meaning formations of a relatively informal, often oral, body of knowledge. No doubt, there are several ways of so doing; however, I am particularly concerned with indeterminate ethical precepts through which criminal accusation (implicitly or otherwise) enunciates how to exist with others. The ethical dimensions of criminal accusation's Lore cannot be formulated as essential, necessary, universal, or ontologically fixed. To do so would cancel the fluid ethical arenas at hand; ethics, let us recall, surfaces in undetermined moments that evaluate how to be with others (determinacy rescinds this prospect). An analysis of the ethical meaning horizons of this Lore defies, therefore, those who privilege only empirical or metaphysical approaches, or who remain anchored to a 'metaphysics of presence', and its ancillary investment in realism.[2] Even those tempted by the seemingly open form of 'what is criminal accusation?' are likely to have efforts frustrated by the question's advance (ontological) commitment to the concept queried.

What follows is written against assumptions of predetermined ontology, including the assertions of conventional histories. Even though I do return to erstwhile cases, mine does not claim to be one such history – I do not pretend to have dipped into the archives[3] to represent the reality of past lives. Instead, my aim is to read singular cases of a vast accusatorial archive through current meaning horizons, and to explore them as examples that exemplify and illuminate a broader phenomenon; namely, the ethical dimensions of criminal accusation's Lore. The examples proffer glimpses of a seemingly enduring everyday paradigm for contextual variations on how to accuse someone successfully of a crime. Such a paradigm enables multiple performances that trace the shifting tenets of criminal accusation. In this sense, I address the Lore of criminal accusation not as a being but as a dynamic ethical phenomenon[4]; the possibility requires a relatively open language able to address plural and embedded assertions of how to live collectively. The emphasis on ethical over ontological languages is offered as a deliberate counterweight to the above-mentioned technical fervour of crime-control networks.[5]

Instead, I will address (bring into being) the Lore of criminal accusation heterogeneously by recognizing this as always simultaneously other (*hetero-*) than what is contingently grouped (*-geneity*) as its meaning in context.[6] To be sure, my interpretations are haunted by an impossibly delicate discursive quest, for they require us – in our times at least – to write without the alibi of 'an invincibly transcendental structure' and yet to do so as if there might be such a thing (Derrida, 2002: xxviii). In many ways, the impossibility of addressing traces of accusation without an alibi, as if there were one, is a function of the regimes of truth into which, and yet against which, the following is asserted.[7] The aporia of this almost agnostic gesture is driven by its unique promise: to open to the ethical and political auspices of criminal accusation, and thence crime.

Ethics, grammar, Lore . . .

A Lore of criminal accusation enables fixed images of crime most efficiently when it has no face, when it lies silent in the recesses of assumptive foundation. The relative paucity of attention directed to accusation betrays, perhaps, its paradigmatic centrality to an ethos whose cultures of crime are now cosmic. Exposing the ethical dimensions of that Lore could potentially re-politicize crime by recalling the indeterminate contours of crime's spawning ground. Despite marked variation, the Lore without face defers to a prevalent 'I accuse you of stealing my trinket' sort of syntax, thereby making various (often implicit) claims about 'appropriate' forms of life free of injustice, malice, evil, etc. As discussed in Chapter 5, the grammar of accusation specifies proper uses of words, and the correct arrangement of their mutual deferments. It licenses, for example, ethical calculations that impart local sense to notions of what it is to accuse, who accuses and who is accused.

First example: accusation in action

The disappearance of Frans Joosten, 1714, (Drakenstein Jurisdiction, Cape of Good Hope)[8]

A case concerning the disappearance of Frans Joosten, the 'first' owner of Bartholomeusklip farm, provides glimpses of life at the outer edges of the Dutch East India Company's (VOC) colonial rule over the Cape. On 3 January, a neighbour, Isaac Visagie of the farm Vogelvallei, is out on horseback looking for an absconding slave when he hears that Joosten is missing. He converses with the man's 24-year-old wife, Maria (nee Mouton), and periodically returns to the farm over the next night and day, but there is still no sign of the missing man. Subsequently, Maria reports her husband missing to the VOC's appointed magistrate (*landdros*) of the Drakenstein district, Nicolaas van den Heuvel. He is charged with investigating the disappearance; a situation requiring some delicacy given the prevailing fears of what might befall slave-owners amid runaway slaves.

Jacques Theron, a member of Council of Justice (*Raad van Justisie*), would later depose that sometime in February he rode past Bartholomeusklip where he discovered three men and two women slaves enjoying some wine and bread. He cautioned Maria that, 'It is entirely unseemly to detain other people's slaves and to distract them with wine' (Toerien, 2004: 15).[9] Her response is simply that the noted slaves were visiting 'her' slaves. Nevertheless, Theron reports the incident to the magistrate because he felt that 'something was not quite right'. Maria is therefore questioned before two aldermen (*heemrade*), with two members of the Council of Justice as witnesses. She confidently relates how her husband went out at about 3 pm to look for his cattle, but failed to return when they did so.

This temporarily settles matters even though Theron notes the communal gossip that Maria (who did not mix much with neighbours) might have something to do with Joosten's death. Later, Pieter of Madagascar (an absconding slave) provides information 'without torture and freely' (Toerien, 2004: 22) to magistrate van den Heuvel that implicates one of Joosten's slaves (Titus of Bengale), and accuses Maria of asking him (in exchange for her buying his emancipation) to kill her husband. Fortuyn of Angola, another of Joosten's slaves, confirms the story and van den Heuvel now pursues Titus in earnest, who admits to an affair with Maria. He also confirms Pieter's allegations and then accuses Maria of killing her husband (by hitting Joosten twice with a stick while he lay sleeping), whereupon he, Fortuyn and Maria buried the man in a porcupine den (hole). Maria denies the claim and counter-accuses Fortuyn and Titus.

All three are now taken 70 miles on treacherous roads to the Castle, in what is now Cape Town, to appear before an inquisition conducted by the Council of Justice. Maria must give up her two children to a neighbour. After examining the information before the Council, the judges remain unsure of Joosten's actual killer, and so – as is usual for the time – evoke *ad torturam*, to torture the accused in search of truth. Before the appointed time of reckoning, however, word reaches the Council that Maria's 5-year-old child (who could not have supposed the impact of his words) has deposed the following. Maria and his father argued, his mother turned away – Titus took his master's loaded gun and shot at him, but missed. Joostens struggled for the weapon, whereupon Fortuyn came to the defence of Titus and hit the farmer behind the neck. Both then attacked and killed him. His mother was absent, but when she discovered her husband dead, she ordered the slaves to take him out back and colluded in the cover up.

The accusations, information, testimonies and decisions of the Council are written down in detail, archived for future reference. On 30 August, the Council of Justice reads its written decision of guilty and is about to enunciate its punishments for each when Maria pleads: 'Please send me to another land! Spare my parents the shame' (Toerien, 2004: 48). The punishments? Indicating the extent to which this is not simple 'bare life' that cannot be sacrificed, Maria is to become the target of the sovereign's full force (see Agamben, 1998). She is to be bound to a pole, half-strangled, burned with molten wax and then strangled fully. Equally, Titus will be impaled alive and left to die skewered on a spit; then his head and right hand will be severed and placed on a pole on the border of his master's farm. Fortuyn will be placed on a cross, his right hand severed and his limbs will be broken, while still alive and without coup de grace, from the feet upwards and left to die. Thereafter he will be decapitated and his head and hand placed next to Titus at the farm. Their bodily remains will be dragged to the South East corner of the Castle, a spot known as 'outside law' ['Buitengereg'], to decay in the air and to be consumed by birds.

Much can be made of the events in this case, but reading the ethical elements from a Lore of criminal accusation points us to what it sanctions as legitimate, lawful, ways to be with others. The previous chapters have referred variously to the etymology of accusation as deriving from the Old Latin *acusare*, 'to call someone to account' (Ayto, 1990: 5), and perhaps a 'cry of distress' (Klein, 1966: 372). In short, we might say that accusation through its etymology signalled a collective social alarm, calling specific subjects to account in the interests of a common good; it compelled accuser, accused and witnesses to account for themselves in relation to a specified crime.[10] Theron is the first in this regard, and his standing is key to enunciating the 'interests of the common good', of how best to live with others.

This Lore of criminal accusation is deeply embedded in sovereign lineages, always already there, constituting the opening and emerging fissures that come to assume the mantle of law and order. Ethically ordering 'life' might be a matter of biopower's governance, but the coercive sword of Damocles and the balanced scales of Themis complement its maxims. The Lore of accusation appears to bridge lay ordering of local custom with the ritualized performances of sovereignty and/or legality. Both enable sovereign visions of how to be with others. The accusatorial bell tolls to signal that a presumed order is disrupted and to initiate a confessional sequence of self-accounting and validation quite different from the ordinary, where ordered self-identities are usually negotiated. What emerges from this Lore are ritualized ethico-political assertions of limit formation, displacements that forge boundaries by calling subjects to account on suspicion of disrupting an imagined order.

Such disruptions serve as warrants to connect *order* with *law*, and thereby creatively embody a sovereign's jurisdiction (Agamben, 2005). Law and order in the name of sovereign conceptions of how subjects ought to live with others is a vital creation of criminal accusations such as those directed to Maria, Fortyun and Titus.[11] The Lore calls for written inscriptions to articulate custom and law; it archives the moment where lore becomes a matter of law. The authorized scribe, the magistrate (justice of the peace, constable, alderman, etc.), receives information by writing it down, collating accounts and deciding – making a judgement – about how, or sometimes whether, to channel relational flows into criminal proceedings. A seamless flow to the logic of writing is implied, a circuit that enables the continuous translation and representation of the events in written ethical formulae.

The investigating magistrate van den Heuvel, for example, is responsible for reordering the information received through the depositions of Pieter of Madagascar, the neighbours and the accused. That transposition is profoundly creative, as the written narratives allow law to present events in a limited static 'capture', archiving the claims that an order was disrupted, how this happened and documenting accusations of who is responsible for the situation. Even if the jurisdiction of law is already there, requiring very little reach, the gesture effectively masks the undetermined quality of ethical claims by ritualizing their calculations and distracting those who might be inclined to ask: is this an appropriate way to respond, or is this how we ought to be with others?

The written archive of an accusation serves as a representation in at least two senses. First, it professes accurately to (re-)present what is said about past events through a written narrative presented as a true accounting of events relating to an alleged crime, a morally sullied act. The text's implicit claim is to incarnate, for *ex post facto* processes, an orderly and truthful record that can be re-presented for the future inspections of a grand jury, the trial, historians, or even for readings of the kind presented in this chapter. Second, the writing is positioned to represent the views of those involved in an event. It is made to function as a re-presentation of all subjects' views, including the testimonies of the neighbours, the accused, and the young boy. In both cases, by virtue of representation, the Lore privileges the assumption that subjects exist prior to criminal events, and are the intentional authors of subsequent accusatory narratives. In turn, this reinforced author serves as a basic unit of its ethical calculations: the subject is positioned as the frame around which subsequent images of 'being with' are constructed.

Maria, for example, is the young woman with two children who fraternizes with slaves, has an affair with Titus, helps to cover up her husband's murder and reports her version of events to the magistrate. Equally, Titus and Fortuyn are individualized as subjects ('slaves') who testify, who witness, and author damning narratives. In all cases, the grammatical scheme licenses a subject as antecedent author of meaning, rather than say exploring how such meanings create the very being of 'independent' subjects. Writing thus re-presents the subject as the basic figure of ethical calculations who signals disruptions by enunciating accusations of wrongdoing, who authorizes or corroborates narratives, or who is charged with bearing exclusive moral culpability.

Criminal accusation transposes ethically ordered visions of custom into law; this move is profoundly constitutive for it creates a sense of *order* through legally authorized renderings of rupture (disorder). Through information relays (grand juries, magistrates, justices of the peace, prosecutors, district attorneys, etc.), the Lore licenses accusations not so much as ethical calculation, but as credible practices by which everyday subjects reach out to law. But it is important again to recall that this reaching out is a fraught gesture, for law is already there; for example, it is already within the age-old obligation to accuse if one is witness to, or victim of, a crime.

The Lore of criminal accusation *calls* subjects to account and thereby evinces its ethical calibrations of disrupted everyday relations. The one who accuses initiates the signal: the victim, or the prosecutor as state-authorized agent. All participants – accuser, accused, witness, agent – are to account for themselves and others with respect to an alleged crime. In the above case, Theron recognizes something 'entirely unseemly' in Maria's behaviour: simultaneously, a suspicion and an ethical exhortation that something is not as it should be were morally ordered relations to prevail in context. The putative disruption is almost quelled by Maria's initially confident narration of events before members of the Council of Justice; yet the information of Pieter of Madagascar confirms the relational rupture, and the three accused parties are taken to Cape Town to be questioned.

All parties are called to account, being held morally responsible for not living with others as they ought to do. They are made to stand before the law that has already partially fashioned them from within, and to confess a truth about themselves in relation to allegations of legally framed crimes. The confessions are creative since subjects must identify themselves anew through narrative descriptions of their roles in a criminalized event, and support or challenge statements made by others. Criminal accusation identifies others, defines their situated identities and actions; in the process, it also identifies the selves who confess their accounts in response to the call of an authorized agent, and through prescribed performances. The processes of accusation demand that accusing and accused subjects forgo familiar, everyday techniques of self-creation, and work on themselves as subjects located in the interstitial realms of criminal accusation where one must define oneself by answering accusatory allegations.

Hence, criminal accusation does more than allege; it names an absented order, and defines the otherness against which its putative orders stand. But in so doing it provides a sense of those putative orders. The discursive apparatuses of that stand are framed from within present horizons of inclusion, around moral, normative, legal, religious, scientific precepts, or a combination of these. The successful accusation identifies a tangible embodiment of what is ethically valued and what is to be excreted by the law and order of a given context. If this process thereby identifies what is transgressed, it simultaneously – through the assertion of transgression – defines porous ethical limits. It implicitly specifies contextually defined images of the law and the order that it defends. Transgression is thus appropriated through ordered images of otherness projected through processes that accuse, identify, define, judge and expel an 'offender'. In the above case, the excretion of otherness, that is simultaneously its definition, is symbolized by the punishments inflicted on the accused. The heads of the two slaves and the hand of Fortuyn who struck his owner, are physically positioned on the border of the Joosten's farm. Equally, the bodies of all three are left in an area outside the Castle called 'Buitengereg', or outside of law. The sovereign exclusion has no need to preserve the whole body, to define the individual subject through images of somatic integrity. Depriving the bodies of a proper funeral, and leaving them to be pecked as offal for birds further symbolizes the sovereign's excreted other; this is the effect of the socially triumphant criminal accusations that went before.

The subject as accuser: three examples[12]

Case 1: Trial of Helena Holman for theft: simple grand larceny, 20 May 1795[13]

The accuser, Thomas Dolly, describes himself as a 'publican in Grub-street' who hired Helena Holman, the accused, the previous December. His suspicions were aroused because he 'thought there was a shortness in the money several times, but it was impossible for me to tell the exact amount that was received there'.

On the advice of the Lord Mayor, he marked the money and on 29 April discovered some notes missing. He sent for a constable and thought it appropriate

> to have her searched, as the money was missing, to see whether my suspicions were well founded or not. When she went up stairs to clean herself, I followed her up stairs, and told her I had some reason to suppose that she had robbed me; she said, she had not; says I, if I accuse you wrongfully, I must ask your pardon; she said she had not robbed me; I said, I have a constable below, and I called him up.

He insisted on searching Ms. Holman's 'box', and claims to have found his money there and in her pockets. His daughter, Mary, corroborates the claims and adds:

> [W]hen my father came into the room, she said, there is all the money I have of yours; and if you think I have bought them new clothes with your money, you are welcome to take them, on condition she said that my father would not carry her before them gentlemen.

The constable confirms the accusation in his testimony before the prisoner calls one character witness. The 34-year-old is found guilty and transported for seven years.

Case 2: Charles Coe Kallmeier, theft, 10 September 1823[14]

George Gold Sadler, the prosecutor, describes himself and narrates his charge in this way:

> I am a tailor, and live in Southampton-row, in the parish of St. George, Bloomsbury; the prisoner was a journeyman in my employ. Between the 1st and 22nd of July, I lost 14 yards and five-eighths of blue cloth, worth 15 l. I saw it in the cutting room on the 1st of July, which is at the bottom of my garden, and connected with the dwelling-house, it is all enclosed by one wall. On the 22nd of July, I accused the prisoner of moving some calico, he said he moved it to measure some ferret, this roused my suspicion. I measured my cloths over, and missed this; and went to his lodging, where I found him. Mr. Hall, said in my presence, 'I am come to take you into custody, and where is Mr. Sadler's property;' the prisoner went to a table and delivered up five duplicates, three of them were for the property stolen; he said he was sorry for it, and hoped I would not prosecute him.

This tailor of fixed abode becomes sceptical because of an extraordinary event that 'roused' his suspicion. He seeks authority from a Mr Hall (of the local parish), and buttresses his accusation by presenting a self of noble character: 'I have known him a long time, and have been his friend all through life, and supplied him with money when starving, and introduced him to my friends – I did not lead him into expenses [*sic*].' Conversely, he alleges what would likely have been read as character deficits in the accused: 'I have seen a person who passes as his wife, but cannot say whether he is married.' As well, the accuser seeks to demonstrate the veracity of the claims through measurement, or by alluding to actions that are taken to reflect the accused's guilt (confessions, admissions, etc.). James Sweatman (describes himself as a 'shopman to Mr. Barker, pawnbroker, Holborn') challenges Sadler's testimony by charging that Sadler failed to accurately recognize the missing cloth and insisting that the prisoner 'belongs to a respectable family'. Even this evidence and good character reports from two witnesses do not circumvent the verdict of guilty, and a sentence of death for the 21-year-old Kallmeier (who is nevertheless recommended to mercy).

Case 3: John Hughes, theft: simple grand larceny, 6 December 1809[15]

Thomas Edwards, prosecutor, testifies to living at No. 4, Henrietta-Street, Manchester-Square, where the prisoner used to lodge:

> On the 14th of November I came home, I went into my room and went to the closet. I looked in my hat box and found that my hat was gone, I had put it there the night before; I accused the prisoner, he denied it; I understood from my landlady that he was going the next morning on account of being accused. I instantly took him to the watchhouse. The next morning he said he had stole the hat and took it to Mr. Layton, a pawnbroker in Wardour-street; I went there and found it. I am sure it is mine.

Thomas Baddam, a servant of the said pawnbroker, acknowledges receiving the hat from the prisoner.[16] The prisoner did not call any witnesses, nor did he offer any further defence. The 26-year-old was found guilty and transported for seven years.[17]

Despite markedly different contexts for so doing, a Lore of criminal accusation assumes the existence of a fixed, a priori subject who exists behind, and is the author of, a given accusation. And that author's identity is first and foremost cast in terms of what a man, and sometimes woman, does and where he or she lives (women are in many cases defined in relation to a male, especially if he is perceived to be of some stature). The address situates in a parish and connotes levels of stability, belonging; we are not dealing with vagrants or vagabonds. These are subjects of standing with a fixed abode from whence they address their communities by accusing others for the common good. And the content of their addresses conveys negative ethical calibrations calling for how not to be with others.

If an address situates the speaker, it also locates him/her within significations of inequity comprehensible to participants comprising the context, speaking to matters of wealth, prestige, respectability, ethnicity, religion, and so on.

Whether publican, tailor, landlord, horse trader or 'daughter', the author of an accusation makes clear his or her productive connection to local economies. This condition enables subjects to mount effective accusations that are understood, considered credible and taken seriously by authorities.

The Lore's subject who accuses assumes various historical guises – private person, constable, public agent and even computer node. In general, though, the Lore requires the subject to be an organizer of information, an assembler of meanings, who structures selectively the possible vagaries of given meaning horizons into an ordered ethical narrative. The author assembles an accusatorial story in an ordered sequence relayed according to what became a rather routine grammatical structure.

Having establishing character credibility, the subject describes how he or she came to suspect that an existing relation order had been criminally disrupted. Symbols, events (putative or otherwise), actions, statements, thoughts, gossip, and hearsay are collated as disruptions to commonplace ways of doing things, of proceeding ordinarily and legally with collective life. Mistrust is articulated through the discernment (enunciation) of disjunction; for example, Dolly's perception that monies had gone missing, or Thomas Edwards' missing hat combined with the hearsay of the landlady, or Sadler's perception that moving a roll of calico to measure ferret makes no sense, does not add up, etc. The contextual nuance is all-important, and the accusatorial impulse often initiated by a barely perceptible whim, a sense that something is awry, that traces itself through suspicion, blame to accusation. Through this, images of proper ways to exist with other beings are calibrated.

The narration of events involves selective combinations of words, deferrals and sequences that comprise contextual examples of how to lay an information. A receiving authority inscribes the (typically) oral information (e.g., justice of the peace, magistrate, alderman, and later police officer, detective, public prosecutor, etc.). It is worth noting that the author and authority are blended in such inscriptions; the archived text blends an accusing subject's deposition into the written translations of authority. The delegated authority performs an ethical duty with an almost sacred quality that implies, or rather is partially constitutive of, the sovereignty in whose name it writes.

A key element of the narration is apportioning blame, the articulation of words that assemble, in a profane way, the identity of the accused as the perpetrator of a crime. The assembling of that offending identity takes various forms, but requires the alibi of evidence. Whether it be Dolly's finding marked money, Sadler's 'finds' regarding the calico (and indeed the attempts to discredit the accused), or Edwards' deferrals to the pawnbroker, the accused is blamed through symbols used to isolate blameworthiness, to enable fingers pointing to an individual, or groups of individuals. The collective, the many, is almost indiscernibly constructed by isolating disruptive ones. This quarantining generates a clean slate upon which to write the accused's identity as other, in excess of order.

Cases of calumny as the accused's response

Case 1: Catherine Spiller, indicted for feloniously killing and slaying Mary Elizabeth Landon, 29 November 1832[18]

This case involves the death of a girl, nearly three years old (Mary Elizabeth Landon), suffering from a skin condition that affected her entire body and head. Her mother (also Mary Elizabeth Landon) describes engaging three different surgeons, and reports some improvement after seeing the last: 'she [her daughter] was under Dr. Carter for 6 or 7 weeks; I had no doubt she would get better under him.' Even so, she took the child to see Catherine Spiller, the prisoner, who apparently had a reputation for curing 'scrofula disorders'. The mother continues, 'I took her to the prisoner by my husband's advice; I put on one plaister myself from the ointment he sent; I have kept none of the ointment; she lost her appetite from the first day she went to the prisoner'. Although not a direct accusation, the implication is that the ointment had contributed to the child's untimely demise; the idea is also canvassed by her husband's testimony and partly by a Dr. John Carter who conducted the inquest: 'my opinion is, that the child died from irritation produced by the extensive disease of the scalp, excited by some irritating cause, and that from a recent period – I could not say how recent.'

The accused is brought to trial where she offers a written defence that begins:

> No one can regret more than myself the death of the poor child, but my conscience acquits me of all blame; I used the same remedy I had successfully used to many others, and had hoped the same result, but for the inattention to, and neglect of, my directions.

Accusatory blame is thereby deflected to its source, and the basis for the claim elaborated upon in some detail. The tone of the accused's narrative is sombre, respectful and yet firm in its counter-interpretation of events:

> I told the father he ought to have come on the Friday, he excused himself by saying he was busy on that day, and as Saturday was wet, his wife would not allow him to bring the child out; I then dressed the child's head, and particularly desired the father to come again to me on the Tuesday morning, but my directions were again unattended to, for the child was not brought until near eight o'clock at night, which was cold and foggy . . . I shall call before you many persons who have been relieved and cured by me, and who will tell you how incapable I am of an unkind act.

This narrative is countersigned by 'Eight witnesses who had been under the prisoner's care for scrofula disorders, deposed to her skilful, humane, and kind treatment.' The verdict? Not guilty.[19]

Case 2: Thomas Hunt, James Murphy, theft with violence: highway robbery, 15 January 1812[20]

At about quarter past eleven on 31 December 1811, Mr Greenhill, a watchman of St Brides, responded to a cry of 'murder!' The *Times* newspaper reports that Hunt was taken into custody but 'rescued by several others'.[21] About half an hour later, another murder cry from the same area was raised and he rushed over to see a woman 'knocked down, and cruelly treated' by rapidly fleeing men. The report goes on to note that, 'A young man present pointed out Murphy as one of the assailants'. He and Greenhill apprehended Murphy and 'Hunt came up at the moment; and being recognized by Greenhill as the person just before rescued, he carried him to the watch-house'.[22] The victim, Margaret Rainey (or *Renny* in trial documents), told reporters that five or six men (including the two prisoners) accosted her on her way home from work. They demanded money and when she denied having any they knocked her down, cut her pocket and made off with her day's wages of three shillings. She cried out to the watch for help and one man threatened to murder her, and another 'called to his companion to kill her outright, the old b_'. The report continues that: 'They left her almost naked; and she was positive the two prisoners were of the men.'

Mr. Rogers 'proved the identity of the prisoners' and at the trial he testified thus:

> I am a labourer in the East India Company's employ. On the 31st of December, at twelve at night, I was proceeding towards Gunpowder-alley, leading into Shoe-lane, I heard the cry of murder, I instantly run to where the voice came from, there I saw the prisoner Murphy strike the prosecutrix a blow upon the head, and as she was falling he struck her again; the prisoner Hunt was in company. When me and another advanced towards them they both took different directions; I instantly ran after Murphy, and just by Harp-alley he fell down, and threw me down to; I was up quicker than he was. I brought him back to Gunpowder-alley.

What of the accused and their responses? The *Times* report indicates that both 'solemnly denied all knowledge of the transaction, and protested that they had never seen each other, nor the woman, before they were brought to the watch-house [*sic*]'. They both declare occupations (a shoemaker and journeyman butcher), and Murphy acknowledges 'to have offered the woman a pound note to withdraw her charge at the watch house; but this was to prevent his name being exposed'. He apparently 'begs' to be sent to Newgate, noting that two other men had been previously committed to death on the evidence of this prosecutrix. At the trial, a constable testifies thus:

> I am a constable. I took Hunt, and when I took him in the watchhouse the prosecutrix said, that is the man that cut my pockets off, I insist upon your taking charge of him. I find that the prosecutrix, Margaret Renny, has shifted her lodgings; I have used my endeavour to find her, I cannot.

The accused prisoners are found not guilty.

The Lore of criminal accusation generates the accused as respondent to allegations of criminality – the culpable entity for unethical being. Should the accused's accounts not convince assembled gatherings of innocence, he or she runs the risk of being displaced from ordinary relations with others and excreted as the other. The point to bear in mind is this: images of the accused other are created from within, but made to appear as threats from without. The Lore supports the creation of the vast networks of *displacing* and *displaced* subjects that enable current calculations of criminal accusation. The accuser and accused are basic figures in this ethical drama.

The Lore requires the accused to speak as the displaced, as other, but to signify through law's ordering meaning horizons why the criminal allegations do not hold.[23] When the accused speaks to challenge ethical claims, it is important to do so from within. As discussed, Socrates has become perhaps the iconic figure of an accused that refuses the language and ethical claims of his accusers – the hemlock is his solace (Plato, 1948).[24] Others might be more inclined to impugn the integrity of the accuser, challenge the veracity of the accusation by reinterpreting events and present a different character/identity.

Recalculating ethical images is often dependent upon the accused's ability to adapt to, and abide by, the different codes of conduct appropriate to the various accusatorial proceedings (from the customary settings, depositions, to grand juries, to the trial, etc.). This is all done from within the acceptable rules of conduct of a setting. Catherine Spiller emphasizes, for example, the ways in which the Landons neglected to follow her instructions on at least two occasions (e.g., they carried the child home in an open cart on a wet day), implying their culpability in the death. In her statement, more articulate than that of either Landon, she simultaneously reinterprets the events to redirect the accusation, and follows up with the claim that she will bring forward 'many persons who have been relieved and cured by me'. She thus asserts the finger of blame is falsely directed at her, and attempts to re-present herself as a compassionate woman who is 'incapable' of an 'unkind act' and who regrets the child's death, but whose 'conscience acquits me of all blame'. Murphy and Hunt replicate this deferral strategy by noting that their accuser's evidence had already sent someone to death, challenging the view that they were present at the attack or even knew each other, and by telling the night watch that they have occupations (and in Murphy's case a fixed abode).

Amending the paradigms of criminal accusation

In traversing, by way of examples, the ethical auspices of a Lore that traces criminal accusation, the previous discussion elaborates upon common-sense formulations that appropriate the phenomenon of criminal accusation through a simple syntax: the accusing subject emerges as the author of an accusation that calls another to account for putatively criminal behaviour. From what has been said above, this pervasive grammar enables a sense of criminal accusation grounded on at least two assumptions: (1) the act of accusing involves an authorized subject who charges another with being the intentional subject of a criminal act in the interests of a common order; (2) the subjects (both accuser and accused) are taken to be discrete, established, beings, a priori entities, whose identities shape, rather than being constituted by, accusatorial performances. They also bear moral culpability for their negotiated positions in relations to a putative 'order'. These assumptions are reinforced through the syntactic deferrals of many different inscriptions, including the work of private depositions, police constables, justices of the peace, public prosecutors, grand juries, police computers, detective novels, newspapers, television programmes, movies and everyday conversation. They impart degrees of inevitability to processes from which criminal identification and punishment arise; they also play a central role in fixing 'crime' as an ontological entity per se.

It might then be important to reformulate these two assumptions in efforts to open the Lore's meaning horizons, and so reconsider the very phenomenon of criminal accusation. If this exposure has effect, it could give impetus to the difficult task of re-politicizing crime and returning that reification to its contingent spawning grounds. How so?

Accusing: the co-appearance of order and disorder

Referring to the first assumption, one might contest the way that the verb 'accuse' narrowly appears as the intended action of an authorized subject who charges another with a crime. Framing accusation in this way restricts the activity involved to individual agents, or subjects. This frame eclipses the perhaps more central role that accusing, calling to account, has for constituting collective formations as 'normal societies', 'peaceful communities' and so on. Far from existing *sui generis*, these formations are contingently sustained through perpetual and various regulatory activities that – in a 'singularly plural' fashion, to borrow from Nancy (2000)[25] – delimit porous borders by identifying, for example, the accused 'criminal'.

The verb 'accuse' might, for example, be mobilized as a descriptor for somewhat unique ethical practices designed to isolate and displace what is excessive. Accusation could, specifically, be understood as unleashing ethical practices that: name what is to be viewed as other; specify how transgression is to be alleged; and, thereby generate images of ordered collectivities. Through variable identification procedures, criminal accusation delimits by naming transgression and so indicates what is transgressed (i.e., specifying transgression also defines conformity to the extent that it specifies what is absent from those who conform). By ordering, regulating, displacing, and naming excess, the verb 'accuse' appears as an ethical reckoning whose effect is to generate the co-appearance of disorder and order.

Accusation, thus understood, actively constitutes the identity of the relational complexes in whose name it is recursively deployed. By appropriating the other as an offender, criminal accusation defines an absence and simultaneously renders a specific vision of the common good, the order, present. It presents what a relational setting aspires to lack, a deliberated absence that simultaneously constitutes associations (this or that society, community, the west, etc.); the naming of absence fabricates the porous, and plural–singular, limits of constantly reiterated, permeable and dynamic images of 'orders'. Delineations of excess implicitly isolate borders within – criminal accusation is one of the seldom-discussed foundations, starting points, of a vast crime-control industry directed at securing by designating criminal otherness.

Now, if accusation is considered a displacing, order-forming, activity, and if criminal accusation is understood as the founding moment of criminalizing processes, then the contingent ethical foundations of crime become explicit. That is, crime potentially emerges from accusatorial relations that displace otherness as criminal. This focus on crime, insofar as it delineates how to exist (justly?) with others, is appositely approached through ethical – rather than instrumental, technical and managerial – languages. With great caution, and without underplaying the burden of such entrenched crime-based cultures/structures that define many people today, the promise of refashioning the first assumption is to reclaim the ethical auspices of criminal accusation's displacing activity. The reclamation would go hand in glove with a regenerated political terrain that need not replicate – indeed would contest – the exclusionary impulse of crime-creating processes. In a pursuit of justice without a fundamental attachment to crime, the Lore could detach accusation from crime, and emphasize its broader identity-forming, ethically based functions. More inclusive accusatorial processes might be conceived and enlisted. This, in turn, could enable definitions of just ways to be that are tied neither to fixed orders, nor to orders defined by exclusionary crime-creating processes. The promise here is to pursue forms of 'being with' not delineated through notions of crime, and to recast otherness by recognizing that it is an 'interior' that designates its own excess. If nothing else, this politics should enable governors to face directly, and recognize themselves in, the 'disorders' they enunciate.

Co-appearing accuser and accused

Let us conclude by returning to the Lore's second key assumption. If criminal accusation enables the co-appearance of order and disorder, it is less a tool for pre-established subjects than a process that helps to create subjects of the (dis) orders that accusations singularly and plurally enunciate. The Lore could thus be reformulated to acknowledge the mutual constitution of accuser and accused, each fundamentally responsible for the being of the other. This view echoes those who describe how the ethical subject is always already a response to the call of the other. Levinas (1985: 83–93), for instance, indicates how the 'I' comes to be only as response to an amorphous collective 'face' that calls.

This idea is most immediately evident when the accused, by way of an accusation, is called to account. The call requires a response, and in responding as an accused person, an accused identity unfolds through complex processes of allegation and counter-allegation. Both accuser and accused become by responding: their co-appearance betrays the fundamental – nay, constitutive – responsibility they bear for each other. As reciprocally created identities, they co-appear by participating in the displacement that is the effective work of criminal accusation. The accuser is not the active, intentional subject any more than the accused is simply the passive subject of an accusation; each emerges through responses solicited by the calls of criminal accusation procedures.

Reframing criminal accusation as a verb to describe the displacing of otherness, and generating the co-appearance of accuser and accused (as well as witness, authorized agent, etc.), once again brings ethics and politics to the fore – this time around questions of identity formation. For example, defining the accused as an individual criminal offender, or the accuser as an individual victim, police officer, public prosecutor, etc., are not essential features of accusation per se, but of contingent (admittedly well-entrenched) configurations associated therewith. By altering this assumption, one could reconfigure the politics of criminal accusation, making it feasible to challenge contemporary versions of the co-appearing accuser (mostly police detective, magistrate, prosecutor) and accused (individual criminal offender). This might allow one to pursue the difficult task of recalibrating the co-appearance more inclusively, with less emphasis on criminal displacements and excluded identities. The phenomenon of accusation in this scheme could address injustice variously, in a never-ending promise to fashion just collective associations. Its reflex need not always be to place moral culpability on accused individuals, as in the instances explored above. In many cases, ethical formulae could less exclusively calibrate corporate associations and other non-individual subjects as purveyors of injustice, or examine their roles in creating dominant images of the just. It is important always to recall that despite the attempts at bordering and ordering, accuser and accused are never distinct. A politics of accusation that promises justice cannot lose sight of this co-appearance without thereby forgoing its laudable aspiration.

Acknowledgements

The author would like to thank Charles Barbour, Ronnie Lippens, Peter Fitzpatrick, Erik Claes and Anthony Duff for their helpful comments on a previous version of this chapter. An earlier version was presented at the British Academy on the occasion of a symposium on 'Criminal Law and Philosophy', October 2005, London.

Notes

1 The same dictionary provides another, seemingly more remote definition, as follows: 'lore| . . . noun Zoology; the surface on each side of a bird's head between the eye and the upper base of the beak, or between the eye and nostril in snakes. ORIGIN early nineteenth century, from Latin lorum "strap."' Though the zoological differentiations might seem relatively far removed from our concerns here, there is a *between* law and order to which we will have reason to return.

2 See Derrida (1976, 1979, 1982, 1995).

3 I use the term 'archive' in the sense of playing with the commencement and commandment that this term simultaneously names – the governor's place. But I will resist portraying my role as that of an *archon* with the power to access and interpret the documents with certainty, with authority. The 'impression' of the archive is explored largely as a 'memory of the future' (see Derrida, 1998).

4 This, notwithstanding Nancy's (2000) useful reminder that ontology could be seen as itself making an ethical claim.

5 See Pavlich (2000) for a more detailed analysis of critique as a response to the technical emphases of criminal justice contexts. The critique of crime has some resonances with earlier work by theorists such as Mathiesen (1974) and Hulsman (1986).

6 See Derrida (1977: 13).

7 More specifically, the following chapter gestures toward senses and uses of the word 'accusation' that render governmental performances of displacement meaningful. The emphasis on traces is one that proceeds without the usual securities, the entrenched comforts of empiricism, metaphysics and an associated realism. Akin to Derrida's (2002) gestures elsewhere, my address will take form 'without alibi', but with a specific sense of at least two conditions. First, the 'axiomatics' of the 'sovereign subject and *autonomous* responsibility' is not taken to be present a priori (Derrida, 2002: xxvii). In context, that is, neither accused, accuser, authority nor witness can be presumed to exist as fixed, free and stable subjects who are 'present without alibi'. If there, presence remains a contextual accomplishment forged as shifting residues of temporarily staid deferrals. Addressing such nominal entities is an uncertain gesture, 'without alibi'. Second, when analyzing this Lore, one need not evoke:

> A predeconstructive thinking of pure and untouched presence of every trace, thus of every referral to the elsewhere of the other (place, moment, who, or what), which would come down to saying, 'This presents itself, or I, myself, conscious subject, I present myself intentionally *without alibi*'.
>
> (Derrida, 2002: xxvii–xxviii)

Traces of accusation are not universally present entities to be discovered. Speaking such traces into a different sort of discursive being has its own reasons; such as the political one of spurning a tyranny that comes with allowing a meaning horizon to fix itself as necessary. The meaning of crime, for example, is necessary only to the extent that deferrals to accusatory processes are denied, or the traces sustaining criminal accusation ignored. And yet when trying to address accusatory traces, one is dogged by the 'perhaps'. Accusation thus is always – in this sense, at least – without alibi.

8 My discussion of this case is based on the archival work of Toerien's (2004) *Die Wegraak van Frans Joosten [The Disappearance of Frans Joosten]*. The material for this Afrikaans text defers to the CJ document series, the Council of Justice Records (in old Dutch), housed at the National Archives of South Africa's Cape Town Repository. I wish to thank Johan Van der Walt for his assistance in translating some Afrikaans passages. The role of accusation in the inquisition is clearly central and may question commentators, like O'Connor (1984), who tend to draw a sharp distinction between the two.

9 The Afrikaans is: '*Dit is uiters onfatsoenlik om ander mense se slawe op te hou en met wyn te trakteur.*'

10 See too the etymology discussed in the introduction.

11 The link between law and order aspects of the Lore has a complex lineage. For example, as a way of extending sovereign rule over a kingdom, King Henry's *Assize of Clarendon* instructed justices to discover:

> Whether there be in their hundred or vill any man accused or notoriously suspected of being a robber, murderer or thief, or anyone who is receiver of robbers or murders or thieves since the Lord King has been King. And let the justices inquire among themselves and the sheriffs among themselves.
>
> (cited in O'Connor, 1984: 354).

The importance of accusation for legal discovery and sovereign rule is implicit and spells out the well ensconced duties of accusation, even in an inquisitorial juridical process.

12 In general, references to cases in this section and the next are to the *Old Bailey Proceedings Online* found at www.oldbaileyonline.org (accessed between 1 June and 14 September, 2005).

13 *Old Bailey Proceedings Online*, 20 May 1795, Trial of Helena Holman (Ref: t1795 0520-57). The full charge is listed as follows:

> 298. HELENA HOLMAN was indicted for feloniously stealing, on the 29th of April, one hundred and sixty-nine copper halfpence, value 7s. 2d. 1/2 twelve farthings, value 3d. ten pieces of copper, called medals, value 4d. one hundred and sixty-two halfpence, value 6s. 9d. nine farthings, value 2d. eight half crowns, value 1l. three shillings and five sixpence; two pieces of metal, value 1d. two pieces of silver, value 6d. four metal cloak pins, value 1s. six brass hooks, value 6d. an iron knife with a wooden handle, value 4d. and an iron fork with ditto, value 2d. the goods of Thomas Dolly. (The case opened by Mr. Gurney.)

14 *Old Bailey Proceedings Online*, 10 September 1823, Trial of Charles Coe Kallmeier (Ref: t18230910-44): '1035. CHARLES COE KALLMEIER was indicted for stealing, on the 22d July, at St. George, Bloomsbury; (being servant to George Gold Sadler) in his dwelling-house, 14 yards of woollen cloth, value 15 l., the property of the said George Gold Sadler, his master.'

15 *Old Bailey Proceedings Online*, 6 December 1809, Trial of John Hughes (Ref: t18091206-27). In particular, '26. JOHN HUGHES was indicted for feloniously stealing on the 14th of November, a hat, value 10 s. the property of Thomas Edwards'.

16 Another case of stealing in a domestic setting can be found at *Old Bailey Proceedings Online*, 3 June 1824, Trial of Catharine Keenan (Ref: t18240603-88).

17 A contrasting case in the same year with a different outcome is found in the following: *Old Bailey Proceedings Online*, 1 November 1809, Trial of Samuel Harvey (Ref: t18091101-95). '903. SAMUEL HARVEY was indicted for feloniously stealing on the 10th of October, three pecks of oats, value 3 s., the property of Armand Dyson.' The prosecutor, Dyson, describes himself as a 'horse dealer':

> On the 10th of October I had ten quarter of oats brought in a waggon from Bear key, the prisoner was the carman. After the waggon was unloaded, my man came to me, I came back with him, and went into the waggon, there I saw a bushel measure nearly full of oats, I accused the prisoner of stealing the oats.

It is noted that he is located in Park Lane, and is asked whether he is alone in business; he answers that he is in business with his father and two brothers. The Accused is in this case found not guilty.

18 *Old Bailey Proceedings Online*, 29 November 1832, Trial of Catherine (Ref: t18321129-155).

19 In a not unrelated fashion, a husband who is accused of throwing his wife out of a window offers the same sort of narrative in a different case. His wife, before her death, deposes his innocence, but alleges bad treatment. He, by contrast, testifies thus:

> My Lords, and gentlemen of the jury, trembling under the awful situation in which I am now charged with a crime of the most brutal enormity, appearing before this Honorable Court with all the mischievous consequences created against me by public prints/, &c. I most humbly appeal; confident, however, popular clamor may condemn me, a conviction of my innocence, to which I call God to witness, and of your humane and impartial hearing, that you will permit me to submit to your consideration those matters irresistibly attached to the case, which will convey to the Court the impossibility of my guilt.

He alleges that his wife was unable to 'govern her passions', was often drunk and had placed them in debt. He confidently tempts fate:

> My Lords, and Gentlemen of the Jury, I once more appeal to God that I have set forth the truth, and nothing but the truth, and hope, when you consider the case fully, which I rest satisfied you will, you will easily convince yourselves of the improbability of my being her murderer. God forbid. Were I so, the sooner I quit this earthly career the better. Pardon me.'

He too is found not guilty. See *Old Bailey Proceedings Online*, 16 September 1812, Trial of Francis Evans (Ref: t18120916-52).

20 *Old Bailey Proceedings Online*, 15 January 1812, Trial of Thomas Hunt (Ref: t18120115-31).

21 *The Times*, 2 January 1812, p. 4, Issue 8489, Col. E. (Source: *Times Digital Archive*).

22 The *Times* article refers to a John – rather than Thomas – Hunt.

23 Here one might refer to the 'strange' case of Adolph Beck who was convicted twice (1895 and 1904) on the strength of apparent calumnies and misidentification. The accused's foreignness might have impeded his ability to account for his innocence in both cases (although he is later pardoned) – see Coates (2011).

24 See also Chapters 1 and 3 for accounts of Socrates as the accused.

25 His concept of the 'singular-plural' reinforces the idea that the words 'being', 'singular' and 'plural' are closely interrelated concepts such that:

> Being is singularly plural and plurally singular. Yet, this in itself does not constitute a particular predication of Being, as if Being is or has a certain number of attributes, one of which is that of being singular-plural . . . On the contrary, the singular-plural constitutes the essence of Being, a constitution that undoes or dislocates every single, substantial essence of Being itself.
>
> (Nancy, 2000: 28–9).

References

Agamben, G. (1998). *Homo Sacer: Sovereign Power and Bare Life*. Stanford, CA: Stanford University Press.

——. (2005). *State of Exception*. Chicago, IL: University of Chicago Press.

Ayto, J. (1990). *Dictionary of Word Origins*. New York: Arcade Publishing.

Coates, T. (2011). *The Strange Story of Adolph Beck*. London: Uncovered Editions.

Derrida, J. (1976). *Of Grammatology*. Baltimore, MD: The Johns Hopkins University.

——. (1979). *Writing and Difference*. London: Routledge and Kegan Paul.

——. (1982). *Margins of Philosophy*. Brighton: Harvester Press.

——. (1995). *Points . . . Interviews, 1974–1994*. Stanford, CA: Stanford University Press.

——. (1997). 'The Villanova roundtable', in J. D. Caputo (ed.), *Deconstruction in a Nutshell: A Conversation with Jacques Derrida*. New York: Fordham University Press, pp. 3–28.

——. (1998). *Archive Fever: A Freudian Impression*. London: University of Chicago Press.

——. (2002). *Without Alibi*. Stanford, CA: Stanford University Press.

Hulsman, L. (1986). Critical criminology and the concept of crime. *Contemporary Crises*, 10(1), 63–80.

Klein, D. (1966). *A Comprehensive Etymological Dictionary of the English Language*. Amsterdam: Elsevier.

Levinas, E. (1985). *Ethics and Infinity*. Pittsburgh, PA: Duquesne University Press.

Nancy, J. L. (2000). *Being Singular Plural*. Stanford, CA: Stanford University Press.

Mathiesen, T. (1974). *The Politics of Abolition*. New York: Wiley.

O'Connor, D. (1984). The transition from inquisition to accusation. *Criminal Law Journal*, 8, 351–72.

Pavlich, G. (2000). *Critique and Radical Discourses on Crime*. Aldershot: Ashgate.

Plato. (1948). *Euthyphro, Apology, and Crito and the Death Scene from Phaedo*. F. J. Church & R. Denoon Cumming (eds). New York: The Liberal Arts Press.

Toerien, B. J. (2004). *Die Wegraak Van Frans Joosten*. Pretoria: Protea Books.

Chapter 8

Criminal justice and Cape law's persons

The remarkable growth of crime-control institutions in many Western societies over the past few centuries has sparked a political and cultural preoccupation with crime control in our societies (Garland, 2002; Simon, 2007). The rhetoric behind this growth promised a fundamental diminution of crime, and by implication the attenuation of its punishment. Generations have heard versions of the promise and many have faced the effects of its unfulfilled aspirations (Garland, 1991; Stuntz, 2011). Even with fluctuations in crime rates, as noted, criminal justice arenas have expanded and captured certain groups of subjects disproportionately – the poor, indigenous groups, people of colour, men and so on (e.g., Alexander, 2012; Loury, 2008; Simon & Sparks, 2013; Wacquant, 2009a, 2009b). Such imbalanced representations of people across colonial criminal justice contexts is both striking and persistent, inviting questions about how it emerged and why it continues to dog criminal justice arenas. Of course, one chapter could hardly respond adequately to the social, economic, political, legal and cultural aspects of this far-reaching, multifaceted question. However, I shall focus on a basic, if not always considered, dimension of the matter, namely, colonial law's contribution to a crime-control logic that perpetuates these uneven cohorts.

Analysts have variously pointed to colonial influences that shaped neo- or postcolonial criminal justice arenas (e.g., Chanock, 2001; Hansen & Stepputat, 2005; Ross, 1980, 1993), but few emphasize the politics of law that nurtured such an unequal regulation of crime and punishment (Comaroff & Comaroff, 2006; Pavlich, 2011). Turning to the latter, the following chapter highlights a politics of the accused legal person in ways that fostered unequal criminal justice practices at the Cape of Good Hope circa 1795. Its basic argument is this: the Cape's crime-focused law[1] entrenched a political logic in support of an assumed social hierarchy by assigning unequal categories of legal personhood to subjects of crime and targeting its force differentially to these categories. This political logic was neither initiated by, nor unique to, the Cape (see Santosh, 2011), though it was explicitly addressed in records of its archive. Versions of that logic have resounded over the centuries; using the Cape's rich archive as an illustrative example, one glimpses how differentiated conceptions of the legal person help to sustain basic inequalities of many criminal justice institutions nowadays.

My approach here is explicitly 'genealogical' in the sense previously discussed, charting as it does a colonial political logic behind the tenacity of systemic inequalities in crime-focused governmental arenas (Foucault, 1977: 139ff., 2013: 202–28). Analyzing the Cape judges' emphasis on 'distinctions of persons' within a differentiated version of criminal justice, this chapter suggests not only how stratified categories of person helped to prefigure South Africa's notoriously unequal apartheid legal systems, but also how that political logic remains relevant to inequities of many other criminal justice systems.

Background considerations

One might be tempted to impute a resonant historical failure to such resilient criminal justice inequities. However, we have noted how such claims to failure eclipse this: expanding, unequal criminal justice systems might constitute a success in other terms. Reiman's (2005) 'pyrrhic defeat' theory noted their success in projecting ideologies in favour of elite classes, thereby perpetuating capitalist economic inequalities. Equally Foucault (1979: 277) set the seeming failure of prisons to eliminate crime against triumphs of disciplinary political technologies behind the delinquents and normal individuals of modern 'carceral' societies. The point is that criminal justice institutions successfully deployed vast power–knowledge complexes centred on 'crime', and so regulate contextually allotted categories of persons unequally. As inequalities associated with 'governance through crime' (Simon, 2007) have entrenched themselves, so some groups have found themselves the targets for different intensities of criminal justice management and force.

All well and good, one might say, but why focus on the legal person, and why the Cape? The legal person initially struck me as important in context, because of the emphasis that Cape judges placed on distinguishing categories of person in cases dealing with crime (Theal, 1897). However, on further reflection, its foundational role in the political logic of criminal justice could be concentrated: when defining accused persons, law deploys method for declaring its jurisdiction, for identifying the targets of its gaze (Dorsett & McVeigh, 2012). While this political role is evident in many areas of law, it takes on a special significance in criminal law because the latter operates through depersonalizing processes. These processes arrest everyday subject identities to make way for criminal accusations and guilty prisoners – thus exposing subjects to the punishing force of law (Esposito, 2012a). In context, the judges of the Cape's crime-focused law commenced their investigations by assigning categories of personhood to all those involved with criminal events – accuser, accused and witnesses. The categories were then used to calibrate the seriousness of specific crimes and to determine a 'suitable' legal force (punishment). In other words, as we shall see, hierarchical accusations of 'criminal' persons enabled crime-focused law to settle its gaze differently on distinct categories of persons, and unequally to unleash its punishing violence on those categories. The political logic behind these accusations might have colonial foundations, but its effects continue to shape current criminal justice systems.

I have turned specifically to the Cape circa 1795 not only because its archive contains unique case records that betray its judges' understandings of persons, crime and punishment, but also since that context explicitly reveals its crime-centred political logic. These were extraordinarily unsettled times for the Cape, with the ruling Dutch East India Company (Verenigde Oostindische Compagnie, or VOC) at the brink of financial collapse and facing dissent from various settlements. Napoleon's military successes in Holland and elsewhere had convinced the British to invade the Cape.[2] With significant naval and ground forces deployed on and off the shores of Muizenberg beach, Britain overcame some resistance to end almost 150 years of Dutch rule. Declaring an occupation rather than settlement, the British sanctioned the former Roman–Dutch legal system to persist largely intact and, with limited reforms, reappointed most judges (Boucher & Penn, 1992) of the previous 'council of justice' to its 'new court of justice'. This law was enlisted to quell dissent and establish British sovereignty over the colony (Pavlich, 2011). But political uncertainty persisted and, in 1803, the British ceded the colony to the Batavian Republic only to reoccupy it in 1806.

Such extraordinarily unsettled times produced frank deliberations on how crime-focused law might complement military force to secure order in the name of a British sovereign (Pavlich, 2013a). For example, in an exchange of letters between the commander of the British occupation forces (Major General Craig) and judges of a re-established Cape court of justice, the latter defended their attachment to a hierarchical 'distinction of persons' upon which their openly unequal sense of criminal justice rested.

Their discourses on legal persons indicated a remarkably enduring political logic, wherein criminal justice had in defence of sovereign social orders targeted categories of person differentially and exposed them to various intensities of its violent force. In danger of getting ahead of my argument, it might be appropriate here first to clarify how 'legal persons' will be approached before examining the Cape instance.

An approach to the persons of crime-focused law

This chapter's political and socio-legal approach to discourses that generate the legal person in the Cape context rests on different assumptions from influential jurisprudential perspectives. While the law of persons frames itself according to an internal legal argument (see Hahlo & Kahn, 1968: 343–7), this chapter references a wider sovereignty politics by which crime-focused law contextually enunciates its target, its 'persons' (Naffine, 2003). Attending to the power–knowledge relations involved in generating various concepts of the legal person, it stands opposed to frameworks that assume more or less fixed notions of personhood to which law should direct itself.[3] But it might be less at odds with the elements of legal positivism or realism that consider the person as a 'pure, legal artifice', a technique to help law declare its jurisdiction[4] or as a constitutive 'fiction' that is law's 'primary means of specifying its object' (Fagundes, 2001: 1746).[5] Extending this starting point, one might say that through concepts of legal personhood law, 'law peoples its world' (Esposito, 2012a: 346), and so defines jurisdiction (Dorsett & McVeigh, 2012: 81ff.).[6] As Naffine (2003: 347) puts it, 'Perhaps the greatest political act of law is the making of a legal person . . . And, in the same move, the making of legal non-persons (those who cannot act in law and who are generally thought of as property)'.

Echoing the idea, but with broader perspective, Dayan's (2011) discussion shows how political acts contextually define 'negative persons' outside law, and how these in turn shape what law accepts as persons. This work rightly insists on the value of continuously asking, 'how law encapsulates, sustains, and invigorates philosophies of personhood' (Dayan, 2011: xii). To chart a political logic of persons in the Cape's crime-focused law – as per Foucault's (1980, 2013) lead – one might examine specific 'discourses', or power–knowledge complexes, that framed themselves around and through images of persons involved with crime. That is, attending to selected 'enunciative modalities' that defined Cape legal persons as targets for its crime-focused law, this chapter is concerned with local 'regimes of truth' (Foucault, 1980, 2002: 88ff.). Esposito (2012a, 2012b) adopts a similar tack in his genealogy of the legal person in the West, arguing that its main, if disparate, elements (e.g., body, mind, reason, etc.) emerged from a 'judicial root' in Roman law. Here, power relations forged a specific discursive apparatus – 'dispositif'– of legal persons, and this was accomplished by channelling these disparate elements into the semblance of a unified idea, named the 'person'. Furthermore, he notes that Roman precepts emphasized something directly relevant to Cape crime-focused law with its Roman–Dutch heritage: nobody was considered 'a fully-fledged person from the beginning of life nor did one remain a person forever' (Esposito, 2012a: 24). Instead, this discourse enabled a fluid movement between Roman law's persons, 'semi-persons' and non-persons, allowing for depersonalized framings of criminality and punishment (but also enabling personalizations associated with, say, manumission). Transitions from law-abiding persons to progressive depersonalizations associated with the accused, the guilty criminal and the punished prisoner at once defined the target of law's force and yielded 'zones of indistinction', with 'things' at the margins (Esposito, 2012a: 24). Such transitions were, and indeed still are, essential to criminal justice measures that operate by criminalizing and punishing or correcting subjects.

The politics of criminalized persons at the Cape, circa 1795: colonial 'distinctions of person', crime and punishment

When examining how crime-focused law conceived of persons at the Cape toward the end of the eighteenth century, it is worthwhile recalling this point:

> The colonial legal system, in the main based on principles of Roman-Dutch law, was invested with every Eighteenth Century European notion of the law. Equality before the law did not exist, of course; that concept was a product of Nineteenth Century liberal thought. Colonial law was nevertheless remarkable for the attention it paid to due process, legality and precedent.
>
> (Dooling, 2007: 17)

An exchange of letters between the military commander (Major General Craig) and members of the re-established court of justice at the start of the British occupation highlights a basic inequality that was deemed essential for justice (Dooling, 1992; Pavlich, 2010, 2013b). As per British customs, regulations relating to conquest required that the existing Roman–Dutch legal system remain the law of the land (Giliomee, 1975; Ross, 1999), but the British reduced the size of the court and increased the judges' compensation (Boucher & Penn, 1992: 127).

Even so, Craig found the existing practice of torturing 'blacks', especially when punishing people with slow, agonizing deaths, to be contrary to 'humanity'. In a letter to the judges, he acknowledged his unfamiliarity with 'a Country in which Slavery exists' and noted his intention not to interfere with judicial processes. However, he opined that:

> [W]ith us the privation of life is considered as the extreme of punishment, in the manner of which we know no graduation; while for you the magnitude of crime measures the severity of the mode by which the criminal is put to death.
>
> (Theal, 1897: 297)

Craig found the punishment of gradually draining the life from people of bondage ('slaves') repugnant. In the 'spirit of humanity', which he considered to be universal and essential to the 'happiness' of the King's dominions, he requested that the judges 'experiment' with abandoning the practice. One can only imagine the discussion his letter provoked among the judges who had just been reinstated under the new regime. Confronted with the occupying commander's request to change harsh punishments for 'blacks' (which they read as 'slaves'), one might have expected eager compliance; instead, they stood firm, insisting on an unequal, differentiated conception of persons which, they claimed, required variable punishments.

Specifically, they argued that, 'distinctions . . . do exist between Europeans or free Persons and Slaves in this Colony' (Theal, 1897: 303). While these distinctions of person alone did not as such necessitate differential modes of punishment, the 'maintenance of publick Order and Subordination' demanded that punishments be tied to social context. For them, 'the great number of Slaves and their less civilized dispositions, has introduced the gradations in the severity of punishment in others' crimes committed against free persons' (Theal, 1897: 305).

This somewhat awkward phrasing makes a self-interested point: because of the 'great numbers' and 'less-civilized dispositions' of slaves, settler law had in the interest of deterrence and the preservation of slave society developed different punishments, reserving excruciatingly painful forms for crimes by 'others' against 'free' persons. They appealed to Roman law's clear separation of 'slaves' and 'free persons', and its requirement to punish these categories in specific ways. They also argued that the 'severity' of any punishment had to be based on the 'atrocity of the crime'. The latter was, in turn, to be established by such 'particulars' as: the 'quality of the fact' (i.e., whether the instrument used is normally deadly or not); 'the quantity of the guilt' (i.e., whether there were several victims or the offender had previously offended); 'design in committing the crime' as well as the motives for the crime (was it premeditated?).

But they assumed an overriding issue as the foundation for accusations of crime and the assignment of punishment, namely, 'distinctions of persons'. For them, law had first to attribute a category to the person(s) accused of a crime as well as 'the person upon whom the crime is committed' (Theal, 1897: 303). Drawn from a perceived social hierarchy, this status was used to decide how the law ought to direct its gaze in specific cases. It was also used to calculate the 'atrocity' of specific crimes and exposed subjects of different categories to varying magnitudes of law's force. The judges enunciated their differential punishment practices in two ways. First, they noted that all 'civilized nations' made use of the practice – i.e., the 'distinction of persons is one of the points by which the degree of punishment is measured in most civilised Nations' (Theal, 1897: 304). Second, they argued that distinctions of persons were basic to Imperial Roman law that underwrote legal uncertainties at the Cape. Both justifications were posited as necessary to keep the legal and social status quo intact and to preserve the Cape's slave economy and society.

In addition, as experienced judges, they insisted that good order demanded carefully calibrated punishments to deter all (actual or potential) offenders. Since they ascribed different characteristics to categories of persons, they called for different kinds of punishments to deter specific groups effectively. They felt it was 'necessary to adopt severe measures to deter [slaves] from revolting against the Masters and taking advantage of their Superior Strength' (Theal, 1897: 304). They insisted their version of justice was 'strongly actuated' by humane motives that recognized the contextual inequalities of the human condition in slave societies.

The judges did not seem to regard these distinctions as 'natural'; rather, they echoed late 1700s debates on race (see Bindman, 2002: 151ff.). Slaves and free people were viewed as members of human kind, but with firm 'distinctions' between 'civilized' and 'rude' nations that sprang from differences in climate, politics and societal conditions. As such, 'altho' in general no difference is admitted between free persons and slaves, yet in this some distinction is necessary' (Theal, 1897: 305). They insisted on preserving such distinctions because of their discriminatory views of slaves as:

> For the most part not only destitute of those principles which commonly restrain thinking beings from the commission of atrocious crimes, but they do not have those relations in society which would induce one to suppose that they really valued the preservation of a life, the greater part of which they must spend for the advantage of those to whom they are subject.
>
> (Theal, 1897: 305)

Repeating prevalent European prejudices of the time, they noted that:

> It could hardly be expected that Men brought up in a different Climate, in a barbarous Nature and under a rigid Government, who retain their own ways of thinking, should change their manners, even if the severity of capital punishment were mitigated.
>
> (Theal, 1897: 307)

Despite their patently patronizing idiom, the judges claimed not to advocate a 'bad opinion' of 'our fallen creatures', of 'rude nations', suggesting that in slave societies one might expect enmity against masters; indeed, it would be unusual to find, they asserted, a 'slave' who would not 'rejoice at any mischief that might befall his master' (Theal, 1897: 307). In other words, social imbalances could only be eradicated when slavery itself was abolished – a course of action that would lead to the economic and social ruin of many 'families' (ignoring, of course, those of bondage in their assessment). In effect, they argued that determining the seriousness of a crime and formulating punishments to deter offenders in a slave society required firm distinctions between free and enslaved persons, with hierarchical shades of difference in-between. Conceived thus, their discourse on crime and punishment was tied directly to an imagined social hierarchy that founded their conceptions of legal persons. It also framed various depersonalizations required to move different categories of persons from accused criminals to prisoners that were exposed unequally to law's force. Such unequal transitions were required, they argued, to maintain the Cape's social hierarchy and to secure the sovereign's power over inhabitants. They even note the value of increasing the severity of slaves' death penalties:

> [I]t is more advisable and even more just not to hazard the painfull reflection but rather to aggravate the severity of capital punishments, in order to diminish the frequency of Crimes, whereas by lessening the degrees of severity it would be unjustifiable to run the risk of exposing one innocent Man to the vengeance of the Slaves.
>
> (Theal, 1897: 306)

While acknowledging that it was impossible to know whether an increase in crimes would result from a reduction in the severity of capital punishment, the judges noted that reducing the severity of punishment would be a political mistake in context.

It would generate uncertainty in the public mind and 'could not fail to excite discontent in the Colony' (Theal, 1897: 309) among those who would be negatively affected by slave uprisings. As well, 'malicious persons' could view the 'mitigation of punishments in the wrong light' and may 'impute' to humane reforms a 'desire of lessening the subjection under which Slaves have been kept' (Theal, 1897: 308). In turn, this would likely 'greatly embarrass the legislature of the Colony' (Theal, 1897: 306), signalling that – even with any potential 'humane' benefits derived from Craig's suggestion – it was not the right moment for such legal reforms (Theal, 1897: 323). Their overall conclusion was simple: 'while there are Slaves, proper measures must be pursued for the maintenance of good order amongst them' (Theal, 1897: 309).

Here one detects the judges' clear sense that criminal justice was directly tied to sovereignty politics; crime-focused law did after all seek to protect a social order in the name of the sovereign. To preserve slave society, they proffered a discourse of legal persons hell-bent on defending unequal punishment regimes, uneven visions of persons and a sovereignly sanctioned social hierarchy. Revealingly, Craig's objections were neither directed at eliminating nor redefining the social hierarchy from which the judges' conceptions of legal persons was invented; rather, he sought an amelioration of the severity of punishments directed to one group of persons. The terms of this debate, therefore, did not challenge imagined characteristics of ascribed personhood. It might even have helped to underscore the taken-for-granted extremes of free persons and slaves. In turn, this provided categories of personhood that law could target as its objects, and to which it could differentially unleash its force in the name of British sovereignty that perpetuated a slave-based order. These letters revealed a consensus on juridical thinking behind specific decisions, a logic reflected by case records of the time.

Cases, persons and prisoners

In examining selected court of justices' summary records of the cases for 93 accused people between 1795 and 1803, I was struck by the consistency of this juridical logic.[7] Recorded as Cape law began its shift from inquisitional civil law to more accusatorial forms of English criminal procedure (Dugard, 1977: Chapter 1), these cases all start by ascribing specific notions of personhood to the accused: 'slave'[8]; 'hottentot'[9] 'bastard hottentot'[10]; 'Caffer'[11]; 'free black man'[12]; 'European'[13] and 'burgher'.[14] Such categories[15] marked the judges' 'distinctions of persons' and established the objects of law's gaze in specific criminal matters. These stratified layers of personhood, each requiring specific legal consideration, were enunciated in law using this sort of terminology: 'Hendrik of the Cape Slave to the late Captain of the artillery, Peitr Ulrich Fischer, about 24 years old at present Prisoner' (WCARS, CJ 799, 171); 'the Hottentot Magerman Jager, computed to be 30 years of age, now prisoner of justice' (WCARS, CJ 797, 317); 'The Bastard Hottentot Platje about 15 years of age, at present prisoner'

(WCARS, CJ 799, 304); 'the Hottentot women Sarah, about 18 years of age, Kaatje 20 years, and Sara about 25 years old, at present imprisoned' (WCARS, CJ 798, 41); 'the free Black man named Adam, a native of this Place nearly 40 years of age (WCARS, CJ 798, 111); 'The Burgher Gerrit Bezuidenhout Cornlisge, aged 49 years, prisoner' (WCARS, CJ 799, 218) and so on. This discourse assigned 'distinctions of person' to the accused based on judges' sense of Cape social hierarchy and then rendered them 'prisoners' who had 'freely confessed' to said crimes,[16] thus exposing themselves to the force of law.

This language signalled transitions from everyday to criminalized identities, initiated by criminal accusations and developed through various 'prisoner' personas. These transitions were different for various categories of persons as juridical calibrations of crime seriousness were based on such categories, as was the quality of force deemed necessary in context. Such inequalities were, as noted, particularly pronounced with slaves, and indeed, as Botha notes, at the Cape the 'old Roman law regarding slaves governed the status of and crime committed by a slave' (1962, Vol. 1: 290).[17] This produced an extremely harsh regime, given that crime-focused law was often directed at persons defined as 'slaves', both at the Cape and surrounding districts (see Dooling, 1992).

For instance, in June 1797, a man described as a 'slave' was found guilty of murdering his 'owner', a church deacon. The case record notes that 'February of Bengal, male Slave of the Deacon of the protestant Church, John Matthew Hertzog, about 40 years of age, now detained in prison, has voluntarily confessed' to being insubordinate to and then stabbing Hertzog after an altercation in the kitchen. In finding February guilty, the court, in the name of the British sovereign, denounced his actions in no uncertain terms:

> [S]uch designed attacks of murder, *especially made by a Slave to his master*, cannot be suffered in a country where justice is duly administered but on the contrary . . . such crimes ought to be punished most rigorously, in order to send as example and inspire to others a horror against similar actions.
>
> (WCARS, CJ 797: 225 – emphasis added)

Note that the atrocity of this crime was calculated through the ascription of persons involved; not only was the act of killing denounced but the 'fact' of a 'slave' killing a 'master' was singled out as an additional challenge to the social hierarchy, requiring particularly severe punishment. Consequently, February was sentenced to die slowly in a halter and to hang on the gallows, with his corpse exposed to a demeaning public spectacle.[18] This sentence stands in stark contrast to an unusual case, in 1801, involving a 'European' man accused of seriously mistreating and killing a 'slave'. The official record tells us that 'Carel Hendrik Lewald, a Native of Prussia aged 47 years at present prisoner' was found guilty of 'bad usage' of a 'slave' named Laban who he had 'beaten in such a manner that he died the same Day' (WCARS, CJ 799, 767). Unlike the punishment inflicted on February, also for killing, the judges condemned Lewald, 'to be fixed to the whipping post and having received a Severe flogging in the presence of the Committee to be transported for Ten Ensuing years'. If this differential application of law's force confirms the significance of the personhood categories allotted to offenders and victims, it also conforms to a wider political logic that required law to apply such categories hierarchically as its targets, with 'burgher' or 'European' and 'slave' at the extremes of its contextually imagined order.

Thus, following the logic, the so-called 'hottentots' who offended against 'burgher' or 'European' victims at times secured relatively (and this is the instrumental word) less severe punishments than those designated as 'slaves'. In 1799, for example, four 'hottentot women' found guilty of poisoning their Dutch employers were spared the death penalty but delivered

> into the hands of the common Hangman, to be tied to a pole, and severely flogged on the bare back with rods, that further the Imprisoned shall be placed in Government's Slave Lodge for the term of their Lives and must serve for their maintenance.
>
> (WCARS, CJ 798, 41)

Also, a man Platje (described as a 'bastard Hottentot', age 15) was found guilty of causing the death of a farmer's infant through neglect rather than intent. His punishment was not death, but a flogging, chains and 15 years at the public works (WCARS, CJ 799, 304). In addition, again following the political logic at hand, criminal persons distinguished as 'burghers' or 'Europeans' were the targets of comparatively less severe punishments such as whipping, 'displayed under gallows', scourging, imprisonment, banishment, forfeiture of pay and branding (for highway robbery). Even when found guilty of treason, they might – as with the Dutch supporter Cornelis Edeman in 1800 – be whipped and then banished rather than executed (WCARS, CJ 798, 271).

The court also pronounced (what it considered) lighter sentences when the accused and victims were placed in similar strata of personhood. For instance, 'August of Mozambico Slave of David Engela Burgher, aged 24, Prisoner' was found guilty of assaulting and sexually assaulting a 'Slave Girl' Louisa, who was 'nearly 10 years of age'. The judges described how he 'employed violence, threw the girl upon the ground, stripped and muffled her, and after some struggling became her ravisher' and also 'gave her afterwards some blows in the Face'. The accused claimed to be intoxicated, but the court argued: 'crimes of so hideous a nature cannot pass unpunished, but should on the contrary be most rigorously corrected'. However, in this case, it sentenced the prisoner to be 'placed under the Gallows with a halter round his neck that he shall afterwards be severely flogged on his bare back and marked with a red-hot Iron . . . chained and put to public works for life' (WCARS, CJ 789, 249). One likely wonders about the intersection of patriarchy and race in this case, noting that the outcome would likely have been different had the victim been defined as 'European' or 'burgher'.

Another example of crime within this socially enunciated stratum was reported in 1801. Defined as a 'slave', 'Jan van de Kaap 20 years of age', seemingly fought and stabbed another 'slave' Daniel, causing a bad wound. The court insisted that, 'like Crimes deserve a rigorous punishment if the Law is justly administered', but condemned the prisoner 'to stand underneath the Gallows with a rope round his neck; to be flogged and Branded; to be sent to the public labours, in chains, for life, and to pay the Costs of his Trial' (WCARS, CJ 799, 418). Likewise, a 'Hottentot, named Hendrik Uithaalder, about 30 years of age prisoner' stabbed 'an other hottentot, named Jan Nel', after discovering him in bed with his wife. The man later 'expired', and even with claims for mitigation, the court argued that, 'such excesses cannot pass without a just correction to the Criminal and a Warning to the public'. Its relatively lighter sentence required that the prisoner be placed in chains, serve at the 'public works without receiving any wages' and pay costs of the process (WCARS, CJ 799, 171).

Notwithstanding mitigating circumstances, the judges also determined a non-death sentence when a 'prisoner, named Andries, a hottentot, nearly 25 years of age' tragically, and seemingly in bad jest, pointed his gun at 'a Hottentot Girl named Jannetje'. It apparently discharged accidentally and killed her. The court pronounced that 'such a high degree of imprudence can not pass unpunished, but should be corrected in such a manner that others may take warning of it'. Yet, it did not prescribe the death penalty, ordering instead that Andries be placed 'underneath the gallows with a rope round his neck, and so convey him from thence to a post where, being tied up he shall be severely whipped and burnt on his back, and being put in chains he shall work at public works for life' (WCARS, CJ 798, 313).

In all these cases, one sees the operation of a political logic of persons rendered explicit by the judges' correspondence with Craig, predicated on hierarchical distinctions that were used to determine criminal atrocity and punishment. The records underscore how Cape law's enunciated persons grounded a depersonalizing violence differentially foisted upon its imagined groupings. Rather than working with a universal concept of persons, semi-persons and non-persons, the Cape example highlights a hierarchically arranged order of persons that reflexively supported, deferred to and generated the meanings of one another. Once the judges placed accused persons within a category of person, the law's processes unfolded in ways that reserved its most horrific force for those located at the lower end of the social hierarchy. While all subjects accused and found guilty by the courts were immediately depersonalized as 'prisoners' and 'criminals', those deemed to have offended against others in ways that challenged an imagined social hierarchy were seen to have committed more 'atrocious' crimes, requiring the harshest punishments. Such unequal colonial depersonalizations arose from a political logic that ricocheted to neo- and postcolonial settings. That logic remains embedded in criminal justice mechanisms that continue to sustain disproportions of people captured, and punished, through its systems.

Current criminal justice implications

While Johnson rightly cautions against simply 'leapfrogging' over different political contexts, he also notes that 'the cost of retaining professional silence about the continuities from the colonial to the post-colonial is the suppression of the dialectical interconnectedness of past and present' (2012: 5). In the present discussion, that interconnectedness may elucidate a political logic behind unequal criminal justice systems chronically marked by disproportionate categories of persons. The Cape's colonial discourse on legal persons allows us to understand how categories of personhood – whether formally enunciated or not – established conditions to expose these to variable intensities of law's force. This colonial political logic has left influential imprints on criminal justice institutions today, three of which are especially evident.

First, explicitly or implicitly assigning 'distinctions' to accused persons – even in criminal justice contexts that declare equality – contours who enters, is processed, managed or punished by criminal justice control networks (Reiman, 2005; Simon & Sparks, 2013). The political logic at play helps us to understand the tenacity of the disproportions within criminal justice systems previously noted. From the Cape, we learn that crime-focused law targeted 'distinctions of person' in a social hierarchy, and this logic resounded in the foundations of later apartheid structures, with its racially segregated rights and duties for – as well as the unequal ways in which it unleashed its force on – different categories of persons. The Population Registration Act of 1950 might have employed different names for its categories of personhood, but it certainly did not expunge the historical logic of recognizing subject groupings and exposing them to different concentrations of law, depersonalizations and authorized violence. Indeed, this political logic has tenaciously endured from settler-colonial to neo- or postcolonial settings. Even after modern jurists enunciated notions of equal treatment before the law (at times 'separate but equal'), criminal justice systems have reflected resilient, disproportionate representations of subject categories. Contextually defined groups continue to experience differential practices of criminalization and/or punishment (Simon & Sparks, 2013). Whether distinguished by implicit or explicit conceptions of race, class, gender or ethnicity, most criminal justice systems seem unequally to embrace specific categories of people within their crime-control networks and punishment regimes (e.g., Alexander, 2012; Wacquant, 2009a, 2009b). Even if now submerged, or tacit, new ways to target categories (types) of persons signal the effects of a resilient political rationality of persons that criminal justice arenas have yet to escape.

Second, the primary objects of colonial crime-focused law – its categories of person – were located within an authorized social hierarchy deemed worthy of its protection in the name of the sovereign. On this matter, Esposito observes that elements within discursive apparatuses of persons were never arranged equally: 'Rather than being equal, these elements are actualized in an ordering . . . or more precisely in a *dispositif* that layers or superimposes one under the other'

(2012a: 20–1). This insight rightly suggests that different legal contexts emphasize and privilege specific kinds of persons. However, as seen with crime-focused law at the Cape, the inequalities associated with persons were not confined to elements assigned to person/semi-person/non-person divides. Instead, Cape colonial law operated through stratified layers of Esposito's *dispositif* itself; it emphasized hierarchical distinctions between categories of persons, ascribing different qualities to each category and not simply to persons, semi-persons and non-persons within particular categories.

So, the legal personhood ascribed to 'burghers' was quite different from that assigned to 'hottentots' or 'slaves', just as variously framed persons were deemed to require unique kinds of depersonalization and intensities of law's force. As such, rituals for transitions between persons, semi- or non-persons were dependent upon the category of person ascribed at the outset to accused subjects. Working alongside Esposito's coppice, but with the modulations of a colonial ethos, one might therefore conceptualize the legal person beyond its emergence through Christian and Roman conceptions of a universal person and variants cast in relation to this.[19] In the context of Cape law, and later apartheid South Africa, hierarchical discursive apparatuses emphasized different categories of Esposito's persons. Indeed, Cape judges claimed that an understanding of hierarchical 'distinctions of persons' was essential to securing social order in the colony and that preserving the tiered relations between these groupings had to be maintained as long as a 'slave society' persisted. As such, framed less around person/semi-person/non-person distinctions, Cape law emphasized categories of persons at different stages of 'advancement'. This political logic required crime-focused law to distinguish types of persons and to deploy criminal justice practices that targeted these differently for its criminalizing depersonalizations.

Imagined in relative groupings, as opposed to singular images of personhood with others defined in relation thereto, the subjects of this law were conceptualized through images of nation and then race or other biopolitically framed populations. Although beyond the scope of this chapter, it is useful at least to allude to Foucault-inspired debates which ponder – even if only by default – the degree to which biopolitical technologies stand in contrast to law and sovereign, or indeed governmental, models of power (Agamben, 2010; Esposito, 2008). Our discussion suggests that techniques of biopower alleging different categories are directly implicated in the politics of legal persons; one might here note as much a legalization of biopolitics as a biopoliticization of law, all in the name of defending a social order for a given sovereign. Such law shapes and supports biopolitical orders to which it ties itself (hence, 'law and order') through transitional depersonalizations that unequally – depending on ascribed category – arrest everyday identities and replace them with different versions of the accused, the criminal and the prisoner. Today, criminal justice systems increasingly rely on biopolitics to frame depersonalization that marks their trades. Through biopolitical techniques that accuse persons variously (e.g., profiling when conducting search and seizures), criminalize unevenly (e.g., reference to criminal profiles and types) and punish with different intensities (e.g., the populations deemed fit for supermax incarceration), crime-focused law supports biopolitically fashioned populations in the name of a given sovereign (Esposito, 2008).

Finally, one is left with a clearer sense of the political successes of criminal justice's seeming failure: crime-focused law and the distinctions of persons to which it directs itself have played crucial roles in the politics of modern sovereigns and may ensconce biopolitical technologies tied to that politics. Stated another way, the enduring success of crime-focused law and its distinctions of person resides in an ability to buttress hierarchical social orders while simultaneously upholding a privileged sovereignty politics. Through its idioms and unequal practices, such law recursively helps to generate images of a sovereign and a social order in whose name it claims to operate (Pavlich, 2013b). As Hansen and Stepputat (2005: 32) point out, 'Criminality as a "zone of darkness"' is, in brief, the perennial outside, an unruly and originary source of sovereign life, and thus a necessary condition for any claim to establish and defend social order'. As we have seen, law's idioms ascribe versions of persons through hierarchical categories, using differentially applied force to secure a social order on behalf of a sovereign. Understanding crime-focused law's foundational link to sovereignty, politics could thus open us to analyses beyond discourses that frame themselves around age-old – but antiquated – concepts of crime, punishment or the legal persons that legitimize both.

Notes

1 The phrase 'crime-focused law' used throughout this chapter is intended to signal an umbrella concept designating legal processes directed specifically to matters of 'crime'. It recognizes that around 1795, a Cape law, a colonial version of Roman–Dutch law, relied on inquisitional procedures (Fine, 1991) quite different from the precedence-based, accusatorial procedures formally adopted some decades after by the British (Dugard, 1977). Also, these approaches differed from more recent formulations of 'criminal law' established in later jurisprudence anchored to specific criminal codes. 'Crime-focused law' is used to include all variants through which processes of 'law' are mobilized, legitimated, sustained and focused on various images of 'crime' in specific contexts. This is intended to avoid the pitfall of anachronistically ascribing present understandings of 'criminal law' to past instantiations, emphasizing instead the ways in which specific forms of legal governance attach themselves to 'crime'.

2 See Ross (2008), Giliomee and Mbenga (2007), Davenport and Saunders (2000), Boucher and Penn (1992), Du Toit and Giliomee (1983), Giliomee (1975), Freund (1972) and Bunbury (1969) for analyses of this extraordinary period.

3 See Naffine (2003) and Tur (1987). One might add to these formulations agent-based forms of personhood (Morse, 2007), ethical critiques of person (Sapontzis, 1981), the anthropological approach of Mauss (1985), Esposito's (2012a) critical approach and so on.

4 Kelsen offers an emblematic statement here when he insists that 'the person exists only in so far as he "has" duties and rights; apart from this that person has no existence whatsoever' (1945: 93).

5 As is to be expected from a fiction, there is latitude, which is why legal persons are not always cast as human, just as human subjects are sometimes designated non-persons. Moreover, the Note points out that existing fictions must adapt themselves to technological advances, changing conceptions of humans/animals and new medical definitions

of life and death. No doubt, too, questions about culpability and responsibility in the face of determinist medical or biological claims on persons complicate the voluntarism required of persons in the context of criminal law (Lacey, 2001).

6 Joubert reminds us too of law's relative independence when determining its objects:

> Legal personality is the capacity to be the bearer or subject of rights and duties. It is conferred by the law on whomsoever the law pleases, the being or thing on whom or which it is conferred is in legal terminology a person.
>
> (1951: 226)

7 I wish to thank members of the Western Cape Archives and Records Services (hereafter WCARS) for their help in locating these records, and to Patrick McLane for his able research assistance. These records were chosen from the archive somewhat randomly but subject to my purposive attempt to capture a diversity of persons and types of crime.

8 These include references to 'government slave' and 'slave woman'.

9 This category referred, as Dooling (1992: 30) indicates, ambiguously to indigenous people who were not enslaved, but if they did not have 'means of subsistence' were required to become servants to farmers (see also, Freund, 1971: 29–30). This category of persons was usually distinguished in the cases by gender and sometimes regarding occupation, including 'government worker'. See Viljoen (2006) for a sense of life for persons so designated.

10 As Watson states (2012: 214 at n. 25), this category of person often referred to the children of 'white or Khoisan and slave parents'. See also Ross (1999).

11 Although a version of this term is considered a great insult, it was initially used to refer to men of bondage from Asia who served a policing function relative to other slaves (see Giliomee and Mbenga, 2007: 54) and also to 'Hottentots' employed for policing or military functions (Penn, 2005; van Aswegen, 1990).

12 As Groenewald (2010: 970) indicates, 'free blacks were essentially freed slaves' and were typically not granted the status of burgher – see also Elphick and Malherbe (1992: 216).

13 Persons' full names in this category are often coupled with place of origin (Prussia, Holland) or occupation ('soldier', 'cooper' or 'servant'). Ross (1999) gives a sense of growing claims to superiority of English culture at the Cape, a view reflected in Percival's (1969) account of the time.

14 This category here refers mainly to Dutch settlers who derive this name from being freed from having to work for the Dutch East India Company ('vryburghers') – see Elphick and Malherbe (1992), van Aswegen (1990) and Spilhaus (1949).

15 See Ross (1999) for a sense of the hierarchies at play. In my selected cases, I found no references to 'Bushman' or 'San', which Adhikari (2010: 25) notes were derogatorily referred to as 'bosjemans' by 'trekboer society' (frontier farmers) and when not 'wild' hunter and gatherers were included as 'Hottentots'.

16 A free confession stood in contrast to confession through torture where, if the judges determined that the evidence pointed to a guilty verdict and the accused refused to confess, various forms of torture were employed to secure a confession (Fine, 1991; Worden and Groenewald, 2005) – this practice was eventually abolished in 1797.

17 Echoing the logic asserted by Members of the Court of Justice, his review of cases finds that 'Crimes by slaves against their masters were, however, more severely punished than those against third parties; and where a slave assaulted a master, even without weapons, the penalty was "death without mercy"' (Botha, 1962: Vol. 2, 175).

18 Specifically, he was condemned to be 'punished with the halter and hanged to the gallows, until death ensues; further the corps to be transported to the gallows near saltriver, there to be hung again and remain, until it shall be consumed by the air and the birds of prey'.

19 Here, one might note Esposito's unease about the legal person and its centrality to the formation of modern politics (see 2010, 2012b; Esposito & Parsley, 2009). He tries to neutralize that person by exploring the potential of working with concepts of the 'third person' (see Campbell, 2010). At the same time, he rejects the technically focused framing of modern politics, proposing to explore the prospect of an undetermined realm of the 'impolitical' (or to what he refers to as an 'affirmative biopower'). However, for this chapter, I refer mainly to his discussion of the link between persons and a technical sort of modern politics.

References

Adhikari, M. (2010). *The Anatomy of a South African Genocide: The Extermination of the Cape San People.* Cape Town: University of Cape Town Press.

Agamben, G. (2010). *Identity without the Person.* Stanford, CA: Stanford University Press.

Alexander, M. (2012). *The New Jim Crow: Mass Incarceration in the Age of Colorblindness.* New York: The New Press.

Bindman, D. (2002). *Ape to Apollo: Aesthetics and the Idea of Race in the 18th Century.* Ithaca, NY: Cornell University Press.

Botha, C. G. (1962). *The Collected Works of C. Graham Botha.* Cape Town: C. Struik.

Boucher, M., & Penn, N. (eds). (1992). *Britain at the Cape, 1795–1803.* Johannesburg: Brenthurst.

Bunbury, C. J. F. (1969). *Journal of a Residence at the Cape of Good Hope: With Excursions into the Interior, and Notes on the Natural History, and the Native Tribes.* New York: Negro Universities Press.

Campbell, T. (2010). 'Foucault was not a person': idolatry and the impersonal in Roberto Esposito's third person. *The New Centennial Review*, 10(2), 135–50.

Chanock, M. (2001). *The Making of South African Legal Culture, 1902–1936: Fear, Favour, and Prejudice.* Cambridge: Cambridge University Press.

Comaroff, J., & Comaroff, J. (2006). 'Criminal obsessions after Foucault: postcoloniality, policing and the metaphysics of disorder', in J. Comaroff & J. Comaroff (eds), *Law and Disorder in the Postcolony.* Chicago, IL: The University of Chicago Press, pp. 273–98.

Davenport, T. R. H., & Saunders, C. C. (2000). *South Africa: A Modern History.* New York: St. Martin's Press.

Dayan, C. (2011). *The Law is a White Dog.* Princeton, NJ: Princeton University Press.

Dooling, W. (1992). *Law and Community in a Slave Society: Stellenbosch District, South Africa, c. 1760–1820.* Cape Town: Centre for African Studies, University of Cape Town.

——. (2007). *Slavery, Emancipation and Colonial Rule in South Africa.* Durban: University of KwaZulu-Natal Press.

Dorsett, S., & McVeigh, S. (2012). *Jurisdiction.* New York: Routledge.

Dugard, J. (1977). *South African Criminal Law and Procedure.* Cape Town: Juta.

Du Toit, A., & Giliomee, H. (1983). *Afrikaner Political Thought: Analysis and Documents.* Berkeley, CA: University of California Press.

Elphick, R., & Malherbe, V. C. (1992). 'The Khoisan to 1828', in R. Elphick & H. Giliomee (eds), *The Shaping of South African Society, 1652–1860.* Cape Town: Maskew, Miller, Longman, pp. 7–22.

Esposito, R. (2008). *Bíos: Biopolitics and Philosophy.* Minneapolis, MN: University of Minnesota Press.

——. (2010). For a philosophy of the impersonal. *The New Centenniel Review*, 10(2), 121–34.

——. (2012a). The dispositif of the person. *Law, Culture and the Humanities*, 8(1), 17–30.
——. (2012b). *Third Person: Politics of Life and Philosophy of the Impersonal*. Cambridge: Polity Press.
Esposito, R., & Parsley, C. (2009). Preface to the categories of the impolitical. *Diacritics*, 39(2), 99–115.
Fagundes, D. (2001). Note: what we talk about when we talk about persons: the language of a legal fiction. *Harvard Law Review*, 114, 1746–52.
Fine, H. (1991). *The Administration of Criminal Justice at the Cape of Good Hope*, 1795–1828. (Unpublished Ph.D. thesis.) Cape Town: University of Cape Town.
Foucault, M. (1977). *Language, Counter-Memory, Practice: Selected Essays and Interviews*. Ithaca, NY: Cornell University Press.
——. (1979). *Discipline and Punish: The Birth of the Prison*. New York: Vintage Books.
——. (1980). *Power/Knowledge: Selected Interviews and Other Writings, 1972–1977*. New York: Pantheon Books.
——. (2002). *Archaeology of Knowledge*. London: Routledge.
——. (2013). *Lectures on the Will to Know*. New York: Palgrave Macmillan.
Freund, W. M. (1971). *Society and Government in Dutch South Africa: The Cape and the Batavians, 1803–1806*. New Haven, CT: Yale University Press.
——. (1972). The eastern frontier of the Cape Colony during the Batavian period (1803–1806). *The Journal of African History*, 13(4), 631–45.
Garland, D. (1991). *Punishment and Modern Society: A Study in Social Theory*. Chicago, IL: The University of Chicago Press.
——. (2002). *The Culture of Control: Crime and Social Order in Contemporary Society*. Chicago, IL: The University of Chicago Press.
Giliomee, H. (1975). *Die Kaap Tydens Die Eerste Britse Bewind: 1795–1803*. Cape Town: Hollandsch Afrikaansche Uitgevers.
Giliomee, H. B., & Mbenga, B. (eds). (2007). *New History of South Africa*. Cape Town: Tafelberg.
Groenewald, G. (2010). Slaves and free blacks in VOC Cape Town, 1652–1795. *History Compass*, 8/9, 964–83.
Hahlo, H. R., & Kahn, E. (1968). *The South African Legal System and its Background*. Cape Town: Juta.
Hansen, T. B., & Stepputat, F. (2005). *Sovereign Bodies: Citizens, Migrants, and States in the Postcolonial World*. Princeton, NJ: Princeton University Press.
Johnson, D. (2012). *Imagining the Cape Colony: History, Literature, and the South African Nation*. Edinburgh: Edinburgh University Press.
Joubert, C. P. (1951). *Die stigting in die Romeins-Hollandse reg en die Suid-Afrikaanse reg*. Stellenbosch: University of Stellenbosch, Africana Library.
Kelsen, H. (1945). *General Theory of Law and State*. New York: Russell and Russell.
Lacey, N. (2001). Responsibility and modernity in criminal law. *The Journal of Political Philosophy*, 9(3), 249–79.
Loury, G. C. (2008). *Race, Incarceration, and American Values*. Cambridge, MA: MIT Press.
Mauss, M. (1985). 'The category of the human mind: the notion of person, the notion of self', in M. Carrithers, S. Collins, & S. Lukes (eds), *The Category of the Person: Anthropology, Philosophy, History*. Cambridge, UK: Cambridge University Press, pp. 1–25.
Morse, S. J. (2007). Criminal responsibility and the disappearing person. *Cardozo Law Review*, 28(6), 2545–75.
Naffine, N. (2003). Who are law's persons? From Cheshire cats to responsible subjects. *Modern Law Review*, 66, 346–67.

Pavlich, G. (2010). Legal judgment and Cape colonial law. *Law, Culture and the Humanities*, 7(2), 1–12.
——. (2011). Sustaining sovereignty through the law at the Cape Colony, 1795–1803. *Journal of Forensic Psychology Practice*, 11(2–3), 184–203.
——. (2013a). Cape legal idioms and the colonial sovereign. *International Journal for the Semiotics of Law*, 26, 39–54.
——. (2013b). Sovereign force and crime-focused law at the Cape colony. *Journal of Historical Sociology*, 26(3), 318–38.
Penn, N. (2005). *The Forgotten Frontier: Colonist and Khoisan on the Cape's Northern Frontier in the 18th Century*. Athens, OH: Ohio University Press.
Percival, R. (1969). *An Account of the Cape of Good Hope*. New York: Negro Universities Press.
Reiman, J. H. (2005). *The Rich Get Richer and the Poor Get Prison: Ideology, Class, and Criminal Justice*. Boston, MA: Allyn & Bacon.
Ross, R. (1980). The rule of law at the Cape of Good Hope in the eighteenth century. *Journal of Imperial and Commonwealth History*, 9(1), 5–15.
——. (1993). *Beyond the Pale: Essays on the History of Colonial South Africa*. London: Wesleyan University Press.
——. (1999). *Status and Respectability in the Cape Colony, 1750–1870: A Tragedy of Manners*. Cambridge, UK: Cambridge University Press.
——. (2008). *A Concise History of South Africa*. New York: Cambridge University Press.
Santosh, A. (2011). Colonialism and the making of criminal categories in India. *NALSAR Law Review*, 16(1), 153–65.
Sapontzis, S. F. (1981). A critique of personhood. *Ethics*, 91(4), 607–18.
Simon, J. (2007). *Governing Through Crime: How the War on Crime Transformed American Democracy and Created a Culture of Fear*. Oxford: Oxford University Press.
Simon, J., & Sparks, R. (2013). *The Sage Handbook of Punishment and Society*. London: SAGE.
Spilhaus, M. W. (1949). *The First South Africans and the Law Which Governed Them: To Which is Appended The diary of Adam Tas*. Cape Town: Juta.
Stuntz, W. J. (2011). *The Collapse of American Criminal Justice*. Cambridge, MA: Belknap Press/Harvard University Press.
Theal, G. M. (1897). *Records of the Cape Colony, from February 1793 to 1796*. Vol. 1. London: Printed for the government of the Cape Colony [by W. Clowes and Sons].
Tur, R. (1987). 'The "Person" in law', in A. R. Peacocke & G. Gillett (eds), *Persons and Personality: A Contemporary Inquiry*. New York: Blackwell, pp. 116–22.
van Aswegen, H. J. (1990). *History of South Africa*. Pretoria: van Schaik.
Viljoen, R. S. (2006). *Jan Paerl: A Khoikhoi in Cape Colonial Society, 1761–1851*. Leiden: Brill.
Wacquant, L. J. D. (2009a). *Prisons of Poverty*. Minneapolis, MN: Minnesota University Press.
——. (2009b). *Punishing the Poor: The Neoliberal Government of Social Insecurity*. Durham: Duke University Press.
Watson, R. (2012). *Slave Emancipation and Racial Attitudes in Nineteenth-Century South Africa*. Cambridge, UK: Cambridge University Press.
Worden, N., & Groenewald, G. (2005). *Trials of Slavery*. Cape Town: Van Riebeck Society.

Chapter 9

Forget crime

Accusation, governance and criminology

For all its hackneyed embellishments, facing the close of a century and the dawn of another does give pause for speculative reflection. My discussion proceeds from a view that disciplinary power–knowledge relations, which flourished in nineteenth- and twentieth-century control systems, face the prospect of a significant fall. The analytical objects, methods, claims and policies that occupied privileged positions within modern welfare states, and their discipline-based societies, are increasingly shaped by the priorities of a different, *governmental*, prince. In the process, erstwhile alliances between disciplinary and legal power–knowledge relations have been reordered by the colonizing advances of governmental ratios. These reorderings are substantial and have problematized criminology's aspirations to discover the nature and causes of crime, as well as its quest to legislate corrective remedies. They also signal a wider 'post-disciplinary' condition in which the epistemological foundations of disciplinary power–knowledge relations have become the target of sustained scrutiny. As a result, these foundations no longer operate as unquestioned background assumptions, and so are unable to enforce subtle closures through the stealth of their silent embrace. Disciplinary power–knowledge relations must now openly engage truth struggles to survive. In this knowledge-producing ethos, criminology, like other disciplines, is forced to confront its ambitions, practices and prescriptions directly (Bauman, 1997; Nelken, 1994).[1] Whatever else, this predicament provides a unique moment from which to review critical opportunities created by governmental encroachments into disciplinary crime-control arenas.

The following essay explores aspects of criminology's plight within post-disciplinary conditions, preparing an alternative way of engaging contemporary crime-control contexts. It adds to the fragmentations of 'criminology' by returning to the etymology of that term, to refocus attention on lost traces of criminology's component signs, *logos* and *crimen*. Attending to the issue of *logos*, the analysis points out the value of deconstructive approaches that have made their peace with the ambient uncertainties of post-disciplinary conditions. It prefaces a call for critique beyond the language of disciplinary demarcations of essence, questioning realist criminology's focus on crime as an absolute, incontrovertible entity whose essence, causes, etc., can be discovered. This critique allows one to explore traces of *crimen* beyond dominant concerns centred around 'crime'; for instance, I demonstrate the value of addressing shifting practices of *accusation*. In concert, my efforts allow one to enunciate a deconstructive criminology in terms of a specific *logos* of *crimen*; namely, one that squares off against post-disciplinary epistemological contexts to provide a critical analysis of emerging governmental patterns of accusation.

Criminology and the post-disciplinary

Images of crime, deviance, criminality and even social harm have played a central role in the development of criminology as a discipline. A feature of modern society's administrative technologies, criminology supported existing juridical frameworks by creating a distinct terrain of study. The contours of this terrain were enunciated by the speculative reason of classical theorists, and the scientific allegiances of positivist thinking.[2] In both cases, one detects attempts to unify criminology as a discipline focused on a real problem; namely, crime. This problem domain was developed outside of, but as a complement to, formal legality; criminologists isolated crime (delinquency, deviance) as an extra-legal problem amenable to control through disciplinary power–knowledge complexes. For instance, as Foucault's work indicates, criminological knowledge enunciated new penal classifications, and these extended existing legal taxonomies by creating a new identity; namely, the 'delinquent as a pathologized subject'. However, the process 'that constitutes delinquency as an object of knowledge is one with the political operation that dissociates illegalities and isolates delinquency from them' (Foucault, 1977: 277).

In a complementary gesture, then, criminology isolated its object (delinquency) of analysis from, but without challenging (on the contrary, by bolstering), juridical illegalities. On this account, criminology's success as a discipline depended not so much on a capacity to resolve crime (on this score, as noted, it failed miserably), but on its ability to recast potential threats to a social order in terms of correctable individual abnormalities. With respect to the latter, its successes were formidable over many years; indeed, by the mid-twentieth century the United Nations even declared criminology a central component of its international strategy to defend 'society' (see Walters, 1999).

During the past 40 years, the discipline's unity has been contested by various (critical and radical) attacks on its underlying administrative, correctionalist precepts (see Pavlich, 1999a). The implications of these challenges extend beyond the scope of my analysis here, but let us at least allude to some prominent features. Early critiques of administrative criminology were levelled by labelling and Marxist (e.g., Hirst, 1975) approaches that called dominant assumptions about crime's ontological status into question.[3] This sort of critique continues to strike a rich chord with recent analyses that question whether legal definitions of criminality, or disciplinary images of deviance, are sufficiently stable to serve as points of focus for criminology. For instance, Sumner (1994: 311) stresses the contingency of 'deviance' and elsewhere notes that:

> Given the impossibility of using the social categories of crime and deviance as scientific categories or observational terms with definable and constant behavioural referents, it makes sense to treat them as elements of highly contextualized moral and political discourses.
>
> (1990: 26)

Such challenges to crime's ontology are echoed by other critics who question realist criminology's assumptions regarding the reality of crime.[4] Even some recent neoliberal versions of administrative criminology question the validity of viewing crime as an absolute entity. Here, as Feeley and Simon succinctly observe, 'criminals are no longer the organising referent (or logos) for criminology . . . The new criminal knowledge aims at rationalizing the operation of systems that manage criminals, not dealing with criminality' (1992: 466–7).

In their various ways, these formulations intimate the post-disciplinary dispersal of a discourse that cannot settle upon a precise formulation (essence) of crime and its 'reality' – the very organizing referent for modern criminology's *crimen*.[5] As I see it, this lack of agreement offers valuable possibilities for unhinging post-disciplinary criminologies from a commitment to realist conceptions of crime. Indeed, the call to decentre realist images could also serve as an invitation to apprehend the problems facing modern criminology's power–knowledge commitments.

By way of an all too brief sketch, one could point to profound changes to modern power–knowledge relations from which disciplinary knowledge was enunciated. For one thing, as Lyotard (1984) usefully argues, knowledge is nowadays legitimated and enunciated through radically altered epistemological arenas. No longer are appeals to modern speculative, or even emancipatory, metanarratives capable of justifying specific claims as legitimate knowledge (see B. Smart, 1992; Pavlich, 1999a). In an ethos wracked by diversity, the very idea that universally accepted metanarratives (e.g., working-class emancipation) could found knowledge claims is at best untenable; at worst, it invites imperialist impositions that silence other subjugated voices (Butler, 1992; Bauman, 1997). Without such metanarratives being firmly intact, disciplinary knowledge directed at 'discovering' universally agreed-upon orders becomes unravelled at its seams. This predicament is further exacerbated by the changing fortunes of the authorized enunciator of disciplinary knowledge. That is, as Bauman (1987, 1992) notes, the legislating expert (normalizing judge) of disciplinary knowledge increasingly occupies a discredited role – that of seeking to impose necessary orders over a world popularly perceived as chaotic, contingent and uncertain. Moreover, the expert role is now played out in the ruins of institutions (e.g., universities) that were once exclusively charged with producing disciplinary knowledge (Readings, 1997). Of course, these bare allusions need further discussion (see Pavlich, 1999a), but they are enough to signal the momentous scale of the changes at hand; they also point to the kinds of challenges facing protagonists of disciplinary knowledge formations under post-disciplinary conditions.

This situation is compounded further in the case of criminology where new discourses (e.g., managerial, actuarial, community-based, etc.) herald themselves as providing more efficient ways of controlling 'crime' than is possible through disciplinary rehabilitation, or the tandem quest for normal 'societies of control' (Deleuze, 1992). One description of these changes, which I have noted earlier, suggests that discipline (and the legality it supports) is being recoded by risk-based, governmental priorities (Simon, 1987, 1996; Ericson & Haggerty, 1997; Dean, 1999). Stated differently, one might say that the plight of criminology is significantly affected by shades of neoliberal, or perhaps 'advanced liberal', approaches to power beyond both state and social welfare domains (Rose, 1996, 1999). An important aspect of these changes for criminology lies in a fundamental reconfiguration of key criminological concepts – 'society' and 'the social' (see Dean, 1997; Rose, 1999).[6]

As O'Malley argues, 'The unity and determinacy accorded to the social is, in the emerging scene, fractured or even shattered' (1996a: 28). And with moves away from conceiving collective patterns in terms of the social, criminology accosts different priorities, debates and political struggles that attend uniquely to post-social contexts. One could perhaps also view such changes as reflecting different priorities of governmentalities directed at managing and reconciling selves in communities (Pavlich, 1996, 1999b). A growing reliance upon crime controls framed around profiling, prevention, managing risk, actuarial calculations, security and so on, may be taken to signal a post-disciplinary shift in the exercise of power.[7]

In concert, these various post-disciplinary developments have significantly altered the context against which criminological discourses are now silhouetted. They are especially debilitating for a criminology that continues to define itself as a scientific account (*logos*) of the reality of crime (*crimen*). Indeed, if my account persuades, then post-disciplinary horizons of knowledge are unlikely to sanction criminologists to continue their erstwhile 'business as usual'; they will likely, instead, be required to confront crumbling disciplinary edifices. However, the moment is not simply a destructive one, since it generates new types of fragmentation with new problems (O'Malley, 1996a: 32); it also invites deconstructive approaches to criminology's *logos* as a preface to developing alternate images of its *crimen* (Pavlich, 1999a).

A post-disciplinary *logos*

Envisaging legitimate ways to speak the truth opens questions of *logos*, the etymology of which connotes diverse meanings, including 'ways of speaking', 'logic', and so on (see Partridge, 1958; Klein, 1966; Ayto, 1990). The issue I wish to address here, however, is specific; namely, what mode of address might be appropriate for a post-disciplinary criminology that makes critical knowledge claims within radically altered epistemological environments? My assumption throughout this discussion is that criminology need not enslave itself to the technocratic whims of disciplinary systems. If criminology speaks only to the priorities identified by particular control rationales, it is unlikely to extricate itself from their hold. It is then ill-equipped to apprehend totalitarian dangers lurking behind political decisions that eschew critical challenges, and declare themselves to be necessary, inevitable, and so on. It is unlikely to prove capable of puncturing the horizons generated by given systems of dominance. To accomplish the latter, criminology might prefer to focus on power–knowledge relations surrounding crime-control institutions, prising open key contingent decisions that masquerade as inevitable events. It could pursue such anti-totalitarian aims by continuously seeking to open up the limits of given systems; it would, no doubt, refuse pressures (funding or other) to reinforce the claimed necessities of technical crime-control systems.

At stake here is a criminological *logos* which names its problems and issues in ways that do not assume the validity, or centrality, of dominant power–knowledge relations. Its critical practices, for example, might seek out analytical objects that do not presume the necessity of existing crime-control institutions. While there are multiple ways to address criminal justice fields thus, one could allude to three key tasks for a critical *logos:* (1) loosen the hold of realism; (2) allude to a grammar of critique beyond founded judgement; (3) open deconstructive spaces from which to name political dangers that attend to crime-control practices. Together, these deconstructive gestures could resist attempts by dominant crime-control patterns to assert themselves as inevitable events. As such, the tasks might be predicated upon, and openly contribute toward, a contingent view of history. Let us explore each task in turn.

First, the question of realism can be approached by pointing to Derrida's (1978) interesting challenge to 'logocentrism' in philosophy. Crudely stated, he questions philosophy's tendency to centre its discourses on the logic of arguments and their claims to truth. Everything else in the text is sidelined as sophistry, rhetoric, tangent and so on. This binary opposition between centre and margin, logical and illogical, elevates one form of rational argument to the exclusion of others, yielding limited ways of speaking. Moreover, it establishes a hierarchy that replicates regimes of truth so central to metaphysical thinking. These observations harbour profound implications for metaphysics, but many criminological texts do not hinge – at least in the first instance – rhetorically around 'logocentric' strategies. Rather, as I see it, a key instrument for establishing the centrality of criminological texts is the degree to which they claim convincingly to reflect reality. That is, in criminology, *realism* is privileged to the point that it has become *the* mechanism for isolating central from marginal texts (as in the common derogatory refrain: 'that is just theory'!). Echoing the point, in a different context, Carol Smart (1995) describes criminology as a discipline closely tied to modern versions of positivist science and empiricism directed to the 'reality' of crime (nature, cause, remedy, etc.). Most administrative, and some radical criminologies (e.g., Left Realists), assume crime to be an ontological fact discoverable through rigorous methods. And in so doing, they place criminal realism at the centre of their disciplinary enterprises. We might refer to this as '*centrealism*', as privileging a *logos* centred on the assumed reality of crime. By naming these discursive strategies, one can approach the margins of *centrealism* through other borders (e.g., fictional, cultural, feminist, critical race, anarchist, etc.). In much the same way as Derrida accosts philosophical 'logocentrism', one might offer a post-disciplinary challenge to criminology's *centrealism*.

While this could involve any number of initiatives, all would question images of a primordial ontological reality called 'crime'. This is more than a matter of calling for multiple and diverse ways of speaking, of allowing many flowers to bloom, so to speak. It is a question of how to speak. If one works from the vantage that realities are created through historical scripts (whatever form these might assume – word, text, speech, action, performance, visual cue, etc.), then the organization of particular forms of language becomes crucial. As such, crime could be viewed as a product of given languages and their sign constellations; to assert it as an ontological reality is an epistemological achievement that positions its speakers in favour of a specific power–knowledge regime. To accept any discursive creation as a necessary being is *ipso facto* to endorse, countersign, the languages responsible for its emergence. As discussed before, it may be useful here to heed Nietzsche's advice: 'More strictly: one must admit nothing has being – because then becoming would lose its value . . . Consequently one must ask how the illusion of being could have arisen (was bound to arise)' (1967: 377).

Just as crime has 'become' a reality through – *inter alia* – criminology's discipline, so its formulation is amenable to fundamental revision in post-disciplinary settings. We shall return to the role of accusation processes in creating crime, but one could conceive of a *logos*, mode of address, whose point is to grapple with complex processes by which crime 'becomes'. This strategy would evoke critical mentalities that deconstruct problematic limits governing our present being. These mentalities might defer as much to storytelling, fiction, ethnography, as to positivist science or reasoned inquiry in reconstituting regimes of truth. All such orientating gestures suggest 'ways of speaking', a *logos*, quite different from attempts to uncover the reality of crime.

Second, a *logos* could imply types of critique that are framed differently from common formulations in radical criminology. Elsewhere, I have detailed this particular issue, and so will refer the interested reader to that work (see Pavlich, 1999a, 2000). But, one could appropriate aspects of this material to note that, in the context of the disciplines (e.g., criminology), critique is typically defined through an underlying grammar of authoritative judgement. That is, briefly, critique is heralded as an activity that judges given contexts against founded criteria. It implies establishing (either apodictic or historically grounded) criteria to serve as yardsticks, standards, for authoritative judgement. Critics then describe a given context to judge it against the previously formulated criteria, and to allow them to legislate areas for improvement. Such judgement is often carried out by critics positioned as authoritative (expert) judges of normalizing discipline (see Foucault, 1977).

Now, while a critical grammar of authoritative judgement might stand firm in disciplinary contexts, its position within post-disciplinary contexts is much more tenuous. This leaves critics without a credible voice to bear witness to, or resist, the emerging governmental limits that increasingly shape our present. One could connect this to a previously noted idea; namely, the erosion of modern discipline is related to a concomitant rise in new governmentalities that produce different regimes of truth and demand various ways of conceptualizing resistance. I have thus argued for an alternative *governmental* grammar of critique to contest postmodern patterns of power (Pavlich, 2000). It focuses neither on judging the realities of a present, nor on enunciating *how to govern*; rather, it is concerned with naming and problematizing dangerous governmental limits by exploring *how not to be governed thus* (see Foucault, 1997). Critique, in this sense, need not be focused on the putative 'realities of crime', but could be directed toward reframing, contesting and resisting governmentalities that govern based on knowledge about the cause, actuarial probabilities and 'reality' of crime. It licenses disruptive gestures to contemplate 'crime' from alternate political frontiers, such as through processes of 'accusation'.

This leads to the third aspect of the *logos*, regarding possible spaces for an alternative, post-disciplinary discourse. We have already seen how a post-disciplinary way of approaching 'crime' could embrace elements of Derrida's thoughts on deconstruction (1978, 1992, 1995, 1997). One could explore under-exploited margins, side-lines, of criminology to focus attention on non-central facets of discourses that claim its mantle. Such practices bear traces of feminist critiques that direct attention to criminology's blind-spots, its rhetorical asides and underlying power–knowledge (e.g., patriarchal) commitments (see A. Young, 1996; Naffine, 1997; Carrington, 1998). Focusing on the blind-spots created by criminology's *centrealism* could lead us to explore diverse places, from journals, media rhetoric to clashes at Association meetings, where consequential decisions about crime's reality are made. Deconstructive approaches might attend to these, recognizing the complexly related, contingent and changing practices involved with creating the reality of crime at any given point. For example, while legal edicts, disciplinary judgements of pathology or governmental calculations of risk are often so mobilized, the reality of crime is also very much the product of other cultural practices that organize signs: media portrayals, television dramas, crime fiction, electioneering, and just plain gossip. Such understandings license a *logos* that addresses *crimen* as a dynamic set of complex practices, rather than as a static, fixed reality.[8]

Many other rich seams could be mined from Derrida's work, but let us here explore his constant refusal to allow thought to settle into fixed, comfortable grooves. Such an approach accords well with post-disciplinary conditions where uncertainty emerges not as a problem to be overcome, but as an ambient condition of the times (see Bauman, 1997). In any case, deconstruction gestures openly toward undeconstructable and incalculable promises (e.g., justice, the gift, hospitality, forgiveness, etc.). Promises, as such, are eternal, and so never achievable; yet their calculation from within given historical locations is required (e.g., justice through law, forgiveness through say South Africa's 'Truth and Reconciliation Commission', etc.). As Derrida notes, in his discussion of justice, 'incalculable justice requires us to calculate', but 'this requirement does not properly belong either to justice or law. It belongs to either of these domains by exceeding each one in the direction of the other' (1992: 28).

Thus, while calculations are required, they are never necessary. In this respect, deconstruction actively seeks to prevent language from settling, from fixing its enunciations as absolute necessities. It destabilizes language's tendency to unify, and to define its contingent discursive achievements as necessary events. Transposed to the context of criminology, deconstruction might well be expected to trouble, problematize, realist calculations of justice that herald crime as a fixed reality. It might, for example, point to the margins – the otherness –whose marginality is required to profess some version of crime as a necessary reality (e.g., the designation of women, or Africans, as marginal other whose berated 'inferiority' was required for, say, Lombroso to profess his atavist realities). By constantly disturbing dominant images of presence, reality, deconstructive analysis embraces the undecidable as a valuable domain of thinking, perhaps as the only domain in which critical thinking can occur. In recovering the undecidable, the disordered, it also provides an alternative to technocratic forms of criminology which assume that the problem of crime can be technically solved by manipulating known orders. In this respect:

> Deconstruction is the relentless pursuit of *the* impossible, which means, of things whose possibility is sustained by their impossibility, of things which, instead of being wiped out by their impossibility, are actually nourished and fed by it.
>
> (Caputo, 1997: 32)

Returning to a relevant issue for criminology, one could view justice as an impossible promise whose very impossibility inspires, nay makes possible, our *ongoing* calculations that bear its name. The undecidable quality of this elusive quest is not a problem to be overcome, but an important way of preventing any political (including criminal justice) system from passing itself off as inevitable. The undecidable thus emerges as a realm in which the contingency of decision is embraced, where democracy as a politics of the yet-to-come is sustained (Derrida, 1994).

In concert, these three elements of a *logos* loosen the grip of criminology's *centrealism*, its disciplinary focus on crime as a fixed reality, allowing for the possibility of speaking without assumptions of centre, or without closing limits around crime. This *logos* is concerned with the absences, with impossible horizons, that lie behind present realities. It is directed at recovering the contingencies that create crime, and allows one to accost the existence inspired by its presumed realities. The point is not to reinforce realities, far less to designate them as necessary, or even necessarily better than those that precede. Quite the contrary, this mode of address involves itself, continuously, with transgressing the limits that sustain crime's realities. In an important sense, this approach is a dissociative one that seeks to unhinge a given existence, a present, from its contextual unities – it entertains the possibility of being otherwise. Another way to say this is to speak of a *logos* that welcomes the 'other as other', and remains receptive to unanticipated promises of justice still to come (Derrida, 1992). Here, discourse stands poised on the threshold of what is, glimpsing the (im)possibilities of what is to come. Such ways of speaking imply a deconstructive opening to a promise that itself always leaves room for the other, and so too for the undecidable, for the chance event. It takes seriously a responsibility to absence, otherness, not contained within present horizons (see Critchley, 1992). But to what might such a *logos* direct itself?

Addressing echoes of *crimen*

The previous section indicates how a technocratic preoccupation with the reality of crime could be displaced in favour of a post-disciplinary focus on how 'crime' is discursively assembled as such. This suggestion can also be recovered through a closer look at the etymology of the term *crimen*. Adding to what has already been said of this matter in the introduction, we might recall that the term derives, like many other words (critic, crisis, excrement, etc.), from a Greek verb *krinein*, meaning to decide (see Ayto, 1990: 145). When associated with the Latin root *cenere* (to sift, decide), it assumed the form of a noun, connoting such meanings as verdict, accusation, cry of distress (as in raising the hue and cry), offence and crime.[9] We might then say that images of *crimen* were not always, or only, associated with 'crime' – they referred to such meanings as 'accusation' and 'cries of distress' (Partridge, 1958). There is more to be made of the apparent amnesia that has since allowed an important constellation of phrases associated with the idea of *crimen* to fall silent, and for a discipline of criminology to focus narrowly on the reality of crime. I propose that a post-disciplinary *logos* might usefully recover a lost facet of this etymology by re-conceiving *crimen* as *accusation*, and so focusing attention on how 'others' are initially called to account for their actions (Ayto, 1990: 5).[10]

As we have already seen in other chapters, such calls involve powers that require subjects to confess specified truths about themselves; these, in turn, require subjects to engage technologies of self-formation involved with decisions about whether identities of exclusion are warranted (Cruikshank, 1996; Pavlich, 1996). In general terms, practices of accusation contain important political techniques with which to confer identities of exclusion (e.g., when an accused subject is designated 'criminal'). Accusation creates *other* identities from a given present, and so consolidates the limits of given patterns of association. By creating excluded subjects, it is involved in supporting specific boundaries around given collective identity formations.[11] Through its excretion of otherness, accusation helps to support a specific *status quo*. Accusation therefore engages a politics of exclusion – and all too often a markedly undemocratic one – to differentiate strangers from friends.

Directing a post-disciplinary *logos* to *crimen*, conceived as accusation, opens itself to distinctive lines of inquiry. It could, for example, name and challenge the political rationales, techniques and consequent effects of particular modes of accusation. While accusations of exclusion are made in the name of different stranger identities (the mad, the potentially dangerous, the dole 'bludger', etc.), our focus here is on those that are made in the name of crime. Several lines of inquiry could be opened. First, a post-disciplinary *logos* might discern and chart the complex relations between political rationales through which criminal accusations are made. It need not centre its analysis on an assumed reality, but on tapping deconstructively into accusatory rationales to render taken-for-granted statements problematic. Its analyses could be regarded as provocative fictions, as attempts to engage a politics of accusation. This sort of analysis could – for heuristic purposes – depict three key political rationales (sovereignty, discipline and governance) through which modern, liberal contexts issue accusations in the name of crime. These are complexly, and contradictorily related in different contexts.

However, as discussed more fully in chapter 2, sovereign accusations tend to rely on legal rationales and judgements made against legal persons through pretexts of criminal law (Tie, 1999). By contrast, disciplinary accusations judge abnormal individuals as pathological deviants, or delinquents, based on shifting normative frameworks created through statistical averages (Foucault, 1977). Equally, governmental rationales manage collectives by reconciling singular and totalizing identities for political goals (Foucault, 1981; Pavlich & Ratner, 1996). Most recently, in the context of crime, one could argue that governmental rationales have developed themselves around images of local security, risk management and community participation. Here, one detects an emphasis on profiling for preventive and management purposes; criminal accusations are increasingly directed at those deemed to be at risk of threatening community security, at those profiled and deemed to present known risk factors inclining them toward crime (see Chapter 2). The logic of such political initiatives is to base accusations on actuarial calculations that identify at-risk subjects (Feeley & Simon, 1992, 1994).

A post-disciplinary *logos* might analyse these tendencies as related elements of what Foucault (1991) refers to as a 'triangle' of regulation. The complex associations between the elements affect whether, and how, criminal accusations are made in specific contexts. It is therefore important to analyse how they relate to one another in context. For instance, the entrenched priorities of medieval sovereignty were transfigured by the rise of liberal disciplinary rationales, as the art of government developed haphazardly in the background. However, as notions of risk, efficient management, prevention and personal security within communities are prioritized over legal and norm-based images of crime, a post-disciplinary *logos* might well have to face what we have already described: disciplinary 'societies of control' are in the process of yielding ground to emerging governmental accusatory rationales.

Second, this approach could direct itself to the changing techniques, and emerging political technologies, through which accusations of crime are made. Some have already alluded to the emergence of a postmodern penality (Feeley & Simon, 1992), actuarial justice (Feeley & Simon, 1994), post-disciplinary parole (Simon, 1993), multiple imaginings of crime (A. Young, 1996), prudential calculations of risk (O'Malley, 1996b, 1998), security (Shearing & Stenning, 1983), situational controls (Garland, 1997), dangerousness (Pratt, 1995, 1997), community governance (Crawford, 1998; Pavlich, 1996), and so on. Moreover, accusers nowadays find themselves remotely placed through managerial relays, and in voluntary/private institutional contexts (e.g., community crime-prevention programmes). As such, accusatory techniques are now evoked to complement, supplement, augment, reorganize, replace, etc., legal and disciplinary technologies. Amid these newly emerging, and/or reformulated, accusatory technologies, one can also identify the prioritized use of preventive profiles (e.g., DNA, community crime, offender, recidivist, etc.). In much the same way as the panopticon exemplified many features of disciplinary surveillance, profiling can be analysed as a basic technique for risk-orientated governmental power–knowledge complexes.

For example, profiling risks requires data to be collected about a specifically formulated problem; say, 'street crime' as a threat to community security. Technologies are used to separate out those subjects considered most likely (in actuarial terms) to endanger a given security. Characteristics of known 'offenders' are divided (coded) into factors considered relevant to the problem, and risk profiles are developed accordingly (see Chapter 2). Such knowledge is then used to identify those 'at risk' of committing future offences. Behind this lies a political logic that identifies 'otherness' in subjects through actuarially based information packages and factorial codes.[12] The *corporeality* of subjects, the breathing, pulsating, docile bodies that discipline sought to shape into normalized individuals, is translated into a hyperreal constellation of factors housed in computer data banks (see Bogard, 1996). These hyperrealized profiles, the constellations of coded information, constitute the raw data of governmental accusations made by programmed computers. In the process, the erstwhile priorities of disciplinary technologies of power are both developed and subverted by governmental techniques of accusation. The hyperreal effects of such new developments are easily eclipsed by blind-spots created through criminology's *centrealism*.

Third, a post-disciplinary approach might seek to problematize areas of political accusation differently from the 'problems' identified by dominant mentalities of rule. For example, it would surely question the now prominent assumption that more rigorous profiles are required to prevent criminal breaches to security. There might be instances where such approaches can be justified, but there are also many cases where an unadulterated faith in profiling disallows critical discussion of the founding rationales of actuarial governance. When the logic of profiling is carried to an extreme, governance gains a momentum all of its own. As Bogard (1996) puts it, surveillance becomes something carried out for its own sake, rather than, say, for a corrective purpose;

quite literally, older corporeal surveillance is *simulated* as accusers dream up new ways of constructing, amassing and keeping tabs on virtual (hyperreal) profiles. A danger here could be formulated thus: when one governs by using computers to accuse, expanding the list of profiled risk factors by even one has the potential to massively extend the number of subjects brought within the purview of accusation frameworks. Notwithstanding the ways that this exposes us to old (e.g., human rights) and new (e.g., information access issues) dangers, virtual accusation provides an all-too-easy way for the already vast crime-control industry to recursively perpetuate its own expansion (Christie, 1994). The issue for a critical *logos* is to seek ways of not being governed thus, initiating a form of critical inquiry in search of post-disciplinary resistance to the dangers of an emerging politics of governmental accusation.

Leanings . . .

Assembling the last two sections of this chapter, one can discern a post-disciplinary reconfiguration of criminology. It proposes a deconstructive, critical *logos* of *crimen* that de-centres the *centrealism* of disciplinary criminology. Its precepts need to be understood as moments in the flow of criminology's history, and contributing further to its apparent fragmentation. Whether criminology survives as an integrated discipline is no longer a pressing issue. More importantly, fragmented criminological discourses could aim to arrest the overwhelming weight of new governmental technocracies that will have us believe there is nothing subjects can do about crime, except to expand and render crime-control initiatives more effective.

Such claims inevitably flirt with disastrous totalitarian political closures. For one thing, the politics of accusation are always concerned with establishing singular and collective identities through explicit processes of exclusion. This is not new. But as the priorities of governmental rationales resituate disciplinary and legal technologies, so practices of accusation shift their responsibilities away from defending a 'normal' social order, or even a legal system. Whatever else, this licenses substantive closures, especially when accusation practices are made exclusively responsible to subjects deemed not to be at risk of imperilling amorphous, and context-specific, definitions of community security (e.g., consumers in shopping malls, fans at sporting events, functional families, safety conscious households, etc.). If accusation is mobilized to service a given incarnation of 'security', then the system's responsibility is primarily conceived as being to the (actual or potential) victims of any security breaches. As for the accused, or even those accused of being 'at risk', the key issue simply becomes one of effective management and/or a redistribution of risks to avoid security breaches. Such redefined responsibilities will continue to de-emphasize correctional rehabilitation, and proportionate calculations of punishment, while elevating actuarial profiles to manage enlarged clusters of excluded identities. They also sanction knowledge that serves governmental crime-control systems, and eschew critiques directed at the underlying rationales thereof. For example, what do we mean by security? Which subjects have privileged access to the means of defining security in specific contexts? Is crime necessarily real and amenable to technical resolution? What moral frameworks do actuarial systems implicitly sustain? What responsibilities toward 'otherness' are deflected by governmental practices of accusation? In my view, questions of this variety must remain viable to prevent governmental institutions from deflecting fundamental critique by parading their administrative decisions as ontologically necessary. At stake here are closures that have the potential to fuel totalitarian exclusions, and could lead us to repeat the unforgettable tragedies that have attended to irresponsible processes of accusation.

If nothing else, the previous discussion enlists a critical version of criminology to keep open, through a deconstructive *logos*, the language of governmental systems that now accuse subjects under the mantle of 'crime'. This version of critical practice develops discursive spaces to accost the emerging priorities of post-disciplinary, governmental accusations of crime. One of its chief ambitions is to relentlessly disturb proclaimed orders of being, focusing particularly on decisions that *ex post facto* inscribe themselves as necessary events. The twentieth century provides too many examples of the catastrophic dangers attending to closures brought about by centring given images of 'reality' as necessarily so. One could critically allude to the hierarchical 'realities' of race that ended with enforced sterilization, the gas chambers, or apartheid's bloodbaths. We might also return to Nietzsche's emphasis on processes of becoming to validate the pursuit of justice as endless promise; a pledge that forever affirms the possibility of escaping present limits of being. By preserving realms of the undecided, where promises of a just future are always still to come, one can recover critical practices that address the contingent and haphazard struggles whose product is 'reality'. The fate of critique is here tied to valuing undecided realms over closed orders; infusing its spirit into a deconstructive criminology addressed at governmental accusation is but one attempt to keep the flames of this anti-totalitarian promise burning under post-disciplinary conditions.

Acknowledgement

The author wishes to acknowledge the Royal Society of New Zealand's Marsden Fund for supporting the research project from which this chapter derives. An earlier version was presented to the American Society of Criminology conference, 17–20 November 1999 in Toronto.

Notes

1 However, such challenges should not be seen to spell the demise of the disciplines – they are not likely to vanish without a trace. Rather, as I see it, disciplinary power–knowledge practices, such as those reflected by correctionalist versions of criminology, will likely exert their influence over contemporary regulatory terrains in increasingly fragmented and contradictory ways (e.g., consider the ambiguous and haphazard plight of 'rehabilitation' in correctional services). See, for instance, Ericson and Carriere (1994).

2 Beccaria (1963) nicely exemplifies the first of these, with Quetelet (1842) and Lombroso (Lombroso-Ferrero, 1911) appropriating scientific methods (e.g., statistics, medical empiricism) to develop their explanations. As Beirne (1993) indicates, these approaches were developed contemporaneously rather than in chronological succession.
3 Criminology's focus on crime is evident from a quick pass through introductory text books. Even in radical approaches, as Barak suggests, 'criminologists might agree that criminology entails the study of crime and crime control, crime and punishment, and crime and justice . . . even if they do not have a clear image of what criminology itself is' (1998: 7). Steinert too notes that, 'Usually criminology just knows that a crime is a crime and only studies phenomena that have already been so labelled' (1998: 407). Similarly, for Nelken, criminology is 'the disciplined study of crime and crime control' (1994: 1).
4 For instance, Hulsman (1986), Shearing (1989), Christie (1994), C. Smart (1995) and Pitch (1995) variously ponder the concept's ontological integrity.
5 See Ericson and Carriere (1994), O'Malley (1996a), Pavlich (1999a). Barak (1998) also points to the matter by noting criminology's loose and 'transdisciplinary' character.
6 One should be cautious when using these terms. For Rose (1996) the 'social' of welfare state powers has been recast, while Dean (1997) sees one sort of society making way for another – a way perhaps to redeem sociology. Either way, the point here is that criminology can no longer rely on concepts that were once treated as unquestioned assumptions.
7 For more detail, see Simon (1987), Castel (1991), Ewald (1991), Deleuze (1992), Feeley and Simon (1992, 1994), O'Malley (1996a), Ericson and Haggerty (1997), Pavlich (1999a, 1999b), etc.
8 No doubt, too, such thinking has found its way into the ambit of criminology through feminist analyses (A. Young, 1996; Naffine, 1997), cultural criminology (Ferrell, 1999) and may even be part of a radical lineage (Carrington, 1998; J. Young, 1998).
9 See Negrier-Dormont (1994: 12), Partridge (1958: 130), and Klein (1966: 372).
10 Accusation is also used to suggest processes involved in 'sifting' (Partridge, 1958; Klein, 1966).
11 Steinert alludes to this point in his discussion of twentieth-century administrative criminology's obsession with criminal exclusion; he asks this question: 'whose exclusion is the condition for a certain kind of solidarity?' (1997: 112).
12 For an excellent compilation of debates around risk and crime, see O'Malley (1998). See generally Lupton (1999), and also Hogg (1996), Pavlich (1999b) and Rigakos (1999).

References

Ayto, J. (1990). *Dictionary of Word Origins*. New York: Arcade Publications.

Barak, G. (1998). *Integrating Criminologies*. Boston, MA: Allyn and Bacon.

Bauman, Z. (1987). *Legislators and Interpreters: On Modernity, Post-Modernity and Intellectuals*. Cambridge: Polity Press.

——. (1992). *Intimations of Postmodernity*. London: Routledge.

——. (1997). *Postmodernity and its discontents*. New York: New York University Press.

Beccaria, C. (1963). *On Crimes and Punishments and Other Writings*. New York: Bobbs-Merrill.

Beirne, P. (1993). *Inventing Criminology: Essays on the Rise of 'Homo Criminalis'*. New York: State University of New York Press.

Bogard, W. (1996). *The Simulation of Surveillance: Hypercontrol in Telematic Societies*. Cambridge: Cambridge University Press.

Butler, J. (1992). 'Contingent foundations: feminism and the question of "postmodernism"', in J. Buder & J. W. Scott (eds), *Feminists Theorise the Political*. London: Routledge, pp. 3–21.

Caputo, J. D. (ed.) (1997). *Deconstruction in a Nutshell: A Conversation with Jacques Derrida*. New York: Fordham University Press.

Carrington, K. (1998). 'Postmodernism and feminist criminologies: fragmenting the criminological subject', in P. Walton & J. Young (eds), *The New Criminology Revisited*. New York: St Martin's Press, pp. 76–97.

Castel, R. (1991). 'From dangerousness to risk', in G. Burchell, C. Gordon & P. Miller (eds), *The Foucault Effect: Studies in Governmentality, with Two Lectures by and an Interview with Michel Foucault*. Chicago, IL: The University of Chicago Press, pp. 281–98.

Christie, N. (1994). Crime *Control as Industry: Towards Gulags, Western Style*. London: Routledge.

Crawford, A. (1998). Community safety and the quest for security: holding back the dynamics of social exclusion. *Policy Studies*, 19, 237–53.

Critchley, S. (1992). *The Ethics of Deconstruction: Derrida and Levinas*. Oxford: Blackwell Publishers.

Cruickshank, B. (1996). 'Revolutions within: self-government and self-esteem', in A. Barry, T. Osborne & N. S. Rose (eds), *Foucault and Political Reason: Liberalism, Neo-liberalism, and Rationalities of Government*. Chicago, IL: The University of Chicago Press, pp. 231–52.

Dean, M. (1997). 'Sociology after society', in D. Owen (ed.), *Sociology after Postmodernism*. London: SAGE, pp. 205–28.

——. (1999). *Governmentality: Power and Rule in Modern Society*. London: SAGE.

Deleuze, G. (1992). Postscript on the societies of control. *October*, 59, 3–7.

Derrida, J. (1978). *Writing and Difference*. Chicago, IL: The University of Chicago Press.

——. (1992). 'Force of law: The "mystical foundation of authority"', in D. Cornell, M. Rosenfeld & D. G. Carlson (eds), *Deconstruction and the Possibility of Justice*. New York: Routledge, pp. 3–67.

——. (1994). *Specters of Marx: The State of the Debt, the Work of Mourning, and the New International*. London: Routledge.

——. (1995). *Points . . . Interviews, 1974–1994*. Stanford, CA: Stanford University Press.

——. (1997). *Deconstruction in a Nutshell: A Conversation with Jacques Derrida*. New York: Fordham University Press.

Ericson, R., & Carriere, K. (1994). 'The fragmentation of criminology', in D. Nelken (ed.), *The Futures of Criminology*. London: SAGE, pp. 89–109.

Ericson, R., & Haggerty, K. (1997). *Policing the Risk Society*. Toronto, ON: University of Toronto Press.

Ewald, E. (1991). 'Insurance and risk', in G. Burchell, C. Gordon & P. Miller (eds), *The Foucault Effect: Studies in Governmentality, with Two Lectures by and an Interview with Michel Foucault*. Chicago, IL: The University of Chicago Press, pp. 197–210.

Feeley, M., & Simon, J. (1994). 'Actuarial justice: the emerging new criminal law', in D. Nelken (ed.), *The Futures of Criminology*. London: SAGE, pp. 173–201.

——, & ——. (1992). The new penology: notes on the emerging strategy of corrections and its implications. *Criminology*, 30, 449–74.

Ferrell, J. (1999). 'Anarchist criminology and social justice', in B. Arrigo (ed.), *Social Justice/Criminal Justice*. New York: West/Wadsworth, pp. 93–108.

Foucault, M. (1977). *Discipline and Punish*. New York: Pantheon Books.

——. (1991). 'Governmentality', in G. Burchell, C. Gordon & P. Miller (eds), *The Foucault Effect: Studies in Governmentality, with Two Lectures by and an Interview with Michel Foucault*. Chicago, IL: The University of Chicago Press, pp. 87–104.

Garland, D. (1997). 'Governmentality' and the problem of crime: Foucault, criminology, sociology. *Theoretical Criminology*, 1(2), 173–214.

Hirst, P. Q. (1975). *Law, Socialism and Democracy*. London: Routledge and Kegan Paul.

Hogg, R. (1996). Criminological failure and governmental effect. *Current Issues in Criminal Justice*, 8(1), 43–59.

Hulsman, L. H. C. (1986). Critical criminology and the concept of crime. *Contemporary Crises*, 10(1), 63–80.

Klein, E. (1966). *A Comprehensive Etymological Dictionary of the English Language*. Amsterdam: Elsevier.

Lombroso-Ferrero, G. (1911). *Criminal Man: According to the Classification of Cesare Lombroso*. New York: Putnam.

Lupton, D. (1999). *Risk*. London: Routledge.

Lyotard, J.-F. (1984). *The Postmodern Condition: A Report on Knowledge*. Minneapolis: University of Minnesota Press.

Naffine, N. (1997). *Feminism and Criminology*. Cambridge: Polity Press.

Negrier-Dormont, L. (1994). Criminology: foundations and efficacy. *International Criminal Public Review*, 450, 10–15.

Nelken, D. (ed.). (1994). *The Futures of Criminology*. London: SAGE.

Nietzsche, F. (1967). *The Will to Power*. New York: Vintage Books.

O'Malley, P. (1996a). Post-social criminologies: some implications of current political trends for criminological theory and practice. *Current Issues* in *Criminal Justice*, 8(1), 26–38.

——. (1996b). 'Risk and responsibility', in A. Barry, T. Osborne & N. S. Rose (eds), *Foucault and Political Reason: Liberalism, Neo-liberalism, and Rationalities of Government*. Chicago, IL: The University of Chicago Press, pp. 189–208.

——. (1998). *Crime and the Risk Society*. Aldershot: Ashgate/ Dartmouth.

Partridge, E. (1958). *Origins: A Short Etymological Dictionary of Modern English*. London: Routledge.

Pavlich, G. (1996). The power of community mediation: government and formation of self identity. *Law & Society Review*, 30, 707–33.

——. (1999a). Criticism in criminology: in search of legitimacy. *Theoretical Criminology*, 3(1), 29–50.

——. (1999b). 'Preventing crime: "social" versus "community" governance in Aotearoa/ New Zealand', in R. Smandych (ed.), *Governable Places: Readings on Governmentality and Crime Control*. Aldershot: Ashgate Publishers, pp. 329–409.

——. (2000). *Critique and Radical Discourses on Crime*. Aldershot: Ashgate Publishers.

Pavlich, G., & Ratner, R. S. (1996). '*Omnes et singulatim* in criminological theory', in T. O'Reilly Fleming (ed.), *Post-Critical Criminology*. Ontario: Prentice Hall, pp. 392–409.

Pitch, T. (1995). *Limited Responsibilities*. London: Routledge.

Pratt, J. (1995). Dangerousness, risk and technologies of power. *Australian and New Zealand Journal of Criminology*, 28(1), 3–31.

——. (1997). *Governing the Dangerous*. Sydney: The Federation Press.

Quetelet, A. (1842). *A Treatise on Man*. Edinburgh: Chambers.

Readings, B. (1997). *The University in Ruins*. Cambridge: Harvard University Press.

Rigakos, G. S. (1999). Risk society and actuarial criminology: prospects for a critical discourse. *Canadian Journal of Criminology*, 41, 137–50.

Rose, N. (1996). The death of the social: re-figuring the territory of government. *Economy & Society*, 25(3), 327–56.

——. (1999). *Powers of Freedom: Reframing Political Thought*. Cambridge: Cambridge University Press.

Shearing, C. D. (1989). Decriminalising criminology: reflections on the literal and topological meaning of the term. *Canadian Journal of Criminology*, 31(2), 169–78.

Shearing, C. D., & Stenning, C. (1983). Private security: implications for social control. *Social Problems*, 30(5), 493–506.

Simon, J. (1987). The emergence of a risk society: insurance, law, and the state. *Socialist Review*, 95, 61–89.

——. (1993). *Poor Discipline: Parole and the Social Control of the Underclass, 1890–1990*. Chicago, IL: The University of Chicago Press.

——. (1996). 'Criminology and the recidivist', in D. Shichor & D. K. Sechrest (eds), *Three Strikes and You're Out: Vengeance as Public Policy*. London: SAGE, pp. 24–52.

Smart, B. (1992). *Modern Conditions: Postmodern Controversies*. London: Routledge.

Smart, C. (ed.). (1995). *Law, Crime and Sexuality: Essays in Feminism*. London: SAGE.

Steinert, H. (1997). *Fin de siècle* criminology. *Theoretical Criminology*, 1(1), 111–29.

——. (1998). 'Ideology with human victims', in V. Ruggiero, N. South & I. Taylor (eds), *The New European Criminology: Crime and Social Order in Europe*. London: Routledge, pp. 405–24.

Sumner, C. (ed.). (1990). *Censure, Politics, and Criminal Justice*. Milton Keynes: Open University Press.

——. (1994). *The Sociology of Deviance: An Obituary*. Buckingham: Open University Press.

Tie, W. (1999). *Legal Pluralism: Toward a Multicultural Conception of Law*. Aldershot: Ashgate.

Walters, R. (1999). 'Criminology, social defence, and the United Nations'. *Criminology: Aotearoa/New Zealand*, 12, 12–13.

Young, A. (1996). *Imagining Crime: Textual Outlaws and Criminal Conversations*. London: SAGE.

Young, J. (1998). 'From inclusive to exclusive society: nightmares in the European dream', in V. Ruggiero, N. South & I. Taylor (eds), *The New European Criminology: Crime and Social Order in Europe*. London: Routledge, pp. 64–92.

Chapter 10

The emergence of habitual criminals in nineteenth-century Britain

Implications for criminology

> It is an almost instinctive response on the part of those who are not criminals to look upon those who are as being different. From there it is a short and easy path to the assumption that this difference originates in characteristics peculiar to the transgressor's individuality alone.
>
> (Radzinowicz & Hood, 1990: 3)

This strange passage signals a paradox underlying much criminological thinking. On the one hand, even if 'instinctive response' goes too far, the quotation suggests that social responses create consequential differences such as the contingent, historical creation of the 'habitual criminal'. On the other, it claims a 'short and easy path' to reify that contingent identity as an existing being (e.g., 'those who are [criminals]', or 'the transgressors'). Yet, Radzinowicz and Hood fall prey to that very slip when they view transportation as 'flushing large numbers of criminals to the antipodes' (1990: 231), or speak of a 'number of criminals' (p. 256), or assert that 'between 1922 and 1928 only 31 criminals, on average, were sentenced to preventative detention' (p. 287). Notwithstanding the offensive derogation of the first, these examples appear to hypostatize the 'criminal', even as they offer a comprehensive historical analysis of the contingent ways in which various versions of this identity (the 'habitual criminal', 'juvenile delinquent', etc.) surface in different epistemes. Not without considerable influence, ontological slippages of this kind enable vast industries – from popular crime scene investigator television shows, reality TV on criminals, detective fiction, criminal identification with associated forensic sciences, and, of course, criminological thought directed to the 'criminal'.

Against the predetermined ontological commitments of such tendencies, this chapter focuses on the contingent, discursive lineage that produced the 'habitual criminal' in nineteenth-century Britain. Against Radzinowicz and Hood's emphasis on the regulatory reasons and responses (e.g., indefinite detention) surrounding this identity, one could highlight key discourses that produced the 'habitual criminal' as a meaningful construct in the first place. Such discourses helped to found criminal anthropology's object (the *Homo criminalis*), versions of which remain a focal point of several subsequent criminological approaches.[1]

Even if policy failures did accompany its emergence (see Radzinowicz & Hood, 1990: 261ff.), the successful enunciation of 'habitual criminals' as discrete beings cemented the idea that certain kinds of individuals are inherently different from everyone else, thereby marking out specifically criminal from non-criminal individuals. This provided a major boost for attempts to delineate the 'criminal' as a fixed and contained object, amenable to scientific criminological study.

The following analysis, therefore, selectively highlights various systems of thought that were central to the discursive production – and so possible accusation – of the habitual criminal as a distinct being in nineteenth-century Britain. It proceeds through three related sections. The first examines selected influential British texts that enunciated the 'habitual criminal' as a being *per se*. The second focuses on three conceptual foundations for enunciating the habitual criminal as a discrete entity. These grounds in turn rested on ideas that were combined to: form a specific class of people as distinctly 'criminal'; enunciate members of this class as possessing depraved individual *characters*; and, imbue degenerate *habits* as the cause of this group's criminal predilections. Stated differently, late nineteenth-century images of the 'habitual criminal' drew on, and gained support from, previously developed ideas about a 'criminal class', 'criminal characters' and 'criminal habits'. The focus of the last section is to explore how these ideas overlapped to define the 'habitual criminal' as a distinct being, and to enable an emerging 'scientific criminology' to tap into these discourses in its related quest to define the 'criminal' as a viable object of study. By so pointing to the lineage of the habitual criminal as the basis of criminology's oft asserted 'criminal individual', the chapter reiterates the call of the previous chapter in new ways: enable a politics of justice and a *logos* of *crimen* that directs itself to 'criminal accusation' rather than to a predefined 'individual criminal'.[2]

The habitual criminal surfaces

> There is a population of habitual criminals which forms a class by itself. Habitual criminals are not to be confounded with the working or any other class: they are a set of persons who make crime the object and business of their lives; to commit crime is their trade; they deliberately scoff at honest ways of earning a living, and must accordingly be looked upon as a class of a separate and distinct character from the rest of the community.
>
> (Morrison, in Tobias 1972: 59)

Given the date of this quotation, one might be tempted to accept the usual view that the habitual criminal was a product of later nineteenth-century thinking (Radzinowicz & Hood, 1990; Pratt & Dickson, 1997). However, formative traces of the basic idea were already apparent in previous discourses. In 1833, for example, Wontner offers a classification of prisoners that begins with 'Habitual Offenders who have all their lives been engaged in crime' (1833: 286).[3] He also asserts that there is but a slim chance of reclaiming 'these characters': 'Let us, therefore, first make laws for these men!' (1833: 216). Similarly, in 1838, a Select Committee's evaluation of transportation as a suitable form of punishment referred to 'habitual criminals' who 'compose what is properly called the criminal population of this country' and who 'gain their livelihood by the repetition of offences, and who consequently have lost all feelings of moral aversion to crime, and can only be restrained by fear' (Great Britain, 1838: xx). Evidence from John Ward to that committee extolled the importance of determining, 'whether the criminal belonged to the class of habitual criminals' or was a victim of a 'moment of temptation', an 'accidental criminal' (5 February, 1838: 5). One year later, the Royal Commission's Report separated out 'habitual depredators' from 'other criminals', calling for detailed information to be obtained on 'habitual delinquents'. It reasoned that without such information, there 'can be no observation and none of that most efficient, economical, and constitutional kind of prevention, which consists in the direct watching and guarding of persons known or suspected bad character' (Shaw-Lefevre, 1839: 7).

Though variously nuanced, these references formulate versions of the habitual criminal as a distinct being.[4] By mid-century, Mayhew's (1856: 88) classic study of London's poor suggests that the 'habitual' (at times 'professional') criminal is widely assumed to comprise a category of people distinct from 'occasional' or 'accidental' criminals.[5] He insists that these categories (rather than the legal taxonomies of criminal law) offer more reliable ways to approach crime and its causes. Against the undifferentiated categories of criminal law, he extols the virtues of discriminating between criminal types, noting each type's unique reason for committing crime. Therefore, if one is

> to learn something as to the causes of the crimes, and consequently as to the character and passions of criminals themselves, he must begin *de nevo*; and using official facts, but rejecting the official system of classification, proceed to arrange offences into two classes, according as they are of a professional or casual character, committed by habitual or occasional offenders.
>
> (Mayhew, 1856: 88)

Just over a decade later, this call to new classifications of criminal types appears more as an incontestable fact. For example, reporting on parliamentary discussions dealing with statutory proposals to regulate 'habitual criminals', *The Times* editorial (10 March 1869) declares as 'ludicrous' the 'hesitations and uncertainties of Parliamentary debate' when compared with the 'absolute practical convictions of the police'. The editors of the paper pause to reflect on whether 'there is any test of Habitual Criminality' but quickly reject it as beside the point given that the 'police have got the names, haunts, character, and abodes of these practitioners all on record' (p. 9, col. C). They continue:

> You want to know what a professional criminal is. Take a walk with the police, and they will show you in the class all the varieties as easily as you could be shown the animals in the Zoological Gardens.

These are, so the article alleges, 'the enemies of society of which we wish to rid ourselves'.[6]

Continuing this line of thought, and mounting a specific 'defence' of society, new regulations for habitual criminals were statutorily enacted through the *Habitual Criminals Act* of 1969 (32 & 33 Vict) c.99. With an overtly stated aim to regulate recidivism, this Act defined the habitual criminal as any person who

> is convicted on indictment of any offence specified in the first schedule hereto in England or Ireland, and in the second schedule hereto in Scotland, and he be proved to have been previously convicted of any offence specified in the said schedule.
>
> (Part III, 8)[7]

In this 'two strikes and you're out' ethos, the habitual criminal was singled out as an identity that should be

> subject to the supervision of the police as herein-after mentioned for a period of seven years or such less period as the court shall direct, commencing from the time at which he is convicted, and exclusive of the time during which he is undergoing his punishment.
>
> (op. cit.)[8]

With such projections of difference came concerted attempts to distinguish, accuse and identify uniquely habitual criminals, as well as to subject them to intensive regulation. The *Prevention of Crimes Act, 1871*, for instance, mandated the identification, surveillance and supervision of habitual criminals, and required a 'habitual criminal register' and a 'register of distinctive marks'.[9] Of necessity, such regulatory prescriptions enlisted new methods – beyond personal recognition[10] – for the identification of habitual criminals.[11] As E. R. Spearman, a retired senior civil servant, lamented, 'Personal recognition is, however, the main thing on which the English detective or prison warder relies' (1894: 257), before reiterating the Home Office's ambitions:

> What is wanted is a means of classifying the records of habitual criminal, such that as soon as the particulars of the personality of any prisoner (whether description, measurements, marks, or photographs) are received, it may be possible to ascertain readily, and with certainty, whether his case is in the register, and if so, who he is.
>
> (in Spearman, 1894: 257)

Such aspirations suggest that a subtle but consequential change was afoot: the habitual criminal's contingently fashioned identity was now fixed as absolute. A Home Office Committee Report specifically directed to the 'Identification of Criminals' confirms the point by assuming the existence of identifiable criminals, seeing its task as one of deciding the virtues of two rival identification systems – Bertillon's anthropometry versus Galton's classification system for finger printing (Troup, 1893–94). Touting the findings of this committee, Lee's *A History of Police in England*, echoes Spearman's concern with the unreliability of 'the memories of policemen and prison warders' (1901: 359), but unequivocally heralds the new criminal identification procedures:

> [S]ince the introduction of photography, and especially since the recent adoption of the system of anthropometry which is associated with the name of M. Alphonse Bertillon and Mr Francis Galton, the chance of any miscarriage of justice, due to mistakes in identification has been reduced to a minimum.
>
> (1901: 359)

However dubious such claims might have been, they indicate the degree to which the habitual criminal had by then become a distinct category of being. The question shifted from an ontological one (does something like the habitual criminal exist?) to one of identification (how do we identify the habitual criminal?). Even Herbert Gladstone's Committee (1894) on Prisons – struck for different purposes[12] – noted the difficulties of distinguishing between professional criminals,[13] but it held firm on the idea that the habitual criminal existed and required special regulatory consideration. The image of the habitual or professional criminal here also fades almost imperceptibly into bolder visions of the criminal at large, but all these related conceptions reinforced the view that the criminal was a unique, ontological being. This formidable – if contingent – discursive achievement was enabled, as I shall argue in the next sections, by the prior institution of three supporting discourses – on 'criminal class', 'criminal character' and 'criminal habit'.

Tracing the 'habitual criminal': criminal class

> One central fact dominated nineteenth-century writing about crime – contemporaries were convinced of the existence of a separate criminal class, different in its ideas and behaviour from the honest poor.
>
> (Tobias, 1972: 29)

Tobias's collection of original sources from different moments in the century helps one to appreciate the degree to which this idea of a criminal 'class' was taken as given.[14] Many crime-related discussions assume a putative group of criminal characters that threaten 'decent' society (Tobias, 1967: 59); continental images of the 'dangerous classes'[15] were less influential in Britain where more specific taxonomies of criminal groups focused on those who survived by criminal action.[16] Prostitutes and the vagrants had been considered foundational elements of the classes habitually supporting crime, but with partial regulatory measures enforced

(Walkowitz, 1992; Mahood, 1990). However, with the gradual abolition of the Bloody Code[17] heightened quests to govern differently and more efficiently, required the identification of new governmental targets and 'enclosures' to be disciplined (Foucault, 1977: 141). In such a regulatory ethos, the criminal class surfaced as a conceptual enclosure that was described in the 1830s by the *Fraser's Magazine* in these terms:

> The character of one is the character of the whole class; their manners and notions are all of one pattern and mould, which accounted for by their general acquaintance with each others, and their habits of association. They have a peculiar look of the eye . . . the development of their features is strongly marked with animal propensities . . . They form a distinct class of men by themselves.
>
> (anonymous author in Tobias, 1972: 39–40)[18]

Such markers defined a 'distinct class' and compared it – albeit unfavourably – to vocational or professional clubs with a common purpose.[19] Essentially, this class was said to offer refuge for criminals,[20] helping them to hone necessary skills and feel part of an extended grouping. Here, differences between the 'honest poor' and the 'criminal class' assumed significance: a Royal Commission on Constabulary Forces (Shaw-Lefevre, 1839) thus used pioneering sociological methods[21] to capture the essence of this supposed class – its size, 'habits', practices, and types of member (Appendix 6 entitled 'Practices of Habitual Depredators').[22] Such descriptions marked this 'class' from non-criminal (and petty criminal) people, and attributed a common essence to the group.

By mid-century, the *Edinburgh Review* could assert with unwavering confidence a clear difference between those who '*commit crime*' and those who '*become criminals*' to form a kind of 'criminal race' (in Tobias, 1967: 63). Equally, Symons' (1849) *Tactics for the Times* clarified the nature and best remedy (Christian education) for reducing the 'dangerous classes', just as Mayhew (1956, 1968, 1998)[23] depicted the criminal class as having a fixed essence amenable to careful and precise taxonomy.[24] Likewise Plint's (1851) mid-century treatise on criminality isolated the criminal class as the prime cause of crime, rejecting earlier metaphysical/moral speculation on crime. His overt allegiance to science drew him to (Quetelet's) statistical methods, and an analysis of available crime rates by decade, from 1801 to 1848, led him to the view that crime rates had trended downward between 1831 and 1845. Nevertheless, he remained convinced that this 'happy effect'[25] was sadly offset because the 'portion of all crime committed by the dangerous – the criminal – class must have been on the increase, relatively to the population, throughout the period under review, in densely crowded seats of manufacture' (Plint, 1851: 140). That he could so securely make this speculation in the absence of any evidence – statistical or otherwise – serves to highlight just how far the 'criminal class' had entrenched itself in the discourses of the day.

The prevailing view of this criminal class[26] was framed by Thomas Plint, the Leeds reformer, and other influential voices of the day (e.g., Mary Carpenter (1857), Jelinger Symons (1849), Matthew Davenport Hill (1857) and Henry Mayhew). However, Plint regarded the 'criminal or dangerous classes' as a product of rapid population growth within cities. It included not only the 'professional thief or burglar', but also the 'rabble of the vagrant and dissolute classes, who labour by fits, and eke out subsistence by pilfering, and who are ever on the verge of a more serious breach of the laws' (1851: 144). Moreover, their 'daily subsistence is so much lawlessly abstracted from the earnings of industrious members of society. They contribute nothing to the common stock, but they must take something out of it' (1851: 146).

Like contagion then understood, he worried that criminals might morally infect members of the 'operative classes' by 'vicious contact', creating 'ducts by which the virus of moral poison circulate through and around them' (1851: 146). In his eyes, the criminal class might have been '*in* the community', but they were, 'neither *of* it, nor from it' (1851: 153). Even if a diverse class, he sensed uniformly deleterious effects on moral sensibilities. In unequivocal terms, he described it as a 'pestiferous canker in the heart of every locality where they congregate, offending the sight, revolting the sensibilities, lowering, more or less, the moral status of all who come into contact with them' (1851: 146).

As an expanding 'evil', this group was for him a matter of enormous concern: 'it is not surprising that speculation has been busy on the question of the origin and natural history of the criminal class' and, moreover, 'probably on no other social question has so much been written within the last ten years as this' (1851: 147). Where once there was no more than a vague reference to amorphous 'dangerous classes', Plint now sought to define an absolute, fixed and determined being: 'The first step to the effectual correction . . . of this evil . . . will be the recording with more accuracy and minuteness whatever information can be elicited respecting the criminals who pass through the courts of justice' (1851: 156–7). Such information, he argued, would enable clear descriptions of the specific class of people who could be described as distinctly criminal, and so make them visible for the purposes of control.

Characters 'depraved'

Alongside discourses on the 'criminal class' one finds contemporaneous discussions championing the 'discovery' of a purported 'criminal character'.[27] Ambiguously the idea refers both to the 'character of crime' and the 'character of the criminal'. Though sometimes connected, the latter is of most concern to our discussion where a type of criminal being was posited, and this helped to frame the idea that habitual criminals comprise identifiable subjects responsible for most crime (Wiener, 1994: 46ff.). Moreover, so the reasoning here goes, it is 'character' that in large measure determines criminal action (Tobias, 1967). As Wiener notes, in the early nineteenth century

> [i]t was less the actions than the characters of offenders on which attention came to focus . . . crime was essentially seen as the expression of a fundamental character defect stemming from a refusal or inability to deny wayward impulses or to make proper calculations of long-run self-interest.
>
> (1994: 46)

Further evidence of this claim can be found in the criminal trials at the Old Bailey, where character played a crucial – if often unannounced – role.[28] As Hitchcock and Shoemaker's analysis shows:

> Trials at the Old Bailey were in part about establishing the facts of the case. Almost as important was the character of victim, defendant and witnesses . . . all evidence was judged in light of the character of those who gave it.
>
> (2006: 130)

Thus, Edward Christian's words in his charge to a grand jury at the Isle of Ely were clear: 'The judgements ought to be proportioned to the character and former conduct of the prisoner' (1819: 287). Discourses highlighting the character of criminal offenders assumed some significance in context. Most discussions envisaged an increasingly civilized society bringing unprecedented individual emancipation, but requiring concomitant self-restraint and effective self-governance of animal, brute passions. A specifically criminal character was said to suffer from 'defective self-management' (Wiener, 1994: 49) – a claim inflected with rational, moral (ecclesial), and scientific (statistical) overtones.

Assertions that by addressing failures of responsible self-governance one could prevent crime became somewhat of a calling card with at least two appearances. First, Jeremy Bentham's rational discussions of crime prevention called for two kinds of governance: direct governance from a legislator who operates in the open where 'the evil is attacked in front' (1962: 533); and 'indirect' governance where 'he does not announce his designs: he opens his mines, he consults his spies; he seeks to prevent hostile designs, and to keep in alliance with himself those who might have secret intentions hostile to him' (1962: 533). Bentham counselled legislators to concern themselves specifically with the '*logic of the will*' (1962: 538), before these produced contrary actions. By developing good characters who governed themselves, one could help to restrain wayward wills, encourage pro social visions of duty and so secure the interests of the common good.

Following Bentham, several early nineteenth-century writers sought to shape will, character and instil duty within 'responsible' and 'moral' individuals (see Wiener, 1994: 11).[29] Thus, in 1819, William Roscoe saw crime prevention in these terms:

> Undoubtedly, the best preventative for the commission of crimes is a *correct sense of moral duty*, so strongly inforced [*sic*] by the precepts of Christianity . . . It is only when these feelings are deeply impressed on every individual of the community that society is safe.
>
> (1819: 21)

The call to educate a correct sense of moral duty – and so shape will and character – became a popular position, underscored by the notion that 'it is chiefly education which determines the human character' (Thomson, 1801: 13). A recurring theme in crime-related discourses throughout the century posited that reforming 'criminals' and 'juvenile criminals' required moral education to reshape characters.[30] By mid-century, Alexander Maconochie (once a superintendent of Norfolk Island) formulated a certain 'Mark System' of prison discipline that measured sentence duration 'by labour and good conduct combined' – a sort of early indefinite sentence. 'The purpose of this,' he observed,

> is to make a man's liberation, when he is once convicted of a felony, dependent on subsequent conduct and character evinced by him, rather than on the quality of the original offence. It is in the first that society really has an interest, and on which depends the security with which he can again be released.
> (Appendix M in Symons, 1849: 232)

Policy was then to focus on character over 'original offence'; but this was no simple repudiation of utilitarian free will.[31] In most discourses, ideas of reforming character occurred alongside notions of free will; individuals were regarded as free to choose whether to build character, to develop good habits, or to fall prey to base character traits. Here, the responsible, reliable, moral individual could *choose* to develop a character that curbs animal (childlike, 'savage') impulses and passions, that if ungoverned produced immoral and criminal actions.[32] Hence, F. W. Maitland's (1880: 261) 'preventive theory' of crime emphasized both character *and* the need for punishment to curtail free wills that chose bad habits.[33] Wiener (1994: 49) rightly observes here that, 'the aims of deterrence and moralization seemed by no means incompatible'.[34] Consequently, crime was simultaneously seen as a product of individual free will (hence ideas of individual responsibility and deterrent punishment) and 'defective self-management' (with related ideas of a shaping character to be reformed through education – especially moral education – and other forms of 'character building').[35]

A second, science-based approach to individual criminal character borrowed from Lavater's (1800) earlier physiognomic formulations. The character of a person was discernible from physical traits, a point developed by Spurzheim and Gall in their 'science' of phrenology where character was inferred from skull shapes.[36] Matthew Davenport Hill, the Recorder of Birmingham, was reported by *The Examiner* (19 October 1850) as having to adopt this position on depraved characters:

> The habits of depredation communicate a character to the countenance, and not improbably to the motions of the body, and an experienced police officer becomes so well acquainted with the criminal physiognomy that he can feel satisfied of the nature of a man's avocations when he sees him.
> (in Hill, 1857: 224)

Mayhew and Binny also inferred character from physical appearance in their revealing declaration:

> It did not require much skill in detecting character to pick out the habitual offender from the casual criminal, or to distinguish the simple, broad brown face of the agricultural convict from the knowing, sharp, pale features of the town thief.
>
> (1862: 148)

Through such discourses, criminal characters were identified and distinguished from good characters by referring to predefined physical attributes (Rafter, 1997).

Marmaduke Sampson's (1846) and George Combe's (1854) phrenology-inspired formulations explicitly enunciated the physical determination of character as the cause of criminal behaviour. Interestingly, they also – supporting Foucault's (1977) analysis of disciplinary power – championed prison discipline to correct (treat) criminals, and rallied against punishment, especially capital punishment. For Sampson, 'a person may be fully convinced that he is doing wrong, and yet be unable to resist the tendency' (1846: 9). He alluded to the nature of insanity, and quotes a Mr Woodward to the effect that many people are 'under the influence of uncontrollable propensities' because of their mind and brain functioning. For his part, Combe focused on the supposed shape of criminals' heads, and explicitly linked crime to 'unfavourable natural dispositions and talents, acted upon by adverse circumstances' (1854: 49). Furthermore, he felt that, 'A defective or ill-balanced brain is thus, according to our view, the *primary*, and a defective or vicious training and instruction is the *secondary* cause of criminal action' (1854: 48–9). Combe also noted that people could be retrained, especially if they are not 'mentally unsound', by encouraging moral restraint and seeking ways to break past habits: 'The object of prison discipline is to discover the minutest elements of individual character, to develope [*sic*] the good and suppress the evil . . . to produce self-reliance and the capacity of virtuous individual action' (1854: 91).[37] For him, breaking habits of bad character required that restraint, inner control or self-governance were exercised to ensure morally virtuous ways of living. Those who failed to develop character, and succumbed to the passions of baser instincts, could be expected to commit crime.

In sum, whether commentators endorsed the lesser or greater emphasis on rationalism or science, Jones's overall comment applies:

> The language of character had an important implication which tended to undermine the caricature of rugged and self-reliant individualism. For it insistently highlighted the importance of social circumstances for the prevention of moral qualities, and subtly insinuated into the Victorian consciousness the idea that public agencies had a role to play in creating the sort of environment in which desirable moral qualities might flourish.
>
> (Jones, 2000: 31–2)

And from such insinuations, *habitual criminals* were cast as unique sorts of beings. If the elaboration of that uniqueness was already addressed through discourses on the criminal class and character, it was developed further within allied discourses focused on the idea of 'habit'.

Criminal habits

> Offences of every description have their origin in the vicious and immoral habits of the people, and in the facilities which the state of manners and society, particularly in vulgar life, afford in generating vicious and bad habits.
>
> (Colquhoun, 1800: 311)

> The changed state of Society, the vast extent of moving property, and the unexampled wealth of Metropolis, joined with the depraved *habits* and loose conduct of a great portion of the lower classes of the people.
>
> (Colquhoun: 1800: 1–2; emphasis added)

The association of negative habits with the 'lower orders', and the 'vulgar classes',[38] reflected in Colquhoun's (1800) view that crime was the product of 'bad' habits, assumed various guises. In one form, those who lived lives of idleness, insobriety, immorality, pilfering, profligacy, vagrancy, defrauding, and gambling were destined to immorality; their bad habits would culminate in crime and punishment. For example, Colquhoun noted how gamblers in 'vulgar life'

> are led, step by step, to the point where they lose sight of all moral principle; impelled by a desire to recover what they have lost . . . till at length this species of peculation, by being rendered familiar to their minds, generally terminates in more atrocious crimes.
>
> (1800: 154)

His call to establish a Metropolitan Police force was premised on the view that to prevent crime, good habits of industry, sobriety and morality could and should be instilled by law and regulatory policy.[39] He considered 'habit' therefore as crucial to understanding how to deal with the character of those in the criminal classes, and especially those who were habitually criminal. Working off similar assumptions, Rev. John Burt, who established a prisoner's aid society in Birmingham, echoed this assessment:

> [W]ith habitual offenders there is, from the very fact of habit, a superinduced, and therefore, double depravity. He is *accustomed* to do evil. If ever a moral revolution is to be effected in the character of such men, there must be time allowed for its completion. *Their heads and hearts are filled with licentious ideas and criminal passions.* These springs of crime must be dried up by degrees.
>
> (quoted in Combe, 1854: 64; emphasis in original)

He specifically called for the 'infusion of virtuous ideas' to obliterate 'habitual indulgence', and saw crime prevention's task as breaking bad habits and instilling good ones.[40] This task was to be accomplished by prison discipline, not punishment.[41] Good character could be formed through disciplinary restraints on natural passions, and sealed by the force of habit – but this required social (and legal) initiatives designed to yield self-control.

The overall policy aim was to nurture good habits within the 'criminal class' and so prevent crime by attacking its root. Such aims rendered punishment decidedly secondary – even irrelevant – to the disciplinary correction that focused on inculcating habits of industry. Thus, Maconochie argued that:

> Habits of voluntary industry being formed in prison would preserve [criminals] from recurring to it after discharge. Habits of manly self-reliance being also formed would have their similar appropriate results. Character would be improved; and success would take the place of failure which has undeviatingly followed our other devisings in this field.
>
> (in Symons, 1849: 234–5)

Such corrective prison policy promoted a special sort of prison discipline – i.e., the so-called silent, 'separate system' – because, 'it breaks off, so far as it can be broken by human agency, the former habit of thought and feeling' (Burt, 1852: 49). In short, while the bad habits of 'the criminal classes' spawned 'depraved characters' prone to committing crime, it was possible to reform members of these classes by instilling good habits through discipline and self-governance.

By my reckoning, the axioms of class, character and habit formed a paradigm from which notions of the 'habitual criminal' as a distinct category of persons as objects of criminal regulation could surface. It was only a short leap for the rising 'sciences' of criminal anthropology and criminology to nab notions of the habitual criminal and consecrate them as an object of study: the class of biologically or psychologically determined, individual criminals. When such objects were attached to social evolutionary frameworks, notions of character and habit were reframed in visions of social improvement and growing civility.[42] The habitual criminal was replaced by Lombroso's born criminal, as the fundamentals of eugenic thinking assembled around it.[43] At the cusp of its development, Pike even depicted 'modern habitual criminals' in explicit anthropological terms:

> With the disposition and the habits of uncivilized man which he has inherited from a remote past, he has to live in a country where the majority of inhabitants have learned new lessons of life, and where he is regarded more and more as an outcast in proportion as he strives more and more to fulfil the yearnings of his nature.
>
> (Pike, 1873: 509)

Furthermore, he opined,

> Of a very great number of modern habitual criminals it may be said that they have had the misfortune to live in an age in which their merits are not appreciated. Had they been in the world a sufficient number of generations ago, the strongest might have been chiefs of a tribe.
>
> (Pike, 1873: 509)

'Chiefs of a tribe', indeed! But in consequence of the discourses on criminal class, character and habit, the Habitual Criminal Act of 1869 endorsed what was by then an assumed figure.

As is to be expected, there were voices of disquiet – but they did not necessarily dispute the existence of habitual criminals. For instance, Greenwood (1869) challenged what he regarded as

> a growing inclination to treat the habitual criminal as though he had ceased to be human, and had degenerated into the condition of the meanest and most irreclaimable of predatory animals, fit only to be turned over to the tender mercies of a great body of huntsmen who wear blue coats instead of scarlet, and carry staves and handcuffs in place of whips and horns, and to be pursued to death.
>
> (1869: 92)

The critique was directed not to the existence of habitual criminals per se, but to the portrayals of such beings. Ironically, then, even contemporary critiques reinforce the existence of that being; with its position firmly intact, the habitual criminal became the basic premise for an emerging discipline: empirical criminology.

Ex parte deliberations

In sum, I have argued that Radzinowicz and Hood's analysis of the habitual criminal paradoxically pledges allegiance to the identity of the 'habitual criminal' as a being *sui generis* while simultaneously claiming this identity to be an historical creation of the discourses they examine. Working from the latter approach, I have explored the discursive lineage of the habitual criminal as it emerged in nineteenth-century Britain. By examining three discursive systems of thought (around criminal class, character and habit), the previous discussion highlights foundational elements from which the habitual criminal surfaced. No doubt, the ensuing identity had effects (surveillance, punishments, etc.), but this in no way rescinds its essential contingency and flux. And the latter provides a way to take a different approach to the politics of crime creation that has profound implications for the discipline erected around the criminal identity – criminology. I conclude by highlighting four of these.

First, criminology's tendency to hone in on the individual 'criminal' as its object of analysis should be viewed through images of the 'habitual criminal' that appeared over the course of the nineteenth century.[44] During this time, discourses on the criminal came to exceed classical conceptions (Becarria, Bentham) of the free person who harms society and state by free *actions* that transgress the common law's changing definitions of felony.[45] The habitual criminal, by contrast, appeared as an identity *sui generis*, as someone whose choices made them – by habit – intrinsically different from others. This was not simply a rational being whose choices had led to a criminal action, but a 'criminal class' whose choices generated a 'criminal character' with 'criminal habits'. This habitual criminal provided founding contours for the 'criminal man' that became the object of criminal anthropology and later criminology.[46] That is, criminology's object was constitutively conditioned by the founding discourses of the habitual criminal. One might question the autochthonous, internal histories of criminology's emergence (c.f. Rock, 1994). Beccaria and Bentham, for instance, could be championed *ex post facto* as pioneers of criminological thought, but their writing on crime does not centre on the criminal – they emphasized a *logos* of civil legislation, and an analysis of juridical processes that define felony. Their discourses, that is, are directed to legislators and jurists; not to the 'criminal' as a fundamentally different sort of human being.

On this matter, Beirne (1993) usefully argues that criminology's early development is often incorrectly described as a triumph of positivist science over classical reason (i.e., positivism's determined individual criminal in need of disciplinary correction, or social reform, replaced a classical free will deterred by rationally calibrated punishment.) For one thing, as our analysis shows, free will and determinate character sometimes co-appeared, licensing concurrent calls for punishment *and* disciplinary or social reform. For another, representatives of the so-called classical school were dealing with an incompatibly different object – the legislator. Perhaps then, the complex genealogy of criminology is better understood as a Foucauldian (1973, 1977) tale of rupture between epistemes (or even involving Kuhnian (1968) revolutions and 'gestalt' paradigmatic switches), than a continuous story of progressive science evolving to an empirical criminology directed to the criminal.

Second, discourses on criminal class, criminal character and criminal habit founded the 'habitual criminal' that was to become one of criminology's key objects. These discourses are, in many ways, what Nietzsche might have framed as criminology's 'lowly beginnings'. So, discussions on criminal class defined a unique segment of the 'lower', 'vulgar' or 'working' classes and singled it out as a different, unified grouping. As Emsley (referring to Chadwick) notes, images of the criminal class managed to 'identify a criminal group within the working class, a group which possessed those habits which, to his mind, were the worst habits of the class as a whole. These habits were then offered as the causes of crime' (Emsley, 1996: 56).

As noted, the point applies more generally; images of the habitual criminal were constitutively conditioned by class prejudices such that the derogation of bad habits such as idleness or profligacy, were used to isolate criminal habits among the poor and not the rich (e.g., the idle gentry, the debauchery of courtly life, etc.). And to the extent that this class-differentiated criminal forms the object of criminological study, criminology becomes predicated on attendant class prejudice. The same logic applies to the sexist, patriarchal formulations of the habitual criminal that either ignored women (as in 'criminal man') or fleetingly referred to them in disparaging terms.[47] Equally, the racist imperialism that so flourished in Victorian Britain finds expression in the derogatory castigations of the criminal character, with its purported atavism, 'savage' impulses, 'chiefs of a tribe' mentality, etc.; it also finds 'scientific' expression in the British eugenic movements and social Darwinism behind criminal anthropology and criminology.[48]

Such 'lowly beginnings' distinguished the 'habitual criminal' and provided criminology with a determinate object. The cause of most crime was then attributed to this being and its 'prevention' tied to disciplinary correction. Criminology's paradigm then sustained this ever-elusive individual 'criminal' by differentiating it from other beings. The discursive performances required to brook this feat keeps criminology focused on providing a *logos* of the criminal; as such, it remains anchored to images of that furtive identity. As Smart (1995) and Young (1990) note, attempts to move critical discussions beyond the 'criminal man' leaves criminology in the awkward situation of having no objects and exposing it to a potential collapse into other – more broadly conceived – discourses. The point here is that so long as criminology paradoxically hypostatizes and contingently analyses versions of the 'criminal', it is unlikely to unravel foundational commitments to sustaining discourses that differentiate its key object. In turn, this limits the questions that criminology can raise (see Pavlich, 2000); most of its approaches centre on the individual criminal, thereby eschewing the possibility of wider questions of, say, social justice.

Third, as noted, the successful enunciation of the habitual criminal elicited calls for effective (scientific?) forensic criminal identification (including a Royal Commission – see Troup (1893–94) – on the subject). In many ways, this foreshadowed a vast forensic industry directed to discovering the 'criminal individual' as part of a wider generic type. Subsequent scientific searches for that identity are complex, and involve diverse technologies, from intricate DNA manipulations, retinal scans, various fingerprint schemes, Bertillon's (1977) anthropometry, to Galton's (1891) composite photographs of a 'criminal type' to be discussed in Chapter 11. Such approaches are usually understood as attempts to *discover* a previously existing criminal identity. However, as indicated above, that identity is an historical product of complex discursive processes, including the role played by criminal identification technologies. Consequently, one might argue that criminal identification practices are less discoveries and more creations of specific criminal identities. As such, changes from character-based to scientific assessments of criminal identity that spanned the nineteenth century were directly implicated in creating, as opposed to discovering, the contours of the new 'habitual criminal' identity. No doubt this observation challenges the privilege granted to forensic science in current criminal justice arenas, the cultural obsession with identifying criminals (which is related to burgeoning prison populations), and the ways in which science is used to 'detect' criminals.[49] Recognizing the contingency of criminal identities opens the door to a politics that publicly reflects on the justice of creating criminals rather than burying such discussions under the ruse of neutral scientific discovery.

Finally, from the above, there is political and epistemological utility in refusing criminology's elevation of individual criminals (or on settings that yield individual criminals); criminal justice may be conceived beyond individual notions of criminality. One need not conceptualize a *logos* of *crimen* as necessarily involving individual 'criminals'; but could, as argued before, focus on how people are accused of crime, thereby shifting the gaze away from an 'individual criminal' to diverse processes of accusation. Such a politicized *logos* would avoid Radzinowicz and Hood's paradox by understanding the criminal as a contingently framed identity for one accused of a crime. It would also allow far broader discussions of justice centred on shifting accusatorial structures and identities – from character-based accusations to those that privilege science. Could this allow one to contemplate justice without immediately evoking exclusionary gestures, focused on identifying individual criminals? Would this still be criminology? Probably not as we know it; but then again it would re-centre the politics of crime creation, rather than masking that politics under the pall of technical visions of science. The approach would also explicitly refocus on the justice of criminal accusation procedures, authorized accusers and images of who might legitimately be accused. Such thinking might not empty the gaols, and nor should it necessarily; but it would at least moderate the extreme dangers of our milieu in which the scientific exclusion of criminals has become virtually synonymous with justice.

Acknowledgement

The author wishes to acknowledge the Social Sciences and Humanities Research Council of Canada for supporting this research, and to thank R. A. Sydie for helpful comments on an earlier draft of this chapter.

Notes

1 See Rock (1994), as well as Beirne's rather more careful attention to the ruptures attendant upon the invention of the *Homo criminalis* (1993: 233–7).
2 See, for example, Chapters 1, 2 and 7.
3 It is perhaps useful to note the allied vision of an 'incorrigible rogue' that in the *Vagrancy Act* of 1824 named persistent vagrants (see Barrett & Harrison, 1999: 220–23). It is also noteworthy, for the next section, that in 1808, Henry Clavering should speak of 'incorrigible rogues' in this manner: 'the{*f*}e offenders are ranked in a le{*f*}s criminal cla{*f*}s and are only to be punished as rogues and vagabonds' (1808: 131).
4 See Emsley (1996: 61–7), Radzinowicz and Hood (1990: Chapter 8), Wiener (1994: 300–7, 342–58), Hibbert (1963: part 3), etc.

5 This classification continues to have purchase in 1870 where it is taken up by Cox and Saunders' (1869: xxiii–xxix) analysis of the Habitual Criminals Acts.

6 The significance of this editorial is commented upon, and quoted by, Greenwood (1869: 207–9).

7 Giving some sense of its reception, Wetherell's (1871: 12) letter to the editor praises the Act for its well calculated effort to 'control the predatory habit of the dangerous classes'. The sentiment is echoed in *The Times* editorial of 16 April 1870, p. 9, col. B.

8 Policy analysts interpreted these sections of the Act thus: 'The test of being a Habitual Criminal, as recognized by statute, is that he has been previously convicted' (Cox & Saunders, 1869: xxiv). Or as Edmund DuCane would have it, to ensure 'that an old offender should on re-conviction, be recognized as such, it is necessary to have a good and complete personal record of the members of the criminal classes, accessible to all police forces and courts of justice' (DuCane, 1882: 40).

9 Perhaps ignoring the importance of this formal enunciation for habitual criminal identity, Radzinowicz and Hood argue, 'the only tangible success eventually to emerge from the legislation on habitual criminals was the system of registration and identification' (1990: 261).

10 In this system, as Spearman describes, all those remanded to Holloway Prison are 'inspected by detectives and warders from other Metropolitan prisons to see if they can be identified as old offenders' (1894: 256). He challenges the costs and ineffectiveness of older 'personal recognition' where 'thirty police officers from various quarters of London visit Holloway Prison three times a week', and calculates about 'ninety hours for each identification' (1894: 257).

11 Francis Galton (1879) added his considerable scientific stature to this differentiation through his use of composite photographs that effectively 'morphed' multiple facial images of criminals into what he characterized as a type (see Pavlich, 2000; Broekman, 1995; Sekula, 1986). He also championed a system of fingerprinting in fulfilling this aspiration: 'The hope of the criminal anthropologist is to increase the power of discriminating between the natural and accidental criminal' (Galton, 1890: 66).

12 See Harding (1988).

13 See Radzinowicz and Hood (1990: 266–7).

14 Emsley (1996: 55) elaborates the point further, noting that crime was seen to reside in a section of the 'poorer classes', and it is from this that a 'criminal class' is excavated.

15 This concept was stirred into life by H. A. Frégier's account of the 'dangerous classes' in France (see Radzinowicz & Hood, 1990: 73, at n. 73 and Beirne 1993: 93, 98–9 at n. 15). See also, Symons (1849) for a contemporary British sense of the dangers at hand.

16 For more detail of this development, see Radzinowicz and Hood (1990: 73–84). See also Beier (2005).

17 It is worth noting the intensity of the perceived threat, for at its height this Code listed some 160 crimes for which the death penalty might be applied (see D. Thomas (1998: 5) and E. P. Thompson's (1975) classic study).

18 Excerpt from: 'The Schoolmaster's Experiences in Newgate', *Fraser Magazine* 1832 (vols v and vi).

19 *The Times* later asserts the following: 'Accordingly crime of all kinds is and will remain a recognized vocation, of which the attractions will annually increase in proportion partly to the diminution of its terrors' (Friday, 5 December 1956, p. 6, Col. B).

20 As Tobias notes, the criminal class provided 'entry into an association, informal but none the less real, members of which could be found almost everywhere. In gaol or lodging-house or on the road, criminals could find companions in like situation, could exchange experiences and discover common acquaintanceships' (1967: 108).

21 Edwin Chadwick was one of the three Commissioners and drafted the report. Whatever his role (cf. Emsley (1996: 55) versus Tobias (1972: 58)), the qualitative

survey questions outlined in Appendix 5 bear traces of his hand and give a sense of the systematic and comprehensive ways in which information was solicited.

22 See Tobias (1967: 62–3) and Thomas (1998: 1–8).

23 See also Mayhew and Binny (1862).

24 Mayhew (1856: 89) distinguishes between the 'criminal class', the 'pauper class' and the 'wealthy class', providing detailed descriptions of the differences within the criminal class. For a useful description of Mayhew's contribution to the concept of a criminal class see Radzinowicz and Hood (1990: 77–84).

25 For Plint, such evidence 'incontestably shows that some moral element was operative, in the latter cycles, so mighty as not merely to arrest further progress of crime, but actually to drive back the flood, which all the surrounding elements conspired to swell' (1851: 139–40).

26 For more detail see, for instance, Tobias (1967, 1972: Part two), Emsley (1996: Chapter 3), Thomas (1998: 1–8), and Hibbert (1963: 21–41).

27 Interestingly, Jelinger Symons insists that character is distinct from class; thus, 'Know only . . . that a man belongs to a class, and define the rank he holds in it as accurately as you may, and you are as ignorant as ever of his character' (1849: 12).

28 Starkie (1828: 364), with reference to the US, for example, outlines situations where the 'moral character and conduct of a person in society may be used in proof before a jury'. Also, a contemporary edition of Blackstone's commentaries includes his notion that 'the age, education, and character of the offender; the repetition (or otherwise) of the offence . . . all of these may aggravate or extenuate the crime' (Blackstone, 1820: Book IV: 400). See also Wakefield's (1831: 57) discussion on weighting the character of a witness.

29 See Lacey's (2001: 363ff.) discussion of Wiener's analysis of the refinements of individual will that enable a version of the 'responsible subject'.

30 See, for example, Symons (1949) and Carpenter (1857). Haney (1982) offers a fuller discussion of the basic ideas, though his analysis refers particularly to the US context.

31 So the Report of a Select Committee on Criminal Commitments and Convictions observes that it is difficult to assess 'criminal character' but notes that prison officials often class prisoners 'by character and conduct, not by crime' because 'the most atrocious character may be sent to prison for a very slight offence' (Great Britain, 1827: 9).

32 As Pike (1973: 510) puts it, 'The history of crime . . . is a history of the ever-increasing restraint placed upon savage impulses, and an ever-increasing encouragement to the wider play of sympathy'.

33 Maudsley's slightly different approach, which insists on the value of cure rather than punishment, nevertheless notes that 'though the criminal might be compassionated, it would still be necessary to deprive him of no power of doing further mischief' (1876: 27).

34 Beirne (1993) notes the ways in which this seemingly paradoxical relation between free will and determinism is very much part of the emergence of thinking on crime and crucial to the development of criminology. It also suggests that the weary classical versus positivism distinction is by no means as clear-cut as most introductory criminology texts would have readers believe.

35 Thus Wontner (1833: Chapter VI) argues for the combination of both 'prison discipline' and 'secondary punishment', for dealing with habitual offenders (see p. 286) before (prevention) and after the commission of offences.

36 See Rafter (1997, 2005) and Pick (1989) for overviews of how phrenology tended to view criminals. See Barrett and Harrison (1999: 317ff.) for some original sources on phrenology and crime. Gould (1981) provides a useful overview of phrenology's contributions to 'craniology' and the ensuing 'sciences of man'.

37 Burt too justifies Pentonville prison's use of the separate (Philadelphia) system of confinement. He speaks of the 'depraved passions and lawless aims which possess the

habitual criminal' as meriting 'separate imprisonment' so that 'it breaks off . . . the former habit of thought and feeling' (1852: 49).

38 Colquhoun (1800: 311) articulates the point explicitly when noting that criminal habits are 'peculiar to the lower orders of the Community in the great Metropolis'.

39 As he puts it, if 'lower ranks of society could be gradually led into better habits, much benefit would arise to the State' (1800: 327).

40 See Carpenter (1864: 10) for a parallel discussion on the 'formed habit of crime'.

41 See Foucault's (1977) classic discussion of such developments.

42 See Pick (1989).

43 See Ellis (1890), and Rafter's (1997) analyses of such developments. Also, the influential and controversial Sir Edmond Du Cane (see Radzinowicz and Hood (1990: 526–31) for more on his life and views), in 1895 formulated the essence of the habitual criminal in these atavistic terms:

> [E]ntirely those of the inferior races of mankind – wandering habits, utter laziness, absence of forethought or provision, want of moral sense, cunning, dirt, and instances may be found in which their physical characteristics approach those of lower animals so that they seem to be going back to the type of what Professor Darwin calls 'our arboreal ancestors'.
>
> (quoted in Wiener, 1994: 301)

44 This claim refers to Farmer's (2000) analysis of an under-researched topic – the codification of criminal law in nineteenth-century Britain. This gradually evolving codification only emphasizes the contingent creation of the criminal identity that the present chapter has sought to develop within the context of the habitual criminal.

45 Pike describes the contingent nature of definitions of crime thus:

> Crime . . . is that which the law declares to be crime, or for which the state recognizes a punishment, at any period over which the history extends. The meaning of the term necessarily varies with the laws at various times, but can at any time be determined by reference to the laws which are in force.
>
> (Pike, 1873: 490)

46 See Ellis (1890) who in Chapter 1 describes the various types of criminal; the habitual criminal is assumed and provides the assumptive framework for his elaborations. The latter draw extensively on images of a criminal class, character (physiognomy) and habit.

47 See Smart (1989, 1995), Young (1990) and Naffine (1996).

48 For example, Galton, Ellis, and Goring – see Beirne (1993: 193–213).

49 See Wetzell (2000) for a comparative analysis of the 'invention' of the criminal in German criminological discourses.

References

Ayto, J. (1990). *Dictionary of Word Origins.* New York: Arcade Publishing.

Barrett, A., & Harrison, C. (eds). (1999). *Crime and Punishment in England: A Sourcebook.* London: Routledge.

Beier, A. L. (2005). Identity, language and resistance in the making of the Victorian 'criminal class'. *Journal of British Studies*, 44(3), 499–516.

Beirne, P. (1993). *Inventing Criminology: Essays on the Rise of* Homo Criminalis. New York: State University of New York Press.

Bentham, J. (1962). 'Of indirect means of preventing crimes', in *The Works of Jeremy Bentham*. New York: Russell & Russell Inc., pp. 533–59.
Bertillon, A. (1977). *Alphonse Bertillon's Instructions for Taking Descriptions for the Identification of Criminals, and Others.* New York: AMS Press.
Blackstone, W. (1820). Sir William Blackstone's commentaries on the law and constitution of England: abridged for the use of students, and adapted to modern statutes and decisions. *The Making of Modern Law*, Thomson Gale (access date: March 4, 2006).
Broekmann, A. (1995). *A Visual Economy of Individuals: The Use of Portrait Photography in the Nineteenth-Century Human Sciences.* Unpublished PhD thesis. University of East Anglia.
Burt, J. T. (1852). Results of the system of separate confinement as administered at the Pentonville Prison. *The Making of Modern Law*, Thomson Gale (access date: April 28, 2006).
Carpenter, M. (1857). On the importance of statistics to the reformatory movement, with returns from female reformatories, and remarks on them. *Journal of the Statistical Society of London*, 20(1), 33–40.
——. (1864). Our Convicts. Vol. 1. *The Making of Modern Law*, Thomson Gale (access date: January 3, 2006).
Christian, E. (1819). Charges delivered to grand juries in the Isle of Ely, upon libels, vagrants, criminal law, religion, rebellious assemblies, &c., &c.: for the use of magistrates and students of the law, with large additions. *The Making of Modern Law*, Thomson Gale (access date: January 8, 2007).
Clavering, H. (1808). The new and complete parish officer, or a perfect guide to churchwork, overseers, constables, headboroughs, tithingmen . . . . *The Making of Modern Law*, Thomson Gale (cited March 7, 2007).
Colquhoun, P. (1800). A treatise on the police of the metropolis: containing detail of the various crimes and misdemeanours by which public and private property and security are, at present, injured and endangered and suggesting remedies for their prevention. *The Making of Modern Law*, Thomson Gale (access date: August 8, 2006).
Combe, G. (1854). Remarks on the principles of criminal legislation, and the practice of prison discipline. *The Making of Modern Law*, Thomson Gale (access date: June 6, 2006).
Cox, E. W., & Saunders, T. W. (1869). The criminal law consolidation acts: with notes on cases decided on their construction. *The Making of Modern Law*, Thomson Gale (access date: April 28, 2006).
Du Cane, E. F. (1882). An account of the manner in which sentences of penal servitude are carried out in England. *The Making of Modern Law*, Thomson Gale (access date: January 7, 2007).
Ellis, H. (1890). *The Criminal.* London: Walter Scott.
Emsley, C. (1996). *Crime and Society in England, 1750–1900* (2nd edn). Themes in British Social History. London: Longman.
Farmer, L. (2000). Reconstructing the English codification debate: the criminal law commissioners, 1833–45. *Law and History Review*, 18(2), 397–425.
Foucault, M. (1973). *The Order of Things: An Archaeology of the Human Sciences.* New York: Vintage Books.
——. (1977). *Discipline and Punish: The Birth of the Prison.* New York: Pantheon Books.
Galton, F. (1879). Composite portraits, made by combining those of many different persons into a singular resultant figure. *Journal of the Anthropological Institute of Great Britain and Ireland*, 8, 132–44.

——. (1890). Criminal anthropology. *Nature*, 42(1073), 75–6.

——. Identification by fingertips. *Nineteenth Century*, 30(1891), 303–11.

Gould, S. J. (1981). *The Mismeasure of Man* (1st edn). New York: Norton.

Great Britain, House of Commons. (1827). Report from the Select Committee on Criminal Commitments and Convictions. House of Commons Parliamentary Papers Online, ProQuest.

——. (1838). Report from the Select Committee on Transportation. *House of Commons Parliamentary Papers Online*, ProQuest.

Greenwood, J. (1869). The seven curses of London. *The Making of Modern Law*, Thomson Gale (access date: April 28, 2006).

Haney, C. (1982). Criminal justice and the nineteenth-century paradigm: the triumph of psychological individualism in the 'formative era'. *Law and Human Behaviour*, 6(3/4), 191–235.

Harding, C. (1988). 'The inevitable end of a discredited system?' The origins of the Gladstone Committee Report on Prisons, 1895. *The Historical Journal*, 31(3), 591–608.

Hibbert, C. (1963). *The Roots of Evil: A Social History of Crime and Punishment.* Gloucestershire: Sutton Publishing.

Hill, M. D. (1857). Suggestions for the repression of crime: contained in charges delivered to grand juries of Birmingham. *The Making of Modern Law*, Thomson Gale (access date: March 23, 2006).

Hitchcock, T., & Shoemaker, R. B. (2006). *Tales from the Hanging Court.* London: Hodder Arnold.

Jones, H. S. (2000). *Victorian Political Thought.* London: Macmillan Press.

Kuhn, T. S. (1968). *The Structure of Scientific Revolutions/Thomas S. Kuhn.* Chicago, IL: The University of Chicago Press.

Lacey, N. (2001). In search of the responsible subject: history, philosophy and social sciences in criminal law theory. *The Modern Law Review*, 64(3), 350–71.

Lavater, J. C. (1800). Physiognomy; or the corresponding analogy between the conformation of the features, and the ruling passions of the mind English Short Title Catalogue. *The Making of Modern Law*, Thomson Gale (access date: February 12, 2007).

Lee, W. L. M. (1901). *A History of Police in England.* London: Methuen.

Mahood, L. (1990). *The Magdelenes: Prostitution in the Nineteenth Century.* London: Routledge.

Maitland, F. W. (1880). The relation of punishment to temptation. *Mind*, 5(18), 259–64.

Maudsley, H. (1876). Responsibility in mental disease. *The Making of Modern Law*, Thomson Gale (access date: July 5, 2006).

Mayhew, H. (1856). The great world of London. *The Making of Modern Law*, Thomson Gale (access date: April 5, 2006).

——. (1868). *London Labour and the London Poor.* New York: Dover.

——. (1998). *The Victorian Underworld.* Donald Serrell Thomas (ed.). New York: New York University Press.

Mayhew, H., & Binny, J. (1862). The criminal prisons of London and scenes of prison life. *The Making of Modern Law*, Thomson Gale (access date: May 5, 2006).

Naffine, N. (1996). *Feminism and Criminology.* Philadelphia, PA: Temple University Press.

Pavlich, G. (2000). *Critique and Radical Discourses on Crime.* Aldershot: Ashgate.

Pick, D. (1989). *Faces of Degeneration: A European Disorder, c.1848–c.1918.* Cambridge: Cambridge University Press.

Pike, L. O. (1873). A history of crime in England: illustrating the changes of the laws in the progress of civilisation: written from the public records and other contemporary evidence. Vol. 1. *The Making of Modern Law*, Thomson Gale (access date: April 28, 2006).

Plint, T. (1851). Crime in England: its relation, character, and extent, as developed from 1801 to 1848. *The Making of Modern Law*, Thomson Gale (access date: April 28, 2006).

Pratt, J., & Dickson, M. (1997). Dangerous, inadequate, invisible, out: episodes in the criminological career of habitual criminals. *Theoretical Criminology*, 1(3), 363–84.

Radzinowicz, L., & Hood, R. G. (1990). *The Emergence of Penal Policy in Victorian and Edwardian England. Vol. 5, A History of English Criminal Law and Its Administration from 1750.* Oxford: Clarendon Press.

Rafter, N. H. (1997). *Creating Born Criminals.* Urbana, IL: University of Illinois Press.

—— (2005). The murderous Dutch fiddler: criminology, history and the problem of phrenology. *Theoretical Criminology*, 9(1), 65–96.

Rock, P. E. (1994). *History of Criminology.* Aldershot: Dartmouth, Pub. Co.

Roscoe, W. (1819). Observations on penal jurisprudence and the reformation of criminals: With an appendix, containing the latest reports of the state-prisons or penitentiaries of Philadelphia, New York, and Massachusettes, and other documents. *The Making of Modern Law*, Thomson Gale (access date: March 30, 2006).

Sampson, M. (1846). Rationale of crime, and its appropriate treatment: being a treatise on criminal jurisprudence considered in relation to a cerebral organization. *The Making of Modern Law*, Thomson Gale (access date: April 17, 2006).

Sekula, A. (1986). The body and the archive. *October*, 39, 3–64.

Shaw-Lefevre, C. (1839). Royal Commission on establishing efficient constabulary force in Counties of England and Wales, First Report. *House of Commons Parliamentary Papers Online*, ProQuest.

Smart, C. (1989). *Feminism and the Power of Law.* London: Routledge.

——. (1995). *Law, Crime and Sexuality: Essays in Feminism.* London: SAGE.

Spearman, E. (1894 [1999]). 'Identifying suspects, 1894', in A. Barrett & C. Harrison (eds), *Crime and Punishment in England: A Sourcebook.* London: Routledge, pp. 256–7.

Starkie, T. (1828). A practical treatise on the law of evidence: and digest of proofs in civil and criminal proceedings: with reference to American decisions. *The Making of Modern Law*, Thomson Gale (access date: March 3, 2007).

Symons, J. C. (1849). Tactics for the times: as regards the condition and treatment of the dangerous classes. *The Making of Modern Law*, Thomson Gale (access date: February 5, 2006).

Thomas, D. (1998). *The Victorian Underworld.* London: John Murray.

Thompson, E. P. (1975). *Whigs and Hunters: The Origin of the Black Act.* London: Allen Lane.

Thomson, J. (1801). An enquiry, concerning the liberty, and licentiousness of the press, and the uncontroulable nature of the human mind: containing an investigation of the right which government have to controul the free expression of public opinion, addressed to the people of the U. States. *The Making of Modern Law*, Thomson Gale (access date: March 3, 2007).

Tobias, J. J. (1967). *Crime and Industrial Society in the 19th Century.* London: Batsford.

——. (1972). *Nineteenth-century Crime in England: Prevention and Punishment.* New York: Barnes and Noble.

Troup, C. E. (1893–4). Dept. Committee to inquire into the best means for identifying habitual criminals. Report, minutes of evidence, appendices. *House of Commons Parliamentary Papers Online*, ProQuest.

Wakefield, E. G. (1831). Facts relating to the punishment of death in the metropolis. *The Making of Modern Law*, Thomson Gale (access date: February 14, 2007).

Walkowitz, J. (1992). *City of Dreadful Delight*. Chicago, IL: The University of Chicago Press.

Wetherell, J. (1871). Habitual Criminals Act. *The Times*, July 7, p. 12.

Wetzell, R. F. (2000). *Inventing the Criminal: A History of German Criminology, 1880–1945*. Chapel Hill, NV: University of North Carolina Press.

Wiener, M. (1994). *Reconstructing the Criminal: Culture, Law, and Policy in England, 1830–1914*. Cambridge: Cambridge University Press.

Wontner, T. (1833). Old Bailey experience: criminal jurisprudence and the actual working of our penal code of laws: also, an essay on prison discipline, to which is added a history of the crimes committed by offenders in the present day. *The Making of Modern Law*, Thomson Gale (access date: February 5, 2006).

Young, A. (1990). *Femininity in Dissent*. London: Routledge.

——. (1996). *Imagining Crime: Textual Outlaws and Criminal Conversations*. London: SAGE.

The Times Editorials,

'What is an 'Habitual Criminal?' *The Times*, March 10, 1869, p. 9.

'Habitual Criminals Acts was passed.' *The Times*, April 16, 1870, p. 9.

'Our Criminals.' *The Times*, March 30, 1861, p. 7.

Chapter 11

The subjects of criminal identification

Accusing someone of a crime based on scientific evidence might seem perfectly ordinary nowadays, but this is a relatively recent phenomenon. Even murder ('killing'), for instance, had long depended on, as Gaskill (2000: 242) puts it, 'people passing information to unpaid, untrained law officers, or what together they gleaned from pretrial investigations conducted informally in the community'. By the late eighteenth century, however, a 'judicial insistence' on 'higher evidential standards' encouraged 'more thorough investigative methods'. Testimony from community members was surpassed by 'the development of detective policing and the routine presentation of forensic medical evidence by expert witnesses' (2000: 242). Throughout the nineteenth century, 'science' – rather than inquisitorial or religious procedures – was increasingly called upon to validate accusations and, amid fears of rising crime waves, to identify criminals (Radzinowicz & Hood, 1990). As seen in the previous chapter, This was especially so where persistent criminals were distinguished as incorrigible delinquents that collectively formed a discrete 'criminal class' with debased habits of character.[1] Those habits were said to render them 'habitually criminal', requiring special control measures, including precise identification methods.

Taking its cue from these developments, this chapter focuses on a late nineteenth-century regulatory ethos in England that called for a 'science' of criminal identification. It examines specifically the influential contributions of Alphonse Bertillon's techniques for measuring bodies and Francis Galton's composite portraiture. The argument begins with a brief outline of the administrative 'problem' to which their 'scientific' criminal identification technologies responded. Thereafter, it draws on selected science study debates[2] to describe key differences in the techniques and visions of 'science' respectively embraced by the two men. By emphasizing the significance of these differences, the discussion discerns unique dangers associated with each approach. On the one hand, Bertillon's anthropometry troublingly, if unintentionally, promotes the narrow view that merely identifying (punishing or rehabilitating) individual criminals justly deals with crime. On the other, Galton's search for a 'criminal type' involves an exclusive (eugenic) science of others born from dangerous imperialist, class-based, sexist and racist prejudices of his time. Despite the proliferation of new criminal identification techniques (DNA 'fingerprinting' or profiling, genetic typing, behavioural genetics, neuroscientific imaging, etc.), the two distinctive dangers associated with Bertillon and Galton continue to plague attempts either to trace, or foretell, criminal individuals (Cole, 2001: 48ff.).[3] In turn, their persistence is implicated in the cultural, political and social practices that currently sustain an undemocratic 'crime complex' (Garland, 2001) that instinctively 'governs through crime' (Simon, 2007).

Without denying the importance of resorting to criminal identification in some circumstances, I argue that current compulsions to identify individual criminals, or criminal types, have inordinately constrained attempts to consider other – more democratic – ways to govern harmful behaviour. As Simon (2007: 4) rightly observes, 'Crime has become so central to the exercise of authority in America, by everyone from the president of the United States to the classroom teacher, that it will take a concerted effort . . . to dislodge it'. Resonant with critical criminology's search for inclusive ways to govern,[4] that resists creating 'criminals' as a reflex response to harmful action, the following analysis urges that criminal identification be considered for what it is: a sociopolitical *creation*, not an impartial *discovery*. By so doing, it suggests a way to re-politicize current practices of criminalization, challenge the legitimacy accorded to supposedly neutral criminal identification practices and explore techniques of just governance beyond the exclusionary impulse to create criminals.

Identifying 'habitual criminals': an administrative solution of sorts

Depicting a regulatory context that fostered scientifically inspired criminal identification technologies in late nineteenth-century England is no small undertaking. Without pretending to do that here, or denying parallel developments in other countries,[5] this section briefly outlines a particular administrative ethos in which Bertillon and Galton were seen to offer credible 'solutions'. In England, as discussed in more detail in Chapter 10, early criminal identification efforts were generally directed to the 'problem' of the 'habitual criminal'. This figure was officially recognized in the late 1830s by a *British Parliament Select Committee Report on Transportation*; it described 'habitual criminals' as repeat offenders in need of special regulatory attention (Great Britain, 1838: xx). Over a decade later, Mayhew and Binny's taxonomic study further differentiated 'habitual criminals' from 'casual', 'occasional', 'accidental' offenders or law-abiding citizens (Mayhew & Binny, 1856: 88). As the shadowy outlines of this emerging concept congealed into a veritable being, its popular meaning suggested a distinct group needing particular controls. In November 1860, *The Times* newspaper noted that 'With regard to men habitually addicted to crime, who make a trade of it, and who are lost to shame, all light punishments are nonsensical.' It urged 'long sentences on habitual criminals' noting that, 'where offenders belong to the class of incorrigible delinquents they are formidable and dangerous to mix with others'.[6]

By 1864, concerns about this 'habitual criminal' spurred the maintenance of basic records and photographs of all imprisoned offenders (Spearman, 1999[1894]). Some five years later, new laws appeared. *The Habitual Criminals Act, 1869* and *The Prevention of Crimes Act, 1871* required that all habitual criminals be recorded and identified (Radzinowicz & Hood, 1990: 261ff.). Also, elaborate personal recognition systems surfaced; for example, people remanded to Holloway Prison were, 'inspected by detectives and warders from other Metropolitan prisons to see if they can be identified as old offenders' (Spearman, 1999[1894]: 256). This practice was resource intensive, with numerous enforcers having to dedicate considerable time to the operation: 'thirty police officers from various quarters of London visit Holloway Prison three times a week', noted a contemporary observer, who also calculated that about an average of 'ninety hours' was required for 'each identification' (Spearman, 1999[1894]: 257). In response to these identification systems, many candidates for the habitual criminal label – with its harsher punishments – assumed false names, new appearances and worked across jurisdictions to defy detection (Wiener, 1994: 300–6; Cole, 2001: 12–16). Their apparent success was of considerable administrative concern and led an important Parliamentary Committee to call for

> a means of classifying the records of habitual criminals, such that as soon as the particulars of the personality of any prisoner (whether description, measurements, marks, or photographs) are received, it may be possible to ascertain readily, and with certainty, whether his case is in the register, and if so, who he is.
>
> (quoted in Spearman, 1999[1894]: 257)

And science was seen as the best means for so doing. Yet, from the outset, administrators ambiguously enlisted science to identify both specific recidivists and potential habitual criminals. As Cole (2001: 3) puts it, 'the search for a way to identify criminals retrospectively . . . remained closely bound up with the search for a way to identify criminal potentiality, by finding some visible biological marker of latent criminality'. So, on the one hand, an applied science promised a precise measurement system to detect repeat offenders. On the other, senior administrators called for a more basic science to discover unique features of those individuals with a predilection for crime. For example, the influential Director for Prisons in Britain, Edmund Du Cane, argued that crime should be tracked to its 'source' to prevent its future occurrence (Du Cane, 1882).[7] He speculated that 'the hereditary disposition' would become 'one of the most important' such sources (quoted in Galton, 1879a: 143), and offered Galton access to prison populations to develop his promising research on composite photography. In this administrative context, two distinctive criminal identification technologies surfaced as plausible responses – one adapted from France, the other homegrown (see Troup, 1893–4).

Two techniques for identifying criminals

Bertillon, clerk and later Director of the Identification Bureau of the Paris Prefecture of Police, created the first widely used identification system (Bertillon, 1977; see also Rhodes, 1968). Influenced by his father's anthropological research on individual-specific elements of human skeletons, the young Bertillon sought uniform ways to photograph, describe and measure distinctive facets of individual criminal bodies. For example, he standardized procedures for photographing criminals (Thomas, 1999: 121), and ways to narrate unique bodily features through *portrait parlé*, or 'speaking likeness' (Sekula, 1986: 30). His system required trained technicians, standard instruments and uniform techniques to measure bodies, avoiding the 'subjective' mistakes of untrained police officers, prison wardens and spies.

As is well known, the photographs, descriptions and measurements were carefully recorded onto cards using standard notations (Cole, 2001: 32–59; Sengoopta, 2003: 9–36). Anthropometry started with primary measurements of skeletal structures that – he argued – did not change after the age of 20 (e.g., head width, head length, cubit, etc.). Each primary measure was classed as, say, small, medium or large. So, a person's head width might be classed as small, head length medium, cubit large and so on. Filing clerks filed completed cards at a unique place within a specially arranged system; for Bertillon, the retrievable card guarded 'the trace of the real, actual presence of the person' and provided 'proof of identity' (in Thomas, 1999: 122). By the late 1890s, his techniques were refined and adopted in France, as well as other parts of the world (Rhodes, 1968).[8]

Around the same time, Francis Galton (Charles Darwin's cousin) proposed another criminal identification technology.[9] He worked from two basic assumptions. First, science could be used to discover hereditary 'pure types' of human species just as it did, say, different tree species (Galton, 1879b). These types would enable one to identify individual species members and typical behaviour patterns – for example, an elm tree is identifiable from generic images of that type of tree and, like other members of the species, behaves in typical ways (e.g., withstands low temperatures). Second, he assumed hereditary 'habitual criminals' comprise a discrete human species and bemoaned the 'unhappy fact' that 'fairly distinct types of criminal breeding true to their kind have become established, and are one of the saddest disfigurements of modern civilization' (1883: 15). He actively pursued ways to capture a generic type of this habitual criminal species. While praising Quetelet's innovative 'social mechanics' for its use of statistical means to typify a group (especially his concept of the 'average man', see Beirne, 1993: 75–92), Galton felt that averages could never precisely represent types. He thus turned to photography to provide mechanically precise images of this 'generic type' (Galton, 1878, 1879b).

With Du Cane's help, he photographed similarly sized and scaled faces of men convicted of murder, manslaughter and violent robbery. Aligned on one side of a special apparatus (Figure 11.1), each portrait was equally exposed to one photographic plate (Figure 11.2) to produce a 'composite' photograph of all portraits (Figure 11.3).

Figure 11.1 Aligned portrait (Galton, 1879a: 133)

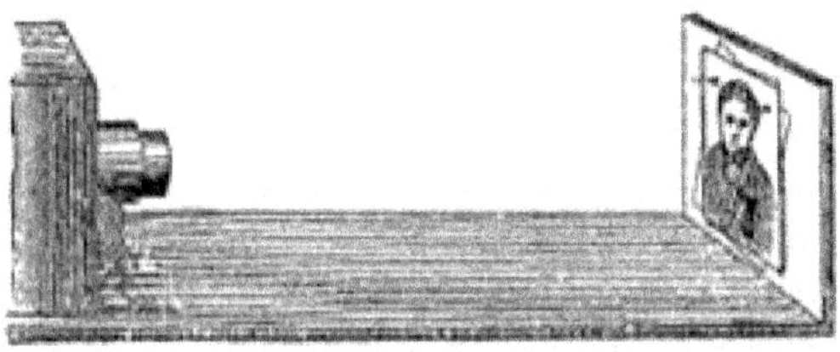

Figure 11.2 Galton's apparatus for creating composite portraits (Galton, 1879a: 134)

Figure 11.3 Francis Galton: composite portraits of 'criminals' (1885)

(with permission, Galton Archive, University College London)

Galton (1879a: 132–3) immodestly claimed that the composite portrait

> enables us to obtain with mechanical precision a generalized picture; one that represents no man in particular, but portrays an imaginary figure possessing the average features of any given group of men. Nobody who glanced at one of them for the first time, would doubt its being the likeness of a living person, yet . . . it is no such thing; it is the portrait of a type and not of an individual.

The aspiration here is clear: by representing a generic type of habitual criminal species, one could identify individual members and predict their inherited behaviour patterns (Galton, 1879b).

Two criminal identification sciences

Galton's techniques differed markedly from Bertillon's measurements, and unsurprisingly they appropriated quite different images of 'science'. In analysing their visual effects, Sekula (1986: 18) differentiates anthropometry as a technical science ('criminalistics') from Galton's basic 'criminological' science. Although it is crucial to distinguish their appropriations of science, Sekula's terminology is anachronistic: when Bertillon and Galton devised these technologies, neither 'criminalistics' nor 'criminology' provided established discursive platforms. This oversight eclipses the sway of other discourses – for example, physical anthropology and Spencer's social Darwinism (Broekmann, 1995) – on their ideas; it might also explain Sekula's curious inattention to the imperialist, civilizing and racist discursive backdrop on which criminal identification sciences surfaced (Hutchings, 2001). Not by coincidence Bertillon named 'signaletics' anthropometry, and Galton served a four-year presidency for the *Anthropological Society* (Forrest, 1974: 207, 180–3). Sharing an interest in scientifically studying 'others', both piggybacked on established discourses to assert scientific pretensions (Cole, 2001: 57).

Bertillon did so literally, claiming to further anthropology's 'systematic study of the physical signs of uniqueness' (Valier, 2004: 29). By contrast, Galton urged anthropologists to detect character from physiognomy (Forrest, 1974: 138). He insisted that 'intellectual and moral gifts are as strictly matters of inheritance as any purely physical qualities' (Galton, 1872: 176), and thus called on science to investigate '"problems" of inheritance and anthropometry informed by Darwinism' (Pick, 1989: 199). Both their sciences, however, emerged from imperial discursive contexts that championed concepts such as precision and measurement, but also savagery, purity, social evolution, civilization, racial inferiority and progress (Jackson & Weidman, 2004). It is worth keeping this in mind when examining Bertillon and Galton's different conceptions of science.

Bertillon's science: transcribing bodies

Bertillon's science created uniform ways to transcribe, classify and retrospectively identify a specific body (Sengoopta, 2003). As Thomas (1999: 223) succinctly writes, he assumed that, 'the body betrays the truth about the criminal in the form of an automatic anatomical writing that is legible to the trained expert'. Moreover, as Sekula (1986: 30) adds: 'For Bertillon, the criminal body expressed nothing. No characterological secrets were hidden beneath the surface of this body. Rather, the surface and the skeleton were indices of a more strictly material sort.' As a science, anthropometry merely claimed a technical capacity to measure precisely static body surfaces, record its results uniformly and develop effective filing systems. The emphasis on exact measurement, uniform taxonomy and systematic retrieval made overtures toward ordinary science, but never pledged to verify general theory by observing individual cases (Ginzburg, 1979). The archived cards served as filters through which all individuals could pass, except the habitual criminal. The real identities of bodies could be transcribed – sometimes coercively (Valier, 2004: 30) – into the language of 'signaletics'. This transcription reduced 'human identity to a language of notation which could be organized and accessed at will' (Cole, 2001: 49). Anthropometry captured raw corporeality using the standard taxonomies of signaletics; these enabled comparisons between new cases and previously recorded cards. The filed cards were treated as the Archimedean reference points of a notated language that was impervious to the deceptions of habitual criminals in search of lighter punishments. The science lay in the details – calliper-assisted measurements, uniform transcriptions and methodically filed taxonomies designed to identify individuals with calibrated accuracy. Bertillon's approach lies behind much current criminal identification thinking, and has been expanded through a battery of forensic sciences that are now standard elements of law enforcement practices (Saferstein, 2004). Cole (2001) and Sengoopta (2003) show how his approach has contoured practices of fingerprinting as a law enforcement technique. However, as they imply, the influence is far greater, having helped to propagate an approach behind many criminal identification techniques that transcribe corporeality into data units (now mostly digital), and store transcriptions for later comparison to determine authentic individual identity. The logic of this approach is evident in all manner of forensic techniques (DNA extraction, CCTV monitoring with face recognition techniques, speech analysis, fingerprinting, etc.). Perhaps, most noteworthy, is the increasing emphasis criminal justice systems now place on DNA identification as a way to isolate individual identity (see Lazer, 2004), and the rising 'science' of face recognition that adds an important identification twist to the panoptic techniques that mark law enforcement through CCTV surveillance (Goold, 2004).

Specifically, for example, Bertillon's approach belies DNA identification techniques where the identity of a particular 'criminal' – rather than a type – is sought. Here, tissue samples are collected from a crime scene, and chemical or physical methods are used to remove intact DNA molecules (see Lazer, 2004: 28ff.). Next, DNA molecules from areas of the genome statistically identified as having 'stable inherited variation' (Lazer, 2004: 29) – are 'amplified' (e.g., through polymerase chain reactions) to ensure sufficient 'material' for analysis. The base-pair sequences of the DNA are then 'captured' digitally, and compared with digital DNA databases, or samples taken from individuals, to determine a statistically probable match (Wasserman & Wachbroit, 2001). Such techniques clearly differ from Bertillon's measurements but the underlying quest to reduce individual identity to a notational classification system remains constant. As Cole (2001: 49) insightfully observes:

> It is the same quest that has grounded the technology of criminal identification through the present day. What, after all, is DNA identification, if not the reduction of complete identities to sentences expressed in the specialized four-letter language (A,G,T,C) of genetics?

In a similar fashion, one could note the ghost of anthropometry behind the rising forensic 'science' that makes use of CCTV surveillance to identify criminals by means of digital 'face recognition'. The technical obstacles to, and gains of, this new technology are outlined in Zhao *et al.*'s (2003) review of that literature. Here, one finds Bertillon's basic approach – capturing an individual's unique features in standard ways and comparing these to a standardized database to determine identity – in a digital form. The binary sequences that produce CCTV images of a face (say, near a crime scene) are isolated and enhanced. These are then compared with digitized databases of 'facial images' to 'recognize' identity. Again, despite vastly different technologies, the aspiration to isolate scientifically and identify an individual criminal by comparing a captured measure (digital sequence) to a pre-existing database replicates Bertillon's anthropometric logic. It might be interesting to observe in passing that face recognition technologies also have the potential to intensify Foucault's (1977) disciplinary, panoptic gaze beyond corrective hierarchical surveillance into hyperreal, digital realms, where 'identification' enables governors to accumulate unprecedented quanta of governmental knowledge created, generated, analysed and reported digitally. Computer science in the service of Bertillon's anthropometric logic has intensified law enforcement through digital criminal identification (see Goold, 2004).

Galton's science of criminal types

Galton's early work on composites had other ambitions: science was to discover a generic type of the 'habitual criminal' species. He put it thus: 'I propose to speak of the study of those groups of men who are sufficiently similar in their mental characters or in their physiognomy, or in both, to admit of classification' (1877: 344). He wanted to 'learn how far the more obvious physical characteristics may be correlated with certain mental ones', adding that, 'The particular group of men I have in view are the criminals of England, who have been condemned to long terms of penal servitude for various heinous offences' (1877: 344). The 'obvious fact' that adverse circumstances propelled some criminals did not mean that 'the convict class' excludes many 'consummate scoundrels' with a 'prevalence of the truly criminal characteristics' (1877: 345). The 'ideal criminal', he continued, 'has three peculiarities of character; his conscience is almost deficient, his instincts are vicious, and his power of self-control is very weak' (1877: 346).

Weak self-control, he argued, is allied with 'ungovernable temper', 'passion' or 'mere imbecility'. However, the 'vicious instincts' and weak conscience are more complex. They are not mere 'perversions' because

> they may be strictly in accordance with the healthy nature of the man, and, being transmissible by inheritance, may become the normal characteristics of a healthy race, just as the sheep-dog, the retriever, the pointer, and the bull-dog have their several instincts
>
> (1877: 346)

Echoing criminal anthropology's pivotal theme, Galton (1877: 346, and 1883: 43) argued:

> A man who is counted as an atrocious criminal by society, and is punished as such by the law, may nevertheless have acted in strict accordance with his instincts. The ideal criminal is deficient in qualities that oppose his vicious instincts; he has neither the natural regard for others which lies at the base of conscience, nor has he sufficient self-control to enable him to consider his own selfish interests in the long run.

Galton urged anthropologists to research the 'life-history' of the 'criminal class' in order to investigate 'its perpetuation by heredity'. But he acknowledged the difficulties of the task, given the 'vagrant habits of the criminal classes, their illegitimate unions, and extreme untruthfulness' (1877: 347). Reviewing Ellis's (1890) criminal anthropology and its search for inborn criminal characteristics, Galton (1890: 76) seemingly applauded this aspiration:

> The hope of the criminal anthropologist is to increase the power of discriminating between the natural and the accidental criminal. He aims at being able to say with well-founded confidence of certain men that it is impossible to make them safe members of a free society by any reasonable amount of discipline . . . and must be locked up wholly out the way.

Several aspects of Galton's approach to science are worthy of note. First, unlike Bertillon, and gesturing toward physiognomy and phrenology, Galton's habitual criminal type made inferences about criminal character from physical appearance. His aim was not to isolate individuals from a mass, but to do exactly the opposite: represent the 'generic type' of a species by fusing the physiognomies of each member. As noted, he did not consider statistical averages up to the task because, 'The physiognomic difference between different men being so numerous and small, it is impossible to measure and compare them each to each, and to discover by ordinary statistical methods the true physiognomy of a race' (1883: 5).

By contrast, composite portraits pledged a robust 'statistical picture' of the type, representing as they did *all* members of a species.

This approach, however, is tautological: the members comprising Galton's generic type were defined in advance by juridical means. That is, instead of investigating whether a distinct species of 'habitual criminals' actually exists, Galton's science starts with 'known criminals', assuming the criminal justice system's labelling thereof. His scientific project was then of a second order, predicated on definitional work performed elsewhere. Its recursive logic allowed a significant ontological slip in which contingent juridical definitions of the 'criminal' unobtrusively reappear as the *de facto* members of the species that Galton's science set out to discern. While his composites no longer hold much sway, his underlying approach is replicated by current attempts to generate 'profiles' (generic?) of criminal types by studying groups already so defined (e.g., Hicks & Sales, 2006). The whole 'science' of criminal profiling rests upon this recursive logic, and yet claims a predictive capacity. The purpose of a criminal profile, like Galton's types, is to identify members of a species who will act in predictable ways – but it is worth repeating that the underlying identity is defined in advance of the science (Feeley & Simon, 1994).

Second, for Galton (1878, 1879a), scientific knowledge progresses only by discovering generic impressions of the world based on individual observations. He (1883: 229) marvelled at a human capacity to abstract generic ideas of, say, 'dogness' from 'blended memories' of individual dogs, enabling us to distinguish this cat from that dog. We form 'general impressions' from individual memories, just as composite portraits mechanically integrate individual cases into a pure generic type. The composites promised to operate as a 'perfect mind' (1883: 230), always creating 'vivid images of a truly generic kind, deduced from the whole range of past experiences' (1879b: 168–9). When a large enough composite portrait set provided a clear image with only slight distortions of image (the 'ghosts and shades' of variation), it could be said to capture a hereditary type of a species (Galton, 1878: 237). Although (as we shall see) his composite portraits never yielded such a criminal type, Galton continued to think that evidence of a hereditary corporeal type could be located (hence his later studies on fingerprinting), and that these would explain individual tendencies toward criminal behaviour.

Galton's quest for generic impressions continues partly to inspire 'biobehavioural' perspectives on criminal behaviour, as Fishbein's (2001) extensive review suggests (see also Hacking, 2006). Fishbein outlines how this approach seeks to uncover biological elements common to individuals who engage in criminal behaviour. A key assumption here is that '[a]ll human behaviour has a genetic component' but with the rider that 'the expression of genetic and biological traits can be modified by the environment' (Fishbein, 2001: 33). Some might argue that this 'softens' Galton's call for a generic type, but I would argue that it merely expands and includes more 'factors' (e.g., the 'environment') in developing a determining criminal profile (type). Now the determining generic species is to be discovered beyond physiognomy, out of a combination of genetic make-up, brain chemistry, brain activity, personality, socio-environmental conditions and so on. Various combinations of these factors are now isolated as the basis of a generic type that promises to predict a propensity for various sorts of criminal behaviour (see Jones, 2006: 100). Such perspectives expand Galton's corporeal thinking of the 'criminal type', and echo his faith that science could identify determining criminal profiles ('generic ideas') to foresee criminal behaviour (see also Greenspan, 2001; DeLisi & Conis, 2008).

Finally, Galton's later work framed ideas of a criminal race within a 'science' of eugenics – the 'science' that for him sought to improve 'the inborn qualities of a race' (Galton, 1904). Although Galton's identification research replaced composite photography with fingerprinting (Cole, 2001; Sengoopta, 2003), he continued to see the value of separating habitual criminals. As late as 1909 he wrote, 'Public opinion is beginning to regard with favour the project of a prolonged segregation of habitual criminals, for the purpose of restricting their opportunities for (1) continuing their depredations, and (2) producing low class offspring' (1909: 62).

He argued that eugenics could investigate such popular opinions in scientific ways by noting the habitual criminal's supposed 'degeneracy', and encouraging racial 'improvement' through managed social evolution (Pick, 1989: ch. 6). Working with the idea that a criminal type inherited 'savage' or 'childlike' instincts, Galton (1877: 346) framed his version of Lombroso's 'atavism': the habitual criminal acted in 'strict accordance with instincts' of people in 'less civilised societies' being an insufficiently evolved individual (1883: 43). The imputed 'degeneracy' of habitual criminals was Galton's reason for limiting opportunities for unfettered reproduction to secure viable evolutionary paths toward social improvement (Pick, 1989: 198).

Galton's search for a distinct criminal type proved to be a lasting element of British criminological thinking on criminal identification. As Davie (2005: 23) persuasively argues:

> The search for a distinctive criminal-type – for a set of physical and mental traits believed to be common to all criminals, or at least certain kinds of them – would in fact prove to be an enduring feature of British criminological discourse during the whole period from 1860–1918, despite wide-ranging changes to the socio-economic, political and intellectual climate in which this search was grounded, and despite the currency of comments expressing the precise opposite.

And that search is by no means dead (see Hacking, 2006; Rose, 2007).

However, we should recall Forrest's (1974) and Rabinow's (1996) caution that Galton never successfully identified a criminal type from physical appearance. A sufficiently committed scientist, he acknowledged that neither his early work on composite photographs, nor his later studies on fingerprints, produced any evidence that a generic criminal type could be detected from physiognomic representations. This is why, reflecting on the composite portraits of criminals, he observed that 'the features of the composites are much better looking than those of the components'. More specifically,

> the special villainous irregularities in the latter have disappeared, and the common humanity that underlies them has prevailed. They represent, not the criminal, *but the man who is liable to fall into crime.* All composites are better looking than their components, because the averaged portrait of many persons is free from the irregularities that variously blemish the looks of each of them
>
> (1879a: 135; emphasis added)

If colleagues at the Anthropological Institute were disappointed by what seemed like an admitted failure to discover a distinct criminal type (Forrest, 1974: 139), Galton salvaged an equally ostentatious project: *identifying from the normal (natural) population those people who are 'liable to fall into crime'*. That is, even if no pure habitual criminal type had yet been found, Galton felt it possible to identify a criminogenic nucleus within individuals of normal populations that inclines some, more than others, to commit criminal acts (Wiener, 1994: 253). His search for the pure criminal type was now to continue through a science seeking to discover factors that determine criminal propensity; namely, that which makes some people liable to a life of crime.

Galton's reframed approach, perhaps even more so than his quest for a generic, physiognomic criminal type, has influenced a range of probabilistically based 'sciences' that variously identify propensities (i.e., those 'liable') to engage in criminal behaviour. For example, various ways of defining that propensity include: risk-based profiles (e.g., Hicks & Sales, 2006: 157ff.), genetic markers (Wasserman & Wachbroit, 2001; DeLisi & Conis, 2008), biochemistry (Fishbein, 2001), personality (Fishbein, 2001), population heritability (Gibbard, 2001), predisposing neurological states (Jones, 2006) and so on. In each case, an individual's propensity to engage in criminal behaviour is framed via a probabilistic profile, an increased potential to, as Galton might have it, 'fall into crime'.

This sort of logic also at times operates through the previously noted law enforcement techniques – CCTV face recognition and DNA analysis. Now, however, both of these are enlisted for a unique purpose: to identify typical facial expressions/behaviours or genes that are associated with criminal behaviour. In such formulations, Galton's quest to isolate a physiognomy liable to commit crime is reframed through technological refinements, and an acknowledgement that the 'environmental context' often mediates individual determinations. These might even suggest a complex and mediated path – rather than absolute determination – from gene to criminal behaviour (see Rose, 2007: 224–51). Epigenetic formulations appear to complicate the determination even further.

However, these approaches do not, for the most part, escape Galton's overall impulse to infer criminality – one might say in the last instance – from underlying corporeal limits and causes (Duster, 2004; Jones, 2006: 100). To repeat a previous observation, the recognition of mediating (e.g., environmental) factors opens the way to an expanded scientific approach that seeks to uncover probabilities of criminal behaviour through the composite interaction of biological (genetics, neurological) and environmental factors (Cole, 2001; Fishbein, 2001; Lazer, 2004). In this regard, Hacking (2006: 83) rightly notes, Galton's framing presence is reconceived (not overturned) through criminal identification sciences: 'But not only Galton: the entire European tradition of criminal anthropology has been brought back to life, although few dare to mention it because it is thought to be as disreputable as Galton's eugenics.' The disrepute is well justified when one considers the exterminations, sterilizations and base exclusions born from eugenic logics (Pick, 1989; Rafter, 1997).

To reiterate, I have so far distinguished between two criminal identification technologies, and their accompanying versions of science, alluding to their foundational influence on two different genres of criminal identification. By focusing on the differences between these scientific approaches, this discussion adds to an existing literature that analyses the visual (Sekula, 1986), historical (Cole, 2001; Sengoopta, 2003), documentary (Caplan & Torpey, 2001), literary (Hutchings, 2001) and eugenic (Pick, 1989; Rafter, 1997; Valier, 2002) aspects of early criminal identification technologies. But it also insists that very different kinds of danger are associated with the respective versions of science.

Two-fold perils of criminal identification

Bertillon's anthropometric claim that criminal identification impartially 'captures' and/or 'retrieves' real identities betrays a unique danger. Of course, there might be occasions where criminal identification technologies avert harmful events, or prevent innocent people from being punished. However, the pervasive impulse to identify the criminal individual as a *primary* response to 'solving', or even 'preventing', crime, dangerously reduces complex sociopolitical and cultural matters to individual malady (Garland, 2001; Simon, 2007). As critical criminologists have noted, individuals are complexly involved in the intricate relational tapestries that produce crime (Taylor, Walter & Young, 1973; Hulsman, 1986). Without rehearsing these and subsequent debates, one could echo their basic question: what is eclipsed when governmental practices target individual criminals as *the* solution to an amorphous 'crime problem'?

For one thing, the prevalence of such practices discourages thought about other ways to govern the terrains at hand (see Chapter 7 in this volume; Simon, 2007). That is, underlying political processes involved in creating criminals are all but overlooked by a discourse narrowly confined to deciding scientifically which individual has committed what crime.[10] Under the guise of impartial scientific precision, these criminal identification technologies (e.g., DNA identification, face recognition) evade complex ethical questions surrounding crime, ignore their part in wider power–knowledge relations that fabricate criminal individuals, and help to entrench a view of crime as the *artefact of individual offenders.* Consequently, anthropometrically based approaches have tended to assume that identifying habitual perpetrators is key to preventing crime, overlooking the complex interplay between sociopolitical, economic and cultural structures, as well as the crime-creating relations between offenders, victims, police officers, judges and so on. Echoing the critical criminologists previously noted, this is a significant danger, because in the name of science, criminalistics perpetuates the sociopolitical status quo – however unjust it might be – by reducing the politics of crime to *individual* malady (Hulsman, 1986; Christie, 2004). It is now especially urgent – given the hegemonic hold of criminal identification – to broaden the politics of identification beyond the criminalist's restricted frame, and to consider wider power–knowledge formations that contour notions of otherness (Ratner, 2006).

By contrast, Galton's science of criminal identification is beset by dangers that many later criminological currents do not evade. For example, as described, his quest for generic types of habitual criminals involves an ontological slip that confuses its starting and ending points: the 'known criminals' contingently defined by criminal justice systems are taken as a priori beings with a scientifically discoverable essence. New versions of criminal typing (be they genetic, neurological, biosocial or psychological) also start with groups of 'known criminals' of one sort or another in efforts to discover salient factors that represent that group's generic make-up. What dangers lurk here? The aforementioned recursive logic at the base of this approach mysteriously accords the 'criminal' individual, as defined through criminalizing processes, the ontological status of a de facto being. In seeking to identify the determining essence of that 'being', the science of criminal 'types' merely elaborates upon a predetermined identity; it also deflects attention away from processes that create the latter. Concealed by this subtle move is the extent to which the identification of criminal types is contingent upon sociopolitical and ethical forces that spawn particular images of the criminal in the first place (Martel, Hogeveen & Woolford, 2006).

On a related note, Galton's views on the habitual criminal type betray a defence of the ethical prejudices born out of his social standing and the political times in which he lived. The idea of a 'savage', 'primeval' criminal type, with habitually unrestrained passions that thwart social advancement, reflects an historically situated vision of the other against (and through) which the gentleman's ethically infused identity is defined. The criminal type provides a direct contrast to Galton's implied ideal of the imperious, civilized, gentrified, normal man. It also reveals his moral prejudices against the passions of children, colonized people, women, and holds the 'civilized' Englishman as the most advanced specimen of the human race. When considered thus, despite Galton's claims to scientific neutrality, one could surely ask this question: in what possible way is his entire project *not* founded on sociopolitical and ethical claims?

An important lesson is embedded here: under the cloak of scientific neutrality key political and moral claims of a given day unobtrusively emerge as the unquestionable ontological categories for a 'science' of criminal identification.[11] Alleging that a habitual criminal type has this or that feature, without examining the ethics and politics that define criminals in the first place, reveals both the dangers and inordinate faith in a justice system's definitions. No doubt, an added leap of faith is required to describe that criminal 'type' as something inherited, discoverable and determining (even if probably so), to say nothing of the historically situated prejudices that frame such thinking. Placed at some historical distance, it is undemanding to unravel the gendered, racist and classist prejudices in Galton's texts, but this should only make us more vigilant of the biases embedded in now prevalent types, profiles and crime-prevention strategies. The root of this danger lies in the bald assumption that 'criminals' (or identifying profiles) constitute an ontological category; however, the criminal is always a contingent, ethico-political creature. We should keep in mind that 'labelling fashions' come and go, as do associated accusations of crime (Christie, 2004; see for instance Chapters 3–5 above), challenging the ontological standing of putative determinations, be they 'types', 'profiles', 'genes' or 'neurological images'.

Related to this danger one finds another: Galton's unequivocal endorsement of eugenics as a science leading to social advancement through 'pure' evolutionary paths. The English gentry's visions of 'pure' and 'superior' hereditary bloodlines flowing in themselves, and no doubt in their thoroughbred horses and hounds, provided the basic exemplar for this 'science'. Yet, from our historical vantage, a eugenic logic echoes through horrific atrocities of the past century: colonial eradications of indigenous lives, the gas chambers, enforced sterilizations of 'degenerates', 'ethnic cleansings' and repeated genocides (Childers & Caplan, 1993; Rafter, 1997). As Pick (1989) reminds us, this logic – even if its founders declared 'philanthropic' intentions (e.g., Galton, 1904) – always revolved around dangerous ideas of atavism, degeneracy, taint and purity. That logic proposed (anthropological and sociological) visions of advanced (civilized, European) societies evolutionarily stalled by the atavistic natures of born degenerates, who by positive (lineage mating) or negative (sterilization, extermination) means ought to be expunged to secure civilized progress. Again, behind these predictive logics lie historically specific prejudices masked as natural, largely invariable, determinations of who exactly needs to be neutralized, or eliminated, when pursuing progress of one kind or another (Jackson & Weidman, 2004). The extreme danger of such obfuscation is palpably evident from the sheer scale of the misery, bloodshed and killing purveyed in the name of eugenic science; surely, its well-known destructive potential must heighten our vigilance over any and all attempts to typify and neutralize others – whether somatypes, criminal genes, neurological structures, criminal personalities or at-risk profiles.

Highlighting these dangers – even if not comprehensive – indicates the different stakes of anthropometric and type-based sciences of criminal identification. But what do such dangers, in tandem, suggest? One proposal returns us to a basic critical criminological insight: the terrain of criminal identification, despite its neutral scientific pretensions, is a highly charged ethical and political realm. The embedded values of scientific views are consequential, and the hazards they have unleashed suggest why it is so important continuously to re-politicize justice terrains that remain silent on – especially under the guise of neutral identification – their ethico-political roots (O'Connor, 2007). But there is a real problem here: how does one re-evoke such fundamental critique in a social field that more often than not defines justice as the systematic identification and neutralization of criminal individuals, or criminogenic biosocial forces?

Creating criminals: ethico-political openings?

One possibility might be to re-engage a politics of criminal identification by unseating now prevalent visions of identification as a process of discovery. The latter view assumes that criminal identification – in both guises – merely discovers what is already there; the criminal or type exists *sui generis*, independently of the identification procedures that detect its being (however defined). Yet, as we have seen, techniques to identify various images of the habitual criminal are predicated upon prior (and contingent) definitions of criminality, subsequently elaborated upon with 'scientific precision'. Bertillon's datasets – images, *portrait parlé*, measurements (and later fingerprints) – never questioned the existence, or the social implications embedded in legal definitions, of habitual criminals. Anthropometry was content to exact transcriptions from body surfaces to identify the real criminal, and create its two-dimensional, notated representations of individual identity. Equally, Galton's composite photographs morphed multiple portraits of known criminals to produce a singular type. This generic type is certainly a creation, even if it *ex post facto* claims to represent a prior criminal species. In either case, a judicially defined 'habitual criminal' serves as the basis for scientific representations of individual criminals or types; the latter are scientific elaborations of contingent technologies that variously isolate, transcribe, classify and claim to identify predefined criminal subjects.

All this evinces the claim that criminal identification is a *creative process rather than one of discovery*; or, more precisely, criminal identification involves creating criminal identities under the guise of scientific discovery. It is constitutively involved in deploying the very identities it purports to discover; the 'known criminal' is both the starting and ending point of its various methods. Highlighting the contingent processes that produce given versions of the 'criminal' is, of course, hardly a novel idea (e.g., Hulsman, 1986; Beirne, 1993; Christie, 2004). However, by focusing attention on the duality at the heart of criminal identification sciences, one is able to isolate key dangers associated with current cultural and sociopolitical fields that orbit around disingenuous ontologies of criminal subjects. This focus also legitimates the search for ways to govern justly without exclusionary and fixed notions of the individual criminal or criminal type. That is, when examining the criminal identification terrain as a creative governmental venture (rather than one that discovers criminals), analysts can legitimately ask such basic questions as: why govern through crime in this case? Can a politics of justice extend beyond individual visions of crime? Can collective accusations be launched in the name of broader promises of justice? Is justice perverted or furthered by alleging distinctive criminal types? And whose justice creates images of others as criminal beings? Although difficult to conceive of in current climates, it might nevertheless be important to decentre a scientific emphasis on individual 'criminals', types, predictive profiles and the allied technologies of criminal identification. In its place, gesturing toward Christie (2004) and Simon (2007), one might return to talk of governing through crime as one of many possible, contingent (rather than necessary) techniques – even if favoured by specific political circumstances. No necessities demand that we cast criminal others as ontological beings; rather, criminals are always contingent creatures of context. Perhaps any semblance of 'enlightened maturity' in matters of criminal justice involves confronting the stark realization that precepts of justice, like all ethical matters, are by definition neither entirely resolvable, nor determined. If nothing else, this requires of ethical subjects more, not less, critical reckoning, reflection and modest decision making. It also obliges us, once again, to abandon the lazy comforts bestowed by that grandest of illusions: scientific impartiality.

Acknowledgements

The author would like to thank R. S. Ratner, Ros Sydie and two anonymous reviewers for their insightful comments on a previous version of this chapter. Erin Kruger and Rebecca Morrison provided helpful and appreciated research assistance.

Notes

1 Wiener (1994), Emsley (1996) and Davie (2005) describe the rise of this 'criminal class' and Radzinowicz and Hood (1990: 73–84) suggest its relation to earlier concepts of 'the dangerous classes' that flourished on the continent.
2 See especially Sekula (1986), Pick (1989), Wiener (1994), Cole (2001), Valier (2002) and Davie (2005).
3 As Hacking (2001: 143) notes, 'The structure, projects, and moral aims and ethical dilemmas of criminology have been remarkably constant for more than a century.'
4 See Pavlich (2000), Martel *et al.* (2006) and Ratner (2006).
5 Although there are consequential differences in criminal identification systems across contexts (France, Germany, the USA, Argentina, etc.), there are also significant parallels (see Caplan & Torpey, 2001; but also Rhodes, 1968; Beirne, 1993).
6 *The Times*, Monday 12 November 1860, p. 4, col. E, 'The Gaol of Newgate' – emphasis added.
7 For more on Du Cane's controversial life and influence at that time, see Radzinowicz and Hood (1990: 526–31).
8 Even though anthropometry was deployed to identify habitual criminals for harsher punishment, it should be noted that it also distinguished first-time offenders for less punitive measures.

9 Galton was well aware of Bertillon's work; he visited him in Paris, and in 1884 set up his own Anthropometric Laboratory in London (Forrest, 1974: 180, 209–10).

10 Whatever reservations one might have about restorative justice, some protagonists urge the opening of that compacted political terrain, seeking ways to govern less through 'crime', and looking for wider paths to justice (see Pavlich, 2005).

11 This is a more general issue that many social sciences face, as outlined by O'Connor (2007).

References

Beirne, P. (1993). *Inventing Criminology: Essays on the Rise of 'Homo Criminalis'*. New York: SUNY Press.

Bertillon, A. (1977). *Alphonse Bertillon's Instructions for Taking Descriptions for the Identification of Criminals, and Others.* New York: AMS Press.

Broekmann, A. (1995). *A Visual Economy of Individuals: The Use of Portrait Photography in the Nineteenth-century Human Sciences.* Unpublished PhD Thesis. Norwich: University of East Anglia.

Caplan, J., & Torpey, J. (eds). (2001). *Documenting Individual Identity: The Development of State Practices in the Modern World.* Princeton, NJ: Princeton University Press.

Childers, T., & Caplan, J. (eds). (1993). *Reevaluating the Third Reich.* New York: Holmes & Meier.

Christie, N. (2004). *A Suitable Amount of Crime.* Abingdon: Routledge.

Cole, S. A. (2001). *Suspect Identities: A History of Fingerprinting and Criminal Identification.* Cambridge, MA: Harvard University Press.

Davie, N. (2005). *Tracing the Criminal: The Rise of Scientific Criminology in Britain, 1960–1918.* Oxford: The Bardwell Press.

DeLisi, M., & Conis, P. G. (2008). *Violent Offenders: Theory, Research, Public Policy, and Practice.* Sudbury: Jones & Bartlett Publishers.

Du Cane, E. F. (1882). An account of the manner in which sentences of penal servitude are carried out in England. *The Making of Modern Law.* Retrieved from: www.gale.com/ModernLaw/ (access date: June 2007).

Duster, T. (2004). 'Selective arrests, an ever-expanding DNA forensic database, and the specter of early-twenty-first-century equivalent of phrenology', in D. Lazer (ed.), *DNA and the Criminal Justice System: The Technology of Justice.* Cambridge, MA: MIT Press, pp. 315–34.

Ellis, H. (1890). The criminal. *The Making of Modern Law.* Retrieved from: www.gale.com/ModernLaw/ (access date: July–August 2007).

Emsley, C. (1996). *Crime and Society in England, 1750–1900.* London: Longman.

Feeley, M., & Simon, J. (1994). 'Actuarial justice: the emerging new criminal law', in D. Nelken (ed.), *The Futures of Criminology.* London: SAGE, pp. 173–201.

Fishbein, D. (2001). *Biobehavioural Perspectives in Criminology.* Belmont, CA: Wadsworth.

Forrest, D. W. (1974). *Francis Galton: The Life and Work of a Victorian Genius.* New York: Taplinger Publishing Company.

Foucault, M. (1977). *Discipline and Punish: The Birth of the Prison.* New York: Pantheon Books.

Galton, F. (1872). Blood-relationship. *Nature*, 6 (27 June), 173–6. Retrieved from: www.galton.org.

——. (1877). Address by Francis Galton, FRS. *Nature*, 8(23 August), Section D, Anthropology section: 344–7. Retrieved from: www.galton.org.

——. (1878). *Composite Portraits*. London: Harrison & Sons, St Martin's Lane. Retrieved from: www.galton.org.

——. (1879a). Composite portraits, made by combining those of many different persons into a singular resultant figure. *Journal of the Anthropological Institute of Great Britain and Ireland*, 8, 132–44. Retrieved from: www.galton.org.

——. (1879b). Generic images. *Nineteenth Century*, 6 (6 July), 157–69. Retrieved from: www.galton.org.

——. (1883). *Inquiries into Human Faculty and Its Development*. New York: MacMillan & Co. Retrieved from: www.galton.org.

——. (1890). Criminal anthropology. *Nature*, 42 (22 May), 75–6. Retrieved from: www.galton.org.

——. (1904). Eugenics: its definition, scope and aims. *American Journal of Sociology*, X (26 May), 28. Retrieved from: www.galton.org.

——. (1909). *Essays in Eugenics*. Retrieved from: www.galton.org. (access date: December 5, 2007).

Garland, D. (2001). *The Culture of Crime Control: Crime and Social Order in Contemporary Society*. Chicago, IL: University of Chicago Press.

Gaskill, M. (2000). *Crime and Mentalities in Early Modern England*. Cambridge: Cambridge University Press.

Gibbard, A. (2001). 'Genetic plans, genetic difference, and violence: some chief possibilities', in D. Wasserman & R. S. Wachbroit (eds), *Genetics and Criminal Behavior*. New York: Cambridge University Press, pp. 169–97.

Ginzburg, C. (1979). Clues: the roots of a scientific paradigm. *Theory and Society*, 7(3), 273–88.

Goold, B. J. (2004). *CCTV and Policing: Public Area Surveillance and Police Practices in Britain*. Oxford: Oxford University Press.

Great Britain, House of Commons. (1838). Report from the Select Committee on Transportation. *House of Commons Parliamentary Papers Online*, ProQuest.

Greenspan, P. S. (2001). 'Genes, electrotransmitters and free will', in D. Wasserman & R. S. Wachbroit (eds), *Genetics and Criminal Behavior*. New York: Cambridge University Press, pp. 243–58.

Hacking, I. (2001). 'Degeneracy, criminal behavior, and looping', in D. Wasserman & R. S. Wachbroit (eds), *Genetics and Criminal Behavior*. New York: Cambridge University Press, pp. 141–68.

——. (2006). Genetics, biosocial groups and the future of identity. *Daedelus*, 135(4), 81–95.

Hicks, S. J., & Sales, B. D. (2006). *Criminal Profiling: Developing an Effective Science and Practice*. Washington, DC: American Psychological Association.

Hulsman, L. (1986). 'Critical criminology and the concept of crime', in H. Bianchi & R. van Swaaningan (eds), *Towards a Non-repressive Approach to Crime*. Amsterdam: Free University Press, pp. 25–41.

Hutchings, P. (2001). *The Criminal Subject in Law, Literature and Aesthetics*. New York: Routledge.

Jackson, J. P., & Weidman, N. M. (2004). *Race, Racism, and Science: Social Impact and Interaction*. California: ABC-CLIO.

Jones, O. D. (2006). Behavioral genetics and crime in context. *Law and Contemporary Problems*, 69, 81–100.

Lazer, D. (ed.) (2004). *DNA and the Criminal Justice System: The Technology of Justice*. Cambridge, MA: MIT Press.

Martel, J., Hogeveen, B., & Woolford, A. (2006). The state of critical scholarship in criminology and socio-legal studies in Canada. *Canadian Journal of Criminology and Criminal Justice*, 48(5), 633–46.

Mayhew, H., & Binny, J. (1856). *The Criminal Prisons of London and Scenes of Prison Life.* London: Griffin, Bohn.

O'Connor, A. (2007). *Social Science for What?* New York: Russell Sage Foundation.

Pavlich, G. (2000). *Critique and Radical Discourses on Crime.* Aldershot: Ashgate.

——. (2005). *Governing Paradoxes of Restorative Justice.* London: GlassHouse Press.

Pick, D. (1989). *Faces of Degeneration: A European Disorder, c.1848–c.1918.* New York: Cambridge University Press.

Rabinow, P. (1996). *Essays on the Anthropology of Reason.* Princeton, NJ: Princeton University Press.

Radzinowicz, L., & Hood, R. G. (1990). *A History of English Criminal Law and its Administration from 1750.* Vol. 5. Oxford: Clarendon Press.

Rafter, N. (1997). *Creating Born Criminals.* Urbana, IL: University of Illinois Press.

Ratner, R. S. (2006). Pioneering critical criminology in Canada. *Canadian Journal of Criminology and Criminal Justice*, 48(5), 647–62.

Rhodes, H. T. F. (1968). *Alphonse Bertillon, Father of Scientific Detection.* New York: Greenwood Press.

Rose, N. (2007). *The Politics of Life Itself: Biomedicine, Power, and Subjectivity in the Twenty-First Century.* Princeton, NJ: Princeton University Press.

Saferstein, R. (2004). *Criminalistics: An Introduction to Forensic Science.* Upper Saddle River, NJ: Prentice Hall.

Sekula, A. (1986). The body and the archive. *October*, 39, 3–63.

Sengoopta, C. (2003). *Imprint of the Raj: How Fingerprinting Was Born in Colonial India.* London: Pan.

Simon, J. (2007). *Governing through Crime: How the War on Crime Transformed American Democracy and Created a Culture of Fear.* Oxford: Oxford University Press.

Spearman, E. (1999[1894]). 'Identifying suspects, 1894', in A. Barrett & C. Harrison (eds), *Crime and Punishment in England: A Sourcebook.* London: Routledge, pp. 256–7.

Taylor, I., Walton, P., & Young, J. (1973). *The New Criminology.* London: Routledge & Kegan Paul.

Thomas, R. R. (1999). *Detective Fiction and the Rise of Forensic Science.* New York: Cambridge University Press.

Troup, C. E. (1893–4). Dept. Committee to inquire into the best means for identifying habitual criminals. Report, minutes of evidence, appendices. *House of Commons Parliamentary Papers Online*, ProQuest.

Valier, C. (2002). *Theories of Crime and Punishment.* New York: Longman.

——. (2004). *Crime and Contemporary Culture.* Abingdon: Routledge.

Wasserman, D., & Wachbroit, R. S. (2001). *Genetics and Criminal Behavior.* New York: Cambridge University Press.

Wiener, M. (1994). *Reconstructing the Criminal: Culture, Law, and Policy in England, 1830–1914.* Cambridge: Cambridge University Press.

Zhao, W., Chellappa, R., Phillips, R. J., & Rosenfeld, A. (2003). 'Face recognition: a literature survey'. *ACM Computing Surveys*, 35(4), 399–458.

Afterword

Reading the preceding chapters, one is reminded of Kafka's (1996, 2009) allusions to thresholds of law, identity metamorphosis, and modern punishment technologies. His compelling, if perplexing, inquiries invite us to think beyond law's authorized self-accounting. *The Trial*, for instance, references K's labyrinthine voyage as one arrested and called to account, surfacing as a bewildered, accused subject negotiating a moving identity in response to law's unfolding obscurities. Kafka shows how accusatory processes shape their participants; subjects are hailed into social existence through this 'calling to account' that arrests everyday life and demands that they respond in ways fathomable to the law. Such accusation requires avowals with consequence, and changes *personas* accordingly. Living through such transitions, as we have seen, can be a bewildering experience, as unpredictable accusatory rituals contradict jurisprudential fabrications of rule certainty.

Political rationalities and practices of accusation tied to criminalization, criminal justice and the like have comprised the focus of this book. Within the various chapters, we have encountered 'criminal accusations' through discussions of art, scholastic reasoning, textual narratives and archived case descriptions, ranging from ancient Greece, the Roman Republic, medieval and modern Britain, settler-colonial western Canada to the Cape of Good Hope. Reflecting on accusation's changing modes of address, modified over millennia, they illustrate recurrent juridical demands to explain what are deemed to be disruptive social events. These events typically confuse ordinary, everyday ways of establishing meaning, and open the way for different interpretations. When attempts to 'make sense' of events go the way of criminal accusation, negotiated meanings are channelled through cultural grammars and legally sanctioned rituals that unfold amid fogs of suspicion and blame. Criminal accusations surface from local apprehensions that frame given events as irregular, socially disruptive, harmful, or wrong. They typically pivot out of meanings contoured by legally sanctioned avowals of truth, including complaint, information, deposition, and witness testimony. Such local 'truths' are transcribed, forming legal records for later juridical, or indeed archival, reference; and open those suspected of being criminally culpable to the prospect of accusation, indictment and trial.

If Greek and Roman examples highlight the constitutive role of rhetoric in successfully initiating accusations of criminal and public wrong, they also attune us to the political negotiations that define what is considered 'accusable', who should be accused and who is authorized to accuse. Cicero and contemporaries, as noted, employed rhetorical argots deemed appropriate for accusers, and equally for the accused. They also described the violent, destructive nature of accusatory rhetoric, which was effective only to the extent that it could – depending on one's place in the contest – attack, destroy, defend or uphold people's characters. Regardless of outcome, that violent root often leaves tattered personas and reputations in its wake, as others have shown with accusations of witchcraft, and which serve as a valuable counterpoint to the chapters of this collection (e.g., Douglas, 2013; Larner, 2000; Le Roy Ladurie, 1987).

More broadly, though, rituals of criminal accusation reflect political rationalities of subjection – and simultaneous subject formation – that either create or release an 'accused' from law's hold. Various calls to account for criminality do not hail pre-existing subjects; they shape the accused through modes of address and patterns of (mis)recognition. The historical co-appearance of accused and accusing subjects is then an outcome of, rather than a discovery by, criminal identification and accusation. It is here too that the possibility of a potentially criminal *persona* can flow from visions of the criminally accused (or public wrongdoer) who is deemed to require socio-legal censure. That is, the identities of participants in unfolding rituals of accusation are forged out of the responses (and so responsibilities) they are pressed to offer. The contingent emergence of accusers, the accused and authorized officials is an effect of processes that invite selected persons to explain in specified ways.

In moments that initiate criminalization, one finds regulatory terrains that form entrances, or thresholds, to criminal justice. The genealogies in the chapters illustrate political rationalities through which sovereign and settler-colonial accusations carve out entryways to emerging criminal justice arenas. We have referenced discursive apparatuses that variously embrace sovereign, disciplinary and governmental paradigms of power. Several chapters also explore settler-colonial ideas (in western Canada and the Cape) that expose attachments to criminal accusation as ways to create monopolies of crime-focused law, and to deploy entrances to such law in the name of (dominion or British) sovereigns. These threshold arenas practically defined the scope of colonial quests to assert exclusive criminal jurisdiction. Displacing indigenous forms of law, monopolistic claims over legal violence in such contexts followed from accusations that categorized 'distinctions of person'. These ritually etched categories enabled differential political calculations of: who could be accused of what, the 'atrocity' of inter-category offences, and the punishment deemed appropriate for each category of persons. The ensuing (colonial) criminal law also managed truth-telling rituals through technologies of transcription, documentation and subjection, rendering everyday life translatable to legal process — bridging social right and legal right, lore and law as well as normative rules and sovereign rule. While such conjunctions were often paraded in the name of one, imperial sovereign, we have seen how plural social performances that enacted accusatory entryways to criminal justice were reduced – in publically recorded events and decisions – to singular visions of sovereign command. As such, ritualized performances of criminalization did not so much follow as generate images of political sovereignty. This political and recursive consequence might help us, in part, to understand the continued importance of criminal justice today.

Regardless, criminal accusation is directly involved with the negotiation of social order and its limits, usually claimed at the behest of the sovereign's mighty justice. Such limits are brought into being precisely through the bordering and ordering rituals of accusation. Legally validated truths, transcribed witness accounts or subjections, and authorized processes help to select persons to appear as the accused; they also help to define a local social order circumscribed by law. Criminal accusation is thus an initiating moment of processes that work to secure law and order, thus coupling social ordering and legal bordering. Here we encounter the ethical dimensions of criminal accusation as a mode of address whose grammar is concerned with defining images of who is to be considered other. It enunciates strangers and determines, through truth-telling rationales and rituals, who can be accused to face criminal trials. If this ethical dimension remains a pre-conceptual (even pre-social) matter bound to the very meaning of what it is to accuse, not unrelated to the accusative case in language (as per Levinas), it also alerts us to a basic plurality at the heart of accusation.

With that ethical plurality in mind, one might wonder whether we can, or how to, 'decline' or 'refuse' accusation (Antaki, 2016). Indeed, *pre-conceptual* calls to account are fundamental to sociality; they cannot be declined without self-annihilation. However, I suggest that specific instances of ensuing *conceptual* apparatuses of criminal accusation may be refused. To be sure that task is not an easy one, especially with pervasive (Western) attachments to forms of life (and associated language games) that appear around visions of crime. While it might not be possible to refuse accusation per se, it is possible decline one conception thereof; namely, those apparatuses of accusation that attend to the pursuit of criminals and their punishment.

Critical criminologists, as noted, have challenged mainstream criminology's focus on 'crime', and individual 'criminals' as distinct ontological beings responsible for social disorder. These are ethical creations born to complex conceptualizations that legitimate criminalizing processes initiated by versions of accusation. In refusing a dominant cultural reflex that evokes criminal forms of accusation almost as a matter of course, I have also suggested that discourses like criminology might reject a fixation on crime as a creature, with causes that can be manipulated and punished. Instead of replicating modes of address that criminally accuse individual persons, might we not focus attention on how local rituals contingently call different categories of persons to account in specific circumstances?

This matter is complicated by accusation's historical complicity in generating criminality through law. Agamben's (2008) discussion of Kafka's K as a self-accuser, even if false self-accuser, makes that complicity clear:

> [N]either guilt (which, in ancient law, is not necessary) nor punishment defines the trial, but rather, the accusation. Indeed, the accusation is, perhaps, the juridical 'category' par excellence (*kategoria*, in Greek, means accusation), that without which the entire edifice of the law would crumble: the implication of being in law. The law is, that is to say, in its essence, accusation, 'category'. And the being – implicated, 'accused' in the law – loses its innocence, becomes a *cosa*, that is, a cause, an object of dispute.
>
> (Agamben, 2008: 15)

In other words, juridical guilt or innocence only ever emerges from accusations; there is no criminal law without accusation. The social and political significance of refusing criminal accusation then becomes clearer. However, I remain unconvinced by Agamben's sense that 'the only way to affirm one's innocence before the law (and the powers that represent it: the father, marriage) is, in this sense, to falsely accuse oneself' (2008: 16). Rather, I have argued that it is possible to refuse attachments to accusation as a categorizing, entryway system by pursuing grammars of accusation that work under different, ethically cognizant, auspices.

That is, one might consider other grammars of accusation that recognize their role in limit formation, in categorizing visions of how to be with others. Such grammars of accusation demand much further analysis; but the chapters have shown that accusation need not be exclusively defined through its current incarnations, or necessarily directed at 'criminal' individuals. It could, for instance, be involved with categorizing social auspices and structures that yield unequal distinctions of person (class, race, gender, sexuality, etc.) that flow from unjust ways of being with others. One might, say, accuse not individuals but the associational patterns that have yielded historically problematic subjections. Of course, such open-ended categories would require local historical incarnation; but the aim would be to enable ethically aware accusations that recognize a responsibility as much to the historical 'we' who accuse, as to the accused other. Criminal accusations so directed might then no longer serve as sheer reflex responses to locally perceived wrongdoing. In addition, more ethically and socially encompassing forms of accusation might seek to initiate sociopolitical and cultural alteration by revealing (that is, accusing) unjustifiable subjections, and highlighting assemblies that yield unjust social subjects. Such ethically reflexive forms of accusation might aim broadly to enhance rather than expunge social attachments, and strive to involve each as directly responsible for depersonalizations of others. Perhaps analogies of hospitality would be useful here (Pavlich, 2005).

In concert, though, the above chapters offer a direct challenge to prevalent versions of a 'crime problem'. Seeking to problematize the political context of a status quo that survives through vast crime-control networks focused on the guilt, punishment and banning of wrongdoers, it has asked whether legal criminalization might not be used as a last resort? And relatedly: might we reduce the size and inequitable profile of criminal justice arenas by constraining points of accusatory entry to criminal justice networks? In offering an affirmative 'yes' to both questions, I acknowledge having but intimated a conceptual opening provided by genealogical critique of criminal accusations as social points of entry to criminalizing processes. By grappling with historical, social, cultural and political mechanisms that recognize accused subjects at entrances to law, the chapters problematize the ordinariness of fluid and contingent apparatuses of accusation that over centuries have yielded omniscient criminal justice institutions. They have thereby opened up to the prospect of reformulating accusation through registers other than its criminally focused versions. At stake is no less than the promise of justice that recognizes its ethical auspices, pursuing political rationales and socio-legal practices that enhance, rather than destroy, broad associative attachments. The work previously encountered is driven by that promise, and closes by throwing forth the prospect of its future elaboration.

References

Agamben, G. (2008). 'K', in J. Clemens, N. Heron, & A. Murray (eds), *The Work of Giorgio Agamben: Law, Literature, Life*. New York: Oxford University Press, pp. 13–17.

Antaki, M. (2016). 'Declining accusation', in G Pavlich, & M. Unger (eds), *Accusation: Creating Criminals*. Vancouver: UBC Press, pp. 44–72.

Douglas, M. (2013). *Witchcraft Confessions and Accusations*. Abingdon: Routledge.

Kafka, F. (1996). *The Metamorphosis and Other Stories*. New York: Dover Publications.

Kafka, F. (2009). *The Trial*. New York: Dover Publications.

Larner, C. (2000). *Enemies of God: The Witch-Hunt in Scotland*. Edinburgh: J. Donald.

Le Roy Ladurie, E. (1987). *Jasmin's Witch*. New York: G. Braziller.

Pavlich, G. (2005). Experiencing critique. *Law and Critique*, 16, 95–112.

Index

For Product Safety Concerns and Information please contact our EU representative GPSR@taylorandfrancis.com
Taylor & Francis Verlag GmbH, Kaufingerstraße 24, 80331 München, Germany

www.ingramcontent.com/pod-product-compliance
Ingram Content Group UK Ltd.
Pitfield, Milton Keynes, MK11 3LW, UK
UKHW022132190926
475702UK00013B/1766
9780367185633